FOREST
UNDER
SIEGE

FOREST
UNDER
SIEGE

The Story of Old Growth after Gifford Pinchot

RAND SCHENCK

BASALT
BOOKS

Basalt Books
PO Box 645910
Pullman, Washington 99164-5910
Phone: 800-354-7360
Email: basalt.books@wsu.edu
Website: basaltbooks.wsu.edu

Library of Congress Cataloging-in-Publication Data

Names: Schenck, Rand, 1952– author.
Title: Forest under siege : the story of old growth after Gifford Pinchot /
    Rand Schenck.
Description: Pullman, Washington : Basalt Books, [2024] | Includes
    bibliographical references.
Identifiers: LCCN 2023058044 | ISBN 9781638640257 (paperback)
Subjects: LCSH: Gifford Pinchot National Forest (Wash.) | Gifford Pinchot
    National Forest (Wash.)—History. | Gifford Pinchot National Forest
    (Agency : U.S.)—History. | Forest reserves—Northwest,
    Pacific—Management—History. | Forest policy—Northwest,
    Pacific—History. | Logging—Environmental aspects—Northwest, Pacific.
    | Old growth forest conservation—Northwest, Pacific. | Pinchot,
    Gifford, 1865–1946. | BISAC: NATURE / Environmental Conservation &
    Protection | POLITICAL SCIENCE / Public Policy / Environmental Policy
Classification: LCC SD428.G45 S34 2024 | DDC
    333.75/110979782—dc23/eng/20240301
LC record available at https://lccn.loc.gov/2023058044

Basalt Books is an imprint of Washington State University Press.

The Washington State University Pullman campus is located on the homelands of the Niimíipuu (Nez Perce) Tribe and the Palus people. We acknowledge their presence here since time immemorial and recognize their continuing connection to the land, to the water, and to their ancestors. WSU Press is committed to publishing works that foster a deeper understanding of the Pacific Northwest and the contributions of its Native peoples.

Cover design by Brad Norr Design.

For my wondrous daughters, Katrina and Marta Schenck

Contents

Part III Ecological Management: The Rebirth of the Forest

We all travel the Milky Way together, trees and man. . . . In every walk with nature one receives far more than he seeks. The clearest way into the universe is through a forest wilderness.

—John Muir

Introduction

A cabin in the woods. That dream began when I was a boy living in primitive cabins while attending summer camps near the Pisgah National Forest in the mountains of North Carolina, the same mountains in which Gifford Pinchot, the founder of the US Forest Service, first practiced forestry. As an adolescent I hiked in those mountains, canoed in their waters, and slid down waterfalls in that glorious landscape. As a college student I backpacked in national forests throughout Colorado and climbed 14,000-foot peaks. Over the past forty years, I have volunteered with a variety of environmental organizations to protect and preserve national forests and to increase the amount of wilderness in many national forests so that they are forever protected from logging. At the turn of the millennium, I began an active search for that cabin from my home in Portland, Oregon, and soon found one next to Trapper Creek in the Gifford Pinchot National Forest (GPNF) in southern Washington state. While I own the cabin built in the 1920s, I do not own the land on which it sits, but rather lease a small parcel of land from the US Forest Service. My "backyard" is the 1.3 million surrounding acres that comprise the Gifford Pinchot National Forest.

My cabin is surrounded by old-growth Douglas-fir, western hemlock, and western red cedar. I am blessed to be removed from many distractions of modern life—no cell phone coverage, no electricity, and no internet connection. Rather, the susurrus of Trapper Creek, which is just 30 feet from my back door, beguiles. Douglas-firs 6 feet in diameter rise to majestic heights nearby. Old-growth red cedars are found up and down the riverbank. What prevented these elders of the forest from being harvested by the early foresters eager to take down such giants? The Trapper Creek drainage was saved from the saw by water, more precisely mineral water, hence the name "Mineral Springs."

The mineral springs, which became known as Government Mineral Springs, attracted people from across the region as the mineral waters were believed to possess curative powers and to treat ailments ranging from gallstones to diabetes and anemia. Near the turn of the twentieth century, the Government Mineral Springs Resort was built adjacent to

1

these sought-after springs, which drained into Trapper Creek twenty miles north of the Columbia River. Over the first few decades of the twentieth century, recreation cabins were built along Trapper Creek. The presence of the resort along with the cabins was largely responsible for preservation of the surrounding old-growth forests.

The Trapper Creek drainage now represents an anomaly in the GPNF. Roughly 1,000 acres in size, this drainage contains one of the best-preserved low-elevation old-growth groves in the Pacific Northwest. In 1918, when the Government Mineral Springs Resort was built, the majority of the trees in this national forest were old growth. How much old growth now exists within these 1.3 million acres? Of the nearly 70 percent of old growth found in this national forest a century ago, now only about 5 percent remains. How did this happen? And how did it happen in the forest that was named after the founder of the Forest Service, Gifford Pinchot—the country's first forester, who fervently believed in a sustainable approach to forestry? This extraordinary transformation from a complex, natural forest—replete with trees 8 to 12 feet in diameter, over 250 feet in height, and 300–500+ years old—to a forest more akin to a plantation, then to a forest of mostly young Douglas-firs one to two feet in diameter and ranging in age from thirty to sixty years, took place over a forty-year period after WWII. I will closely examine this transformation. What led leaders of the US Forest Service to believe such a radical transformation was the right thing to do?

My first engagement with the US Forest Service began in the late 1970s when I became an activist and leader with the Sierra Club in North Carolina. Our local group, the Research Triangle Group, began "ground truthing" to assess how the Forest Service was conducting its Roadless Area Review and Evaluation process in national forests in the state. This process was intended to assess roadless areas for inclusion in the National Wilderness Preservation System. We were rightly concerned that areas with potential as future wilderness were being ignored. I also was a member of the first group of activists trained by the Sierra Club in the early 1980s in how to both endorse candidates running for the US Congress, and then, once they were elected, how to effectively lobby them. A key area of focus was their support for wilderness designation of those areas deserving of such protection in our national forests.

I moved from North Carolina to Oregon in 1996 to work as an organization development consultant for Intel. I quickly learned about a group, the Oregon Natural Resources Council (now called Oregon Wild), that was focused on protection of the area's wildlands, wild waters, and wildlife and soon joined their board. Much of my advocacy as a board member involved supporting the organization's efforts both to increase the amount of wilderness in our national forests and to stop destructive logging practices (clear-cutting logging; logging on steep slopes and along streams and rivers) in those forests. As a board member and as a new resident of the Pacific Northwest, I quickly became aware of how little of our old-growth forest remained. Starting in the 2010s, I focused much more of my volunteer efforts on climate change. An all-volunteer group we called MCAT—Mobilizing Climate Action Together—evolved and I served as the Forestry and Natural Lands lead. The science was clear: simply growing trees longer was by far the most effective natural climate solution on the planet. Because most of my leisure time has been spent hiking and backpacking in our national forests, I decided to search for a cabin in one of the few remaining old-growth groves in our national forests in the Northwest. Just after New Year's Day in 2000, I saw a tiny ad in the *Oregonian* newspaper for a rustic cabin in the GPNF. Three days later, I was the owner.

After buying my cabin, I began to explore, hike, and backpack throughout the forests. I quickly became aware of the extent to which rampant logging had decimated what had once been a majestic, biologically diverse landscape—a landscape that now was dominated by single-aged, single-species, biologically impoverished "crops" (crop was the term many foresters used when describing the kind of highly regulated forest they viewed as more desirable) of trees. From the top of Observation Peak, just a 7-mile hike from my cabin, I can see three dramatic glaciated, volcanic peaks imposing themselves on the landscape: Mount Hood, Mount Adams, and Mount St. Helens. But I can also see vast tracts of cutover lands that extend throughout the landscape.

After much reading and research, I realized that Gifford Pinchot was much misunderstood not only by the environmental community but also by foresters themselves. Many in the environmental community viewed him as a forester motivated by utilitarianism—that the best use of the forest is as a resource, a source of wood products that would help the nation and its citizens thrive. Foresters—both those in private industry and especially those leaders within the Forest Service after WWII—saw Pinchot as a champion of producing and using wood products, who would have approved whatever practices would have increased such production. Sadly, both environmentalists and foresters have misunderstood Pinchot.

Pinchot saw forests as much more than a collection of trees awaiting harvest. He viewed them as part of an extensive landscape with an extraordinary interdependence among its streams, soil, fish, wildlife, and other natural resources. His views of forests evolved over his lifetime. Late in life he wrote, "conservation is the foresighted utilization, preservation, and/or renewal of forests, lands, minerals, for the greatest good, of the greatest number for the longest time." While Pinchot described the "greatest good, of the greatest number in the long run" as the mission of the Forest Service in 1905, his later emphasis on preservation and renewal reflects his long-standing core values. How did it happen that Pinchot became so misunderstood, especially after his death?

The Forest Service rightly honored him when it changed the name of the Columbia National Forest to the Gifford Pinchot National Forest soon after his death in 1946. Then, in the succeeding forty years, the Forest Service dishonored Pinchot by cutting down almost all the old growth not only in his namesake forest but also throughout the Pacific Northwest. The result was extensive harm to a centuries-old ecosystem such that species like the spotted owl, marbled murrelet, and salmon were put at risk. I will explore and reflect on this contradiction; one in which, on the one hand, the Forest Service continues to pay homage to its founder, while on the other hand acting in opposition to his vision of sustainable forestry and sustainable communities. This examination of Pinchot's namesake forest provides a lens for better understanding what happened more broadly in national forests throughout the Pacific Northwest.

To tell this story in a way that viscerally captures one hundred years of forestry with a primary focus on the GPNF, I relied on a wide range of resources. Contained within boxes in the National Archives in Seattle were many of the inspection reports that Pinchot insisted be written as his primary tool to ensure accountability in the management of national forests. Inspection reports for what was then the Columbia National Forest—all of which were written by outside auditors—contained invaluable information, both quantitative and qualitative, about the challenges, opportunities, and priorities for foresters during the early decades of the GPNF. In one of the slowly decaying cabins maintained by the Mount Adams District within the GPNF, I discovered the annual reports for the GPNF, which began to appear in the 1950s. These reports, significantly, show how much old growth was logged and how many new miles of roads were built. While the inspection reports written during the first four decades of the Forest Service's existence often did lead to real improvements in management practices, these later annual reports for the GPNF existed primarily as public relations documents intended to win support for forestry practices. Beginning in the 1980s, a wide variety of planning documents were produced in the GPNF as a result of the requirements of the National Forest Management Act. By analyzing and sifting through these many documents, I gained insight into the beliefs and values undergirding the actions of the leaders of the GPNF over the past century. Tragically, many of their actions, especially in the second half of the twentieth century, were directly counter to Gifford Pinchot's hopes, dreams, and vision for how his national forests would be managed. In later chapters, I will discuss how managerial actions such as the ongoing focus on cutting of old growth led to much less resilient, healthy forest.

I also interviewed a wide range of people who have been involved with the Gifford Pinchot National Forest over the past forty years. These interviews included many active Forest Service employees, forestry academics, researchers studying practices on the ground, environmentalists involved in protecting the GPNF, and two past supervisors of the GPNF active during the high-production decades of the 1970s and 1980s. GPNF supervisor Ted Stubblefield, who was active during the turbulent spotted owl period in the late 1980s and early 1990s, had initially agreed to be interviewed but later declined after learning that I had been on the board of an environmental organization. Some twenty-five years after serving as supervisor of the GPNF, he apparently was distrustful of meeting with someone he viewed as an environmentalist. This level of distrust is highly representative of the hard feelings of those on both sides of the timber wars. All of these people had their own stories to tell about the GPNF and what the forest meant to them. All were well-intentioned, yet some were directly responsible for the utter transformation of a biologically diverse natural forest into what they viewed as much more desirable forest, a highly regulated one, one they viewed as a "crop." By listening to these people and by examining their actions on the GPNF, we are able to gain a greater understanding of how forest management was transformed throughout the Pacific Northwest. What happened in the 1.3 million acres of the GPNF was representative of what occurred throughout the almost 25 million acres of national forest across the Pacific Northwest. The irony is that those in control of our national forests over the past century to the present day continued to have an almost worshipful view of Gifford Pinchot while acting in ways that would have caused him much dismay.

Gifford Pinchot was one of the primary originators of the conservation movement in the United States. John Muir was one of the primary origina- tors of the preservation movement in the United States. Both men left this country invaluable, inestimable legacies, yet Muir is held up, especially by the environmental community, as the true champion for how we should manage our public lands, while Pinchot is viewed as one who primarily championed "use." A corrective is needed. Pinchot is equally deserving of our respect and admiration. In this work I will explore why we need to elevate Pinchot as a champion equal to Muir for all those who care about conservation.

In the early 1890s, Gifford Pinchot traipsed through the woods in what became his namesake forest. He saw an ancient forest unlike any he had experienced on the East Coast. Less than fifteen years later, he became the first US Forest Service chief, the person accountable for all of the national forests in the United States. The forests under his stewardship that captured most of his attention were those on the West Coast. They were the most primitive, the wildest, and had the most extensive stands of virgin timber in the entirety of the continental United States.

At the time of Pinchot's death in 1946, the forests throughout the Pacific Northwest were largely unchanged from the woods he walked through some sixty years earlier. But in the brief span of four decades, almost all of the old growth was logged and hauled off the land—initially, at least, one single-log truck after another after another after another. Trees that were three hundred to five hundred-plus years old. Trees that took three to four people to put their arms around. Trees that were taller than most skyscrapers at that time. During the four decades after WWII, most old growth in the Pacific Northwest vanished. We witnessed the "death" of old growth. How this was allowed to happen is a story that, like a complex Persian carpet, has many different patterns, colors, and threads.

The forests in the Pacific Northwest experienced three distinct phases over the past hundred years: life, a nearly forty-year period of stewardship; death, a forty-year period of relentless production; and now twenty-five-plus years that have been trending toward restoration, toward the rebirth of old growth. What will the next hundred years bring to this forest? Will it bring an expanse of uniform plantations, not unlike corn crops, bereft of the complexity that sustains diverse flora and fauna or the restoration of a natural forest in which old growth is abundant? Can the forest once again appear much like it did at the turn of the twentieth century with all its complexity, its primeval mystery, its towering bulk and size? Nothing is certain. The impact of climate change on the forest is, perhaps, the most significant uncertainty in the decades ahead. Just as powerful winds and fires can transform forests in minutes, so too can political decisions thousands of miles away lead to misinformed policy and devastation.

I have no doubt what the vast majority of people across this country want. Anyone who has walked into an ancient forest reveres these inspiring trees, just as they revere their grandparents. They undoubtedly would advocate for restoration, in which efforts are taken to restore degraded forests and landscapes, and preservation. We can restore these forests and once again appreciate an abundance of old growth throughout the Gifford Pinchot National Forest and beyond. My children's children can experience what my grandfather could have experienced a hundred years ago: old-growth groves extending for hundreds of miles in all directions. This will not be an easy transformation, an easy restoration to achieve. The chapter on ecological management illustrates the management actions needed to achieve this transformation. Unlike brutal destruction, this transformation will require relentless care, relentless nurturing, and relentless love. Healthy children are the product of this care. By providing the same kind of care, attention, and nurturance we provide to our children to Pinchot's Forest, we can, over time, ensure the rebirth of old growth throughout the Pacific Northwest.

Part I

Stewardship:
The Life of the Forest

1

The Birth of Forests

For humankind the trees—their roots in the ground, their heads reaching into the sky—have seemed always to bind together the universe.

—George Nakashima

The most likely origin for the word "forests" is the Latin word *foris*, meaning "outside." During the Middle Ages in England, a forest referred to land that was put off-limits by royal decree and was to be preserved in its natural state. These forests were thus not open to cultivation or exploitation. Forests were distinct from parks, which were viewed as spaces that provided opportunities for recreation and leisure. These early rulers viewed forests first and foremost as a habitat for wild animals. The people of the realm were not allowed into these protected lands to hunt or seek firewood. The king decreed these lands as refuges for wildlife where only the king and friends of the realm could hunt. Thus, forests were also seen as a landscape that provided all animals a space for rest.

Among the royal duties the crown was compelled to perform was the preservation of the wilderness character of the forest. The king's subjects, however, were more interested in the forest as a resource that met their needs for firewood and lumber. England's kings prioritized the forests as a resource that provided habitats that sustained wild animals and as landscapes that ensured abundant water resources.

This preservation of wild lands by English kings was a significant shift from the dominant practices of the prior millennium, and even earlier, that led to deforestation across most of Europe and northern Africa. Certainly, the cutting down of forests was an integral part of Neolithic life. Both the Greeks and the Romans practiced a relentless deforestation in their drive to promote their way of life and expand and fuel their societies and empires. As early as the fourth century BCE, Plato was already nostalgic about forest that had previously covered much of southern Europe and northern Africa.

Much of the deforestation resulted from Athens' and Rome's need for wood to build their naval ships. The forests were devastated as these empires expanded. Especially needed in areas of low rainfall, these forests were critical to the health of the land, as they held moisture from winter rains and then slowly released that water in summer, keeping springs from drying out. At the height of the Roman Empire, northern Africa sustained hundreds of cities, some of which were the richest across the empire. Deforestation throughout northern Africa caused the land to dry out and crops to die. The cultivation of wheat was no longer possible. Land was converted into olive groves, although soon even these plantings failed. In time, forests were buried beneath the sand dunes that migrated from the south. Harbors across northern Africa disappeared. And so, with the devastation of the forests came the collapse of the cities.

The conception of forests as a place for rest is vital to our own way of viewing forest. A place for rest is one that can also serve as a sanctuary. Sanctuaries, like medieval cathedrals, are places where people may seek renewal and experience bliss.

Two contrasting mindsets have dominated the Western world's way of seeing forests over the past two thousand years. After the Middle Ages, the view of forest as a productive resource evolved, until, in the second half of the eighteenth century, the new science of forestry began in Germany. Forests began to be viewed in terms of quantifiable mass, in volumes of wood to be harvested and utilized. Utility became the greatest good, and with this belief system, forests were transformed from places with diverse species and diverse ages of trees to groups of uniform plant types and prescribed planting times. Thus, the concept of forests as crops came to be. The ideal forest was no longer complex and random, but rather quantifiable and orderly.

US governmental policies, greatly influenced by the Age of Enlightenment, favored the German model for forests, a data-based approach that subjects North American forests to mathematical models where increased yield, ever greater volume, is the highest goal. In contrast to this utilitarian perspective, others who viewed themselves as descendants of the Romantics (key figures from English literature including Wordsworth, Keats, and Coleridge) preferred knowing and experiencing forests as sanctuaries, as refuges. These contrasting belief systems have been in continuous conflict in our country for hundreds of years.

When the old-growth Douglas-firs in the Pacific Northwest were felled one hundred years ago, what did their concentric rings tell us? These tightly spaced rings held much complex mystery. If we could see history as represented by the centermost concentric ring of an old-growth tree, we might see Native Americans passing through the region that became Pinchot's namesake forest in search of huckleberries, possibly as far back as when Leif Erikson first visited the continent in the first millennium AD. Toward the middlemost concentric ring we would witness the first White men passing just south of what is now Gifford Pinchot National Forest as Lewis and Clark and their party paddled down and then back up the Columbia River. Just as today we preserve the Declaration of Independence and the US Constitution—important documents that represent the best of our history—we also must preserve the 5–10 percent of old growth left in the Pacific Northwest, as that remaining old growth represents our history and holds our stories. Like water itself, those old-growth groves are vital to our own well-being and spiritual nurturance.

Robert Pogue Harrison, who was tenured at Stanford the same year he wrote *Forest: The Shadow of Civilization*, captures well the hidden meaning of those concentric circles: "From the family tree to the tree of knowledge, from the tree of life to the tree of memory, forests have provided an indispensable resource of symbolization in the cultural evolution of humankind . . . even the concept of the circle, we are told, comes from the internal concentric rings laid bare by the felling of trees." This notion of a circle, derived from the concentric rings of felled trees, can now be extended to the circle of our own fragile planet, the "Blue Marble," around our sun, and outward to the circling planets in our solar system.

In many ways, old-growth forests became a symbol and way of understanding the earth itself and all the intricate and profound interdependencies that our very well-being depends on. Our view of our own planet as precious yet vulnerable did not really crystalize until we saw the first photographs of Earth from space and realized that this planet is all that we have. Just as we have come to understand the extraordinary interdependencies that enable healthy old-growth forest, so too have we come to understand the many connected strands in our integrated ecosystems that ensure the health of this marvelous planet.

Robert Pogue Harrison eloquently captures this interdependence, both that which is sublime and that which threatens. "What is true for a particular forest's ecosystem is true for the totality of the biosphere. Humanity begins to appear in a new light: as a species caught in the delicate and diverse web of a forest-like planetary environment. More precisely, we are beginning to appear ourselves as a species of parasite which threatens to destroy the hosting organism as whole." We stand at a precipice with this understanding that with the death of forests we put our planet and ourselves at greater risk as well. Long-term climate change threatens to make our earth uninhabitable.

2

The Early Years
and Gifford Pinchot

Human cultures have encountered Cascade forests for at least twelve
thousand years. . . . Through most of the intervening ages, human
presence must have barely bruised the forest. . . . Then Europeans arrived.

—Bill Yake

Since the end of the last ice age, about eleven thousand years ago,
Pinchot's forest and the rest of the Pacific Northwest forests have
changed in both their composition and structure. The valleys west of the
Cascade mountain range were largely maintained as prairie or savannah
ecosystems as a result of fires set by Native Americans. On occasion,
these human-caused fires moved into the west side of the Cascades and,
when conditions were optimal, burned large tracts of the wetter and
cooler west side forests. Unlike east side forests, where low-intensity fires
burned every eight to fifteen years, forest fires on the west side were less
frequent, with a return interval about 425 years before White settlement
and about 250 years after White settlement. Much of the old growth
found in the Cascades today got its start in the aftermath of catastrophic
fires that occurred between 1400 and 1650, although some very large
wildfires did burn in the southern Washington Cascades in the second
half of the 1800s.

When Columbus landed in North America in 1492, significant
stands of old growth throughout the Cascades were barely in their adolescence. Native American peoples who lived in the Northwest during
the three hundred years after Columbus witnessed the transformation of
much of the landscape surrounding them on the west side of the Cascades from largely young forests to ones that were dominated by old
growth. The rare old growth that remains now is found almost entirely
on federal lands.

Native Americans have lived close to what is now the Gifford Pinchot National Forest for more than twelve thousand years. The Columbia River, which runs along the southern border of the GPNF, has long been a major transportation corridor. Villages and trade markets could be found up and down the river as well as innumerable trails radiating away from the river and into the mountains. Hunters travelled throughout Pinchot's forest in search of game, especially bear, elk, and deer. Berry gatherers sought out the many meadows found scattered throughout these forests in search of huckleberries and other fruit. Native Americans thrived in this environment for thousands of years. However, by the time Lewis and Clark travelled through the region in 1804–1805, many of the once prosperous Native American tribes and villages had already been severely impacted by European diseases such as smallpox, malaria, and viral influenza.

The Native American challenges of adapting to the economic, social, and political norms of the settlers who transformed the Northwest can best be summed up by the declaration of Smohalla, a Native American spiritual leader who lived during most of the nineteenth century: "You ask me to plow the ground! Shall I take a knife and tear my mother's bosom? Then when I die she will not take me to her bosom to rest. You ask me to dig for stone! Shall I dig under her skin for her bones? Then when I die I cannot enter her body to be born again. You ask me to cut grass and make hay and sell it and be rich like white men! But how dare I cut off my mother's hair?" This belief system in the face of the global expansion of market capitalism led to resistance, and ultimately, the experience of terrible harms to Native American peoples and their culture in the nineteenth century.

This expansion of market capitalism throughout the United States and especially in the Pacific Northwest was driven to a great extent by the extraction of natural resources. The most valuable natural resource in the Northwest available for extraction was not gold or silver as in California and Nevada, but rather timber. The old-growth trees that dominated the forests of the Cascades were almost certainly viewed by Native Americans much as they viewed the volcanic snow-capped mountains: as immovable, powerful, and sacred, as Smohalla made clear in expressing his beliefs about the ways of "white men." For the many thousands of years in which Native Americans lived in and near the Cascades, they rarely cut down old-growth trees in those forests. That was not true on the coast, where some small-in-number ancient cedars were harvested to build cedar plank houses and canoes. Fire, though, was used to open forests especially in the central valleys for the grasses, herbs, and small trees favored by the browsing animals Native Americans hunted. These fires sometimes did enter into old-growth groves in the Cascades and burned significant acreage around three hundred and five hundred years ago.

Unlike Native Americans, most early American settlers viewed the wilderness as a threatening and terrifying place. Early fur traders working in the Northwest described the old-growth-dominated landscapes as gloomy and dreary. The outlook of Europeans and their descendants who settled in the Northwest was radically different from that of Native Americans. First and foremost, Cascade forests were feared, as they appeared impenetrable and highly challenging to navigate through. They also presented major obstacles to farming and grazing. Only with backbreaking work could they be cleared for crops and pasture. The early settlers who moved to the Northwest to farm viewed the wilderness as more of an obstacle than a resource. Their attitude was one of disregard, if not hostility, as their dominant concern was easy access to farmable land.

From their perspective, these settlers were bringing civilization to the region; they were bringing order to chaos, transforming evil into good. Wilderness was the villain and the pioneer the hero. The old growth in the heart of the Cascades was largely ignored as settlers first settled in the broad valleys to the west of the mountain range. Logging during most of the nineteenth century had little impact on the environment, due to the low level of technology that was applied. Cutting down old growth was simply too laborious.

After much of the old growth on the East Coast and then in the Midwest had been logged, timber needs were met by turning to the Northwest. A seemingly endless supply of the country's largest trees lay waiting for the saw. More than any other, one man ensured that those Northwest forests did not experience the same cut-and-run forest devastation that had occurred elsewhere: Gifford Pinchot. When Pinchot was in his teens, his father encouraged him to become a forester. At the time, in the 1880s, forestry did not exist as an occupation in the United States; there were no professional foresters. Pinchot's father was aware of the European model of forestry and likely believed his son could bring more effective approaches to forest management in the United States. Perhaps the senior Pinchot also felt a sense of guilt as a result of the deforestation that his own ancestors had contributed to, which was a significant factor in his own wealth, and abhorrence at the cut-and-run type of forestry that was dominant throughout the East Coast.

The senior Pinchot communicated a set of expectations that readily blossomed and took root in his son: that he adopt a highly disciplined life, that rationality and order serve as his dominant guide to decision-making, and that he use his energies and his time as efficiently as possible. These values were fully reinforced for Gifford Pinchot at his chosen educational venue for becoming a forester: the L'Ecole Nationale Forestiére in Nancy, France. In the 1880s, the only place one could learn forestry was in Europe. The first school of forestry in the United States was established in 1900 and was endowed at Yale by the Pinchot family.

In France, the dominant approach to forestry as a profession was based on rational planning, structure, and efficiency. These values dovetailed nicely with those the senior Pinchot sought to inculcate in his son. From this perspective, forests that were diverse in age, tree types, sizes—in short, forests that were seemingly chaotic like those in the Northwest—were viewed as antithetical to a well-managed forest. The European approach preferred a forest that could be managed as easily as one managed an agricultural crop, in which regular, tidy, administrative grids were dominant. This system was readily adopted by the young Pinchot and reinforced his sense that a utilitarian approach to forestry was one that could most readily and successfully transfer to the United States.

The two insights that Pinchot gained in Europe and that he carried with him throughout his life were that a utilitarian approach to forestry depended on the oversight and control by an "imperishable guardian," the national government, and that unlike corn or wheat, a forest could not be harvested annually. The national government must retain ownership of this resource as only it could exercise the patience and foresight required to ensure trees matured and were harvested at a rate that was sustainable.

After completing his schooling in forestry in Europe, Pinchot returned to a country where, as he put it, "forest devastation was going like a runaway locomotive" while forest protection "was pursuing it like a manpowered handcar and falling further behind with every mile." Pinchot recognized that those practices would need to change if forests were to become a sustainable resource. He also realized that, as one of the first practitioners of the new science of forestry, he would need to blaze his own trail. Because what he called the "denudatics" were destroying the forest without regard for the future, and because countervailing forces acting for preservation were largely missing, Pinchot took upon himself the Herculean task of changing this country's mindset about the forest.

Largely through family connections, Pinchot was hired by Cornelius Vanderbilt in 1892 to serve as forester for the Vanderbilts' Biltmore estate in Asheville, North Carolina, which eventually grew to over 125,000 acres and later became the heart of the Pisgah National Forest. Almost all of the old-growth forests throughout the East Coast had been cut by the late 1800s, and this was true of the Biltmore estate forests as well. This reality on the ground did not deter the young Pinchot. Rather, this despoiled landscape provided just the kind of outdoor laboratory he was looking for to make his mark, to prove that forestry was a profession that could be practiced in a way that was both economically profitable and sustainable over the long term. In 1893, Pinchot published a pamphlet for the Chicago's World Fair in which he declared false the claim that "it is necessary to destroy a forest to make it pay."

Pinchot rarely (if ever) doubted his ability to accomplish what he professed. His confidence at times could be seen as arrogance, his resolution as stubbornness, his grit as lack of insight. The actual outcomes on the ground at Biltmore may not have matched Pinchot's rhetoric. Char Miller, his biographer, wrote, "Biltmore had in effect offered up America's first below cost timber sale." If the Biltmore estate is viewed as a laboratory where Pinchot practiced what he learned in France for the first time, then one may more charitably view his actions there as an opportunity to experiment and learn from his mistakes and his failures.

One of Pinchot's first real experiments in active forestry took place near Brevard, North Carolina, on the Mills River, a tributary of the French Broad River, on which had been built a Vanderbilt mill for raw timber. One of the challenges all foresters face is transporting downed logs to a mill site as cheaply as possible. The bigger the tree, the greater the challenge, especially before the advent of logging trucks. Pinchot developed a plan that relied on the use of temporary splash dams in rivers, behind which a reservoir of water would build up. Immense trees in the vicinity of the Mills River were felled and moved to the area behind the dam. After heavy rains filled the area with water, creating a reservoir, the splash dam would be destroyed and the immense logs behind it released to float down the Mills River drainage into the French Broad River and finally to the timber mill. According to Pinchot, this project realized a profit for Vanderbilt, at a cost that Vanderbilt likely cared little about, but one that Pinchot himself was unwilling to acknowledge, perhaps in his fervor to demonstrate that his approach to forestry was solid and sound and should be adopted by others. The reality was that the massive logs floating down the river knocked out bridges, scoured out river sediments, overran the river's banks, and damaged farmers' fields, leaving a scene of devastation in the Mills River drainage. German forester Carl Schenck [no relation], who partnered with Pinchot at Vanderbilt, later wrote, "The bed of Big Creek, arched with rhododendrons, green with moss-covered rocks, and replete with brook trout, was made a ruined run, a veritable arroyo of torn shores and skimmed stones . . . where has it not been true that forestry, superimposed upon the primeval, has destroyed nature's gorgeous beauty at the first stroke of the ax." Pinchot's experiences on Vanderbilt's lands likely played a significant role in his growing recognition of the need to log in a way that would sustain the resource over the long term.

These two needs—to prove that forestry could be both profitable and sustainable—bring to mind Oscar Wilde's statement that the test of a first-rate intelligence is the ability to keep two opposing thoughts in mind at the same time and still be able to function. Never was anyone who knew Pinchot in doubt of his possessing a first-rate intelligence. These two often opposing ideas were a lifelong dilemma for Pinchot. One of the first documents he produced as chief of the US Forest Service was called *The Use Book of the National Forest Reserves*. At the same time the leaders of the USFS were concerned that they were facing a future timber famine, Pinchot sought to prove that production and conservation were compatible.

Pinchot felt intensely the need to prove himself and to develop an entirely new profession. This conviction, as we shall see, was pivotal in the creation of the US Forest Service itself and in its early years, when its very existence was periodically threatened by political forces that wanted to eliminate it as an agency of the government.

3

Muir and Pinchot: Protecting the Forest

Because forests predate us, they certainly can appear, disappear, and thrive without us. Perhaps that is what wild means: life thriving without human attention.

—Bill Yake

The Pacific Forest Reserve, which contained what eventually became the Gifford Pinchot National Forest, was first established in 1893 by President William Henry Harrison and then expanded by President Grover Cleveland in 1897. Cleveland renamed these protected lands the Mount Rainier Forest Reserve, which then became the largest preserve in the United States, encompassing almost 4.5 million acres and stretching 235 miles in length centered on the crest of the Cascades. The 1891 legislation that authorized the establishment of these reserves read, "The President of the United States may, from time to time, set apart and reserve, in any State or Territory having public lands bearing forest, in any part of the public lands wholly or in part covered with timbers or undergrowth, whether of commercial value or not, as public reservation, and the President shall by public proclamation, declare the establishment of such reservation and the limits thereof." This legislation, however, provided no means for administering and managing these lands, nor did it state what kind of uses could take place within them. While the term "reserves" implied protection, that was not the intent of Congress. Significant protest by those wanting to extract value from these reserves, whether from mining or logging, led to Congress passing the Organic Act of 1897, which clarified the purposes of these reserves: to ensure forest improvement and protection, to protect water flow, and to ensure a continuous supply of timber. This first aim regarding improvement and protection, which later was subsumed by the term "sustainable practices," was in potential conflict with the third aim, timber production. Those two conflicting goals were in near perpetual war for the next one hundred years. The Organic Act clarified that the US government had the authority to use the forests and that the forests were not to be seen as preserves.

One of the first legislative acts to impact settlement and logging in the Northwest was the Timber and Stone Act of 1878, which allowed settlers to acquire up to 160 acres of timber or mineral lands. Robert Ficken writes in *The Forested Land* that the primary purpose of the act was to address fraud by mill companies, which were buying up large parcels of land, but the act led to even greater fraud as lumbermen used agents to file claims on the best timberlands. Ficken notes that in many cases private citizens paid paltry sums to acquire claims that were then turned over to mill companies who thus were able to secure vast expanses of land "at prices so low that lumbermen marveled at their audacity in taking advantage of the law."

One of the drivers for Pinchot's later work to establish the US Forest Service was his awareness of how timber companies were engaged in fraud to acquire timbered lands. He felt strongly that only the US government was capable both of protecting these forested resources in the Northwest and making use of the resource in a sustainable fashion. As a forester, he felt that his "job was not to stop the ax, but to regulate its use . . . that a nation utterly absorbed in the present had to be brought to consider the future." In many ways, Pinchot was reacting to what he viewed as the greed and short-sightedness that dominated the timber industry; he railed against the fact that vast tracts of land were falling into the "crooked, mercenary, and speculative hands of companies, corporations, and monopolies."

Early settlers on the East Coast, at the time when Pinchot's father was involved in early logging, described a landscape in which a squirrel could travel from the Atlantic Ocean to the Mississippi River along the treetops, never touching the ground, so vast were the forests. The dominant belief about forests were that they were boundless, a resource that could never be depleted. By the second half of the nineteenth century, this viewpoint, at least on the East Coast, with its once expansive hardwoods of chestnut, oak, hickory, and poplar, was in tatters. One of the few mid-nineteenth century Americans to recognize the stark reality that our forests, like those of northern Egypt during the Roman era, could be cut down and not return, was George Perkins Marsh. He foresaw that the level of logging across the country was not sustainable. "We have now felled forest enough everywhere in many districts far too much. Let us restore this one element of material life to its normal proportion and devise a means for maintaining the permanence of its relations to the fields, the meadows, and the pasture, to the rain and the dews of heaven, to the springs, and rivulets with which it waters the earth."

Had Pinchot met Marsh, he likely would have been in full agreement with him. As a forester, Pinchot was keen to exercise his influence on future forest policy. He used his family connections to become a member of the 1896 National Forest Commission, which was established to answer three fundamental questions regarding the public lands out West:

- "Is it desirable and practical to preserve from fire and to maintain permanently as forestlands those portions of the public domain now bearing wood growth for the supply of timber?
- How far does the influence of forest upon climate, soil, and water conditions make desirable a policy of forest conservation in regions where the public domain is principally situated?
- What specific legislation should be enacted to remedy the evils now confessedly existing?"

It was in that role that Pinchot first set foot in the Cascade mountains and what became his namesake forest. After assessing the Cascades, Pinchot headed south with the commission where he hiked through immense Sequoia groves in the California Sierras and lamented the "gigantically wasteful lumbering of the great Sequoias, many of whose trunks were so huge that they had to be blown apart before they could be handled. I resented then and I resent now the practice of making vine stakes hardly bigger that walking sticks out of these greatest of all living things."

The forest reserves, which were under the General Land Office and part of the Department of the Interior, were transferred to the Department of Agriculture in 1905. This change led to the establishment of the US Forest Service with Gifford Pinchot as its first chief, although the actual name change, from forest reserves to national forests, did not take place until 1907. Over 63 million acres that had been managed by the Bureau of Forestry were now to be managed by the US Forest Service. Pinchot chose the name "Forest Service" because of the high value he placed on the notion of being in service to the public, to communities, and the country.

From the beginning, a major concern for the Forest Service was the need to pay its own way—to generate enough revenue from timber sales to cover its costs. This need led to an emphasis on production at the expense of protection that became the dominant mindset for the first eighty years of its existence. A countervailing force was at work, however, that prevented this focus on production from becoming a reality on the ground within the national forests until WWII: private interests. Owners of privately held timberlands feared that lumber from national forestlands would drive down the market value of their logs. The Forest Service was responsive to this concern both because of the pressures put on them by private timber interests and because they were concerned at the outset that a timber shortage was just years away. These dual concerns, and the fact of the Great Depression during the 1930s, resulted in very low production of timber on our national forests until WWII when demand skyrocketed. For the first nearly forty years of its existence, the Forest Service, despite its dominant philosophy being to show that forestry could pay its own way, actually left much of the old growth in the Northwest virtually untouched.

The guiding policy for the Forest Service was established in 1905 when Pinchot wrote that these national forests were intended to provide the "greatest good for the greatest number in the long run." This mission, which is still referred to today by employees of the Forest Service, is one of Pinchot's most remarkable and enduring legacies. The mission, however, has built within it an elasticity that allows it to be interpreted based on the particular social/economic context of the time. Thus, the mission could be defined for whatever purposes those in power chose, whether they leaned toward championing conservation or production and utilization.

In 1905, Pinchot issued *The Use Book of the National Forest Reserves*, which thereafter simply became known as the *Use Book*. Under the heading of "To the Public," the *Use Book* states, "The timber, water, pasture, mineral, and other resources of the forest reserves are for the use of the people." Because Pinchot knew that the very existence of the Forest Service was threatened by political forces within the US Congress, he felt that he could defeat those forces by declaring these forests were intended to meet the public's needs. Throughout the *Use Book* he challenged the common conception that these lands were to be set aside as reserves not open to use. Pinchot made clear his driving purpose for these forests early in the *Use Book*: "Forest reserves are for the purpose of preserving a perpetual supply of timber for home industries, preventing destruction of forest cover which regulates the flow of streams, and protecting local residents from unfair competition in the use of forest and range. They are patrolled and protected, at Government expense, for the benefit of the community and the home builder." With this declaration he placed strong emphasis on what we today refer to as the need for sustainable forestry—"preserving a perpetual supply"—and the ongoing need for water. By also referring to benefits to communities and home builders, he was clearly expressing his core Progressive values: that the forests need to help ensure the well-being of the common people.

After ensuring the needs for timber and water were met, Pinchot set the third aim for the national forests: preventing unfair competition. This idea was significantly influenced by the Progressive movement, to a great extent led by both Pinchot and Theodore Roosevelt. It was largely a response to the extraordinary accumulation of resources and wealth by the few as monopolies became the dominant economic force in the second half of the nineteenth century. Pinchot viewed his greatest contribution and most important legacy as the launching and support of the conservation movement. He viewed conservation as "the most effective weapon against monopoly of natural resources and monopoly of resources is the basis for concentration of wealth in the hands of a few. In a democracy that is the fundamental evil." He was aware that extreme wealth inequality was a direct threat to our democracy. Ensuring that the vast forests in the Northwest remained in the public domain served as a direct challenge to the concentration of natural resources in the hands of the few. Our national forests were resources intended for the many and that could only be realized by making them open to and utilized by the public. Pinchot was consistently against large corporate interests. He wrote: "We who took over the Forest Reserves preferred the small man before the big man, because his needs were greater. We preferred him in honor and in privilege, in principle and in practice. No wonder we had trouble."

Pinchot emphasized "use" when the Forest Service was created, which was a necessity to resist the powerful forces within and outside of Washington, DC, that wanted to crush the fledgling agency. Use, however, was counterbalanced by the need for protection of the resources so that they could be maintained in perpetuity. Toward the end of his five-year term as chief of the Forest Service, Pinchot wrote: "The conservation of natural resources is the key to the future, it is the key to the safety and prosperity of the American people." He understood that the forest was not a crop that could be harvested without regard to the future. He did not view conservation and preservation as antithetical but rather, as complementing each other.

The two men primarily responsible for the conservation and preservation movements that emerged in the late nineteenth century were Gifford Pinchot and John Muir. They first met in 1896 when the young Pinchot was a member of the National Forest Commission. John Muir was not an official member of the commission, but he joined the group during part of its travels through the inland West, the Northwest, south into California, and then east to the Grand Canyon. Muir and Pinchot shared a love of tramping and camping in the forests, which enabled them to develop a friendship based on mutual trust and respect that strengthened as they traveled together with the commission. While Muir was in Oregon with Pinchot, he was quoted by the *Oregonian* newspaper as saying: "Simply withdrawing timber lands from [homestead] entry is only the first step. Something must be done to preserve and perpetuate the forests, for the timber must ultimately be used. The forest must be able to yield a perennial supply of timber, without being destroyed or injuriously affecting the rainfall, thus securing all the benefits of a forest, and at the same time a good supply of timber." This view expressed by Muir in 1896 aligns perfectly with Pinchot's view with an emphasis on use within the context of sustainable practices. Both men were also concerned about the impacts of forestry on water resources and on the climate. Clearly, they were extraordinarily prescient in their recognition of how the forests and the climate are connected.

Char Miller wrote about Pinchot's and Muir's strengthening relationship: "The link was forged not only in their shared concern over the deplorable state of the American forest but in lighter ways as well, most visibly in the adolescent bravado with which they displayed their common enthusiasms. One evening in Oregon when their colleagues chose to sleep in a cabin, Muir and Pinchot bedded down under the stars in a nearby field." Later during the tour, the two spent several days camping together and sleeping out among the junipers and pines in the Grand Canyon, while, again, other members of the commission stayed in a comfortable hotel. For the next decade and into the early years of the Forest Service, both men acknowledged the bond that developed between them during that tour of the West. Miller noted that they continued to draw on the "reservoir of goodwill and intense feeling to sustain cordial relations. Camping was a powerful metaphor for a special kind of male bonding."

What brought the two men together and led to their shared view that the vast forests in the Western half of the United States should remain in the public domain was their recognition that to win public and political support they needed to declare that sustainable logging was a primary raison d'être for establishing the Forest Reserves. At the same time, they were quite different in their temperaments, their social milieu, and their ambitions. Muir was the perennial outsider, while Pinchot was the consummate insider. Muir was fiery and poetic, while Pinchot was highly disciplined and bureaucratic. Muir was, perhaps, happiest roaming alone throughout the high Sierras, while Pinchot was most fulfilled in creating and administering the Forest Service in Washington, DC. Each man learned from the other about sources of power and how to wield power, although they took very different paths, especially after the National Forest Commission concluded its work. Muir relied on the power of the pen and became one of the best-known advocates for preservation of wildlands beginning in the 1890s and continuing until the end of his life in 1914. Pinchot also relied on the power of the pen but used a very different approach; he established within the Forest Service one of the most effective public relations programs in the US government.

Muir, undoubtedly, was quite strategic in his early support of logging in our national forests, as he recognized that a sustainable approach to forestry was far superior to the slash-and-burn techniques that led to devastated landscapes first in the forests of the East Coast and then in the Midwest. Muir's support was also critical to Pinchot as he recognized the immense influence Muir exercised through both the use of his pen and the power of his personality. Their paths did increasingly diverge as Muir aligned ever more strongly with the movement he almost single-handedly created: the preservation movement. What many may not know is that, for the first sixty years of his life, Muir was much more closely aligned with the practice of conservation even before the conservation movement was established and championed by Pinchot beginning in the 1890s. This is clear in Muir's writings: "It is impossible, in the nature of things, to stop at preservation. The forest must be, and will be, not only preserved, but used;

and the experience of all civilized countries that have faced and solved the question shows that, over and above all expenses of management under trained officers, the forest, like perennial fountains, may be made to yield a sure harvest of timber, while at the same time all their far-reaching beneficent use may be maintained unimpaired." While Muir later in his life was seen as the premier preservationist, during his earlier life he clearly championed a sustainable approach to forestry.

At heart, Muir was a rebel. Beginning in his teens, he rebelled against his father; he rebelled against societal expectations to settle down and work, instead embarking on his first 1,000-mile walk; and, finally, after much soul-searching, he rebelled against Pinchot's utilitarian ethic in the early 1900s and instead became convinced of the rightness of Thoreau's declaration that "in wildness is the preservation of the world."

What is surprising is not that the two men eventually became adversaries but rather that they were, early on, truly friends. They came from entirely different backgrounds: Muir, having immigrated from Scotland, lived in a state of poverty during his early years; in contrast, Pinchot, born and reared in one of the wealthiest families on the East Coast, was never concerned with economic security. Both men were highly self-confident, well-read, poised, not easily daunted, self-assured, and rarely in doubt of their ability to accomplish whatever they set out to do. That these two driven and often stubborn men became friends and sustained that friendship over many years is surprising. Neither preservation nor conservation were terms that engaged the public in the nineteenth century. That all changed in the twentieth century and resulted from the different paths taken by Muir and Pinchot.

While Pinchot and Muir were friends and allies for nearly two decades, that friendship came to an end during the Hetch Hetchy controversy. Hetch Hetchy is a glaciated valley close to Yosemite Valley. In the early 1900s, Hetch Hetchy was often compared to Yosemite Valley and viewed as equally worthy of protection. However, after the massive earthquake of 1906, which led to the devastation of San Francisco largely as a result of fires, the city's inadequate water supply system was identified as a chief culprit. Damming the Hetch Hetchy Valley would provide San Francisco with a reliable source for its water needs. The battle over this proposal highlighted the distinct philosophies of Muir and Pinchot, especially their differences on preservation and conservation. Muir declared his fervent opposition: "Dam Hetch Hetchy! As well dam for water-tanks the people's cathedrals and churches, for no holier temple has ever been consecrated by the heart of man." Pinchot, however, supported flooding the valley: "The fundamental principle of the whole conservation policy is that of use, to take every part of the land and its resources and put it to that use in which it will serve the most people." This emphasis on use of the resource over preservation guided Pinchot, especially in his early years as a forester. He viewed the resource first through a utilitarian lens. At the same time, Pinchot frequently expressed appreciation of wilderness values and that the idea of preserving Hetch Hetchy Valley did appeal to him, but the value that guided him most was the greatest good for the greatest number for the long run. Providing water to San Francisco, especially in light of the lives lost and destruction of much of the city due to inadequate water for firefighting, was, for Pinchot, the greatest good at that time.

Pinchot's view of conservation was precedent setting and challenged the dominant approach to resource extraction in the West, which focused almost exclusively on profit with little or no regard to impact on the ecosystem. Pinchot was particularly farsighted in calling for a sustainable approach to forestry at a time when forest resources, especially in the Northwest, seemed limitless. The elasticity of the term "greatest good" allowed Pinchot's followers and later chiefs of the Forest Service to define the term in a way that emphasized what became their dominant value post-WWII: production and use of forest resources. The "long run" perspective, which required seeing the forests as an ecosystem and thinking in terms of hundreds of years, was eventually minimized after Pinchot left the Forest Service and a greater emphasis was placed on these subsequent leaders' view of the greatest good. Rather than protection of the ecosystem, the greatest good became all about maximizing yield.

At the turn of the twentieth century, most of the forests in the Cascades were old growth: magnificent, majestic, live trees; immense dying and dead standing snags that served as critical habitat for a wide variety of species; massive fallen trees that decayed over hundreds of years and supported a wide variety of microorganisms; and toppled trees in creeks and streams that created critical habitat for anadromous fish. Old-growth forests are but one stage in the continuum of the life, death, and rebirth that is the forest cycle. Just as the forest progresses through the life cycle, so too did Muir and Pinchot's thinking about the forest change over time.

In both cases, the men's valuing of the forested landscape evolved as they aged. Early in their lives, both men placed much greater emphasis on the need for timber products. John Muir, in fact, helped run a timber mill in what became Yosemite National Park. In their later lives, both Muir and Pinchot prioritized sustaining the forest resources for the longer term, Muir championing preservation and Pinchot waving the banner for conservation.

4

Creation of the US Forest Service

We are left in awe by the nobility of a tree, its eternal patience, its suffering caused by man and sometimes nature, its witness to thousands of years of earth's history, its creations of fabulous beauty. It does nothing but good, with its prodigious ability to serve, it gives off its bounty of oxygen while absorbing gases harmful to other living things. The tree and its pith live on. Its fruit feeds us. Its branches shade and protect us. And, finally, when time and weather bring it down, its body offers timber for our houses and boards for our furniture. The tree lives on.

—George Nakashima

In the nineteenth century, the United States controlled a vast public resource, land, but lacked a strategic aim for what to do with or how to manage this incalculably valuable resource. For much of that century, the dominant philosophy was one of distribution, from the federal government to private individuals for private gain. Toward the end of the century, two alternative approaches to these lands emerged: preservation and conservation. These views were in opposition to disposal of lands for private use and instead professed that they should, in fact, be kept in federal ownership and thus belonged to the public at large.

Some farsighted statesmen in the late nineteenth century recognized that forests in the Northwest were not an infinite resource as further west was the Pacific Ocean and to the north was Canada. They recognized that, unless this resource was protected, the unthinkable could occur: the nation's woodlands would shrink rather than expand. In addition, they were aware of the avaricious practices of unscrupulous land speculators who sought to acquire public lands through bribes and payoffs.

In the 1870s, a popular nature magazine, *Forest and Stream*, predicted that the United States only had a twenty-five-year supply of timber, based on the rate of logging then occurring across the country. In that same decade, the chief of the Forestry Division, Bernhard Fernow, estimated a fifty-year supply remaining. Some of these writers and professionals were influenced by George Perkins Marsh, who had written about the many harms the environment was experiencing as a result of destructive resource extraction practices. What they failed to recognize or anticipate were the many technological changes that led to less reliance on wood products. Beginning in the early twentieth century, coal and petroleum replaced wood as a heating source. Concrete replaced wood as a building resource. Much more efficient use was made of current wood products such as cre-osoted railroad ties that endured much longer as a product. By the 1920s, the fear of a forest famine had largely disappeared.

The Organic Act of 1897 likely provided Pinchot, who had joined the Forestry Division in 1898, the guidance he had been looking for to open up the forest to development as the act gave the Interior Department the power to "regulate the occupancy and use" of the reserves and opened the door for federal managers to enable grazing, commercial logging, and hydroelectric power generation within these reserves. In many ways, the act also repre-sented the birth of the conservation movement with its focus on utilization of resources in contrast to the preservation movement championed by John Muir that focused on preservation of the resource in its natural state. Con-servationists recognized change as inevitable, while preservationists argued for stasis. The former believed that technology was a good and mankind was the shaper of that good, while the latter believed that nature knows best and that mankind was a disrupter of that good. Conservationists were led by empirically minded Progressives in control of the executive branch, especially Theodore Roosevelt and Gifford Pinchot, in the first decade of the twentieth century, while preservationists followed bearded iconoclast John Muir, who loved nothing more than roaming in the wilderness with little more than a blanket and biscuit. The rationalist vs. the romantic.

Gifford Pinchot can rightly be viewed as the father of the conserva-tion movement with his boss, Theodore Roosevelt, as the symbolic leader. Both men had an enduring love of the outdoors. Each came to that love and appreciation through very different paths: Pinchot as the nation's first forester spent much of his early life in the woods and found contentment in fishing and walking in the primeval forest; Roosevelt, on the other hand, chose to face the challenges of ranching and cattle grazing in the wilds of the open West and found confidence in his capabilities and a physical strength that long sustained him. Both were patricians who could easily have taken very different paths in life and become stewards of their family's wealth, but that would not have satisfied their driving ambitions to blaze their own trails and find their own individual glories.

Pinchot first met Roosevelt when Roosevelt was the governor of New York. Pinchot had been invited to dinner and after some initial getting acquainted conversation found himself invited to a wrestling match. Remarkably, the nation's future president and the nation's first future chief forester engaged in a wrestling match in the governor's mansion. Physically, they were opposites. Roosevelt was short, barrel-chested, stout; Pinchot was tall, lean, and rangy. Roosevelt, with his greater skill as a wrestler and boundless energy and strength, won the match. Later, Pinchot challenged Roosevelt to a boxing match, and with his greater skill as a boxer and his longer reach, he won. These early encounters—rare even for two men in the nineteenth century, much less wealthy aristocrats—endeared them to each other early in their relationship and led to enduring mutual admiration and respect.

Pinchot worked assiduously to gain Roosevelt's support and advocacy of the conservation movement and succeeded. Both men believed that the great outdoors was what shaped the "rugged individualist" on which the greatness of their country was founded and which would ensure its continued greatness. Facing and surmounting the challenges of the outdoors developed the kind of character they highly valued: men who were independent, driven, ambitious, tough. For Pinchot, the greatest good was never limited to ensuring a sustainable supply of forest products for the country. Like Roosevelt, he viewed these protected lands as essential to the building and development of the quintessential American character, fearless in the face of adversity, a striver never satisfied with the status quo, a seeker always pushing into the unknown frontier, and a steward of the matchless landscapes the country offered him.

Both men were champions of the Progressive movement, which provided the umbrella under which the conservation movement grew and flourished. Both held a strongly meritocratic perspective that what mattered most were one's capabilities, one's achievements, one's merit, not the nature of one's birth or wealth and inheritances. All the people in their country had the right to these lands; wealth should never be a requirement. Pinchot and Roosevelt were convinced that democracy itself was dependent on people who could handle whatever hardships they might encounter in the natural world. These hardships transformed us into the kind of people needed to sustain their country—strong of body, mind, and spirit.

Theodore Roosevelt established the US Forest Service in 1905 and appointed Gifford Pinchot as the chief forester. Pinchot was determined to transform the widely-held view that federal bureaucrats were simply feeding and enriching themselves at the expense of the public coffers. His aim at the outset was to create an agency that would be trusted by its citizens to act in the interest of the common people, not the interest of the monopolists. In his autobiography, Roosevelt praised his chief forester: "Gifford Pinchot is the man to whom the nation owes most for what has been accomplished as regards the preservation of the natural resources of our country. He led, and indeed during its most vital period embodied, the fight for the preservation through use of our forest. . . . He was the foremost leader in the great struggle to co-ordinate all our social and governmental forces in the effort to secure the adoption of a rational and far-seeing policy for securing the conservation of all our natural resources."

While Pinchot was several levels below Roosevelt on the federal organization chart, from a policy perspective he served as the head of both the Departments of Agriculture and the Interior. Roosevelt viewed Pinchot as one of the most influential members of his administration. This is evident when he wrote of Pinchot that "among the many public officials who under my administration rendered invaluable service to the people of the United States, he, on the whole, stood first." These are exceptional words of praise from a man who could have recognized many other leaders in his administration, yet he chose Pinchot. These words of admiration resulted not only from the close friendship that evolved between these two men that had begun with a wrestling match, but also from recognition of perhaps the most significant accomplishment of Roosevelt's time in office: safeguarding an extraordinary amount of public land. Working together, Roosevelt and Pinchot increased the national forests in size from more than 46 million acres to nearly 151 million acres, protected in 159 units from the Atlantic Ocean to the Pacific, from the country's border with Canada to that with Mexico.

From forest reserves to Forest Service. A tripling in size of protected lands within a span of a few years. What, then, to do with this vast resource?

When Pinchot became the first head of the US Forest Service in 1905, he wrote what became the agency's guiding light:

> In the administration of the forest reserves [the forest reserves were renamed national forests in 1907], it must be clearly borne in mind that all land is to be devoted to its most productive use for the permanent good of the whole people; and not for the temporary benefit of individuals or companies . . . the policy of this department for their protection and use will invariably be guided by this fact, always bearing in mind that the conservative use of these resources in no way conflicts with their permanent value. . . . You will see to it that the water, wood, and forage of the reserves are conserved and wisely used for the benefit of the home-builder first of all, upon who depends the best permanent use of lands and resources alike . . . and where conflicting interests must be reconciled the question will always be decided from the standpoint of the greatest good of the greatest number in the long run.

The actions of forest supervisors and district rangers in charge of millions of acres of woodlands were shaped to a great extent by the key tenets of the Progressive movement—that government policy must be designed to protect the small landholder, the small business owner, the laborers and employees rather than the owners of capital, the holders of great wealth, the monopolists that controlled entire industries. In one of my interviews with Pinchot's grandson, Gifford Pinchot III, he summed up well his grandfather's contribution: "Gifford Pinchot's contract was about social benefits and about this generation and future generations." As a Progressive, Pinchot railed against special interests and those who had special privileges as a result of their wealth. He believed strongly that people should be able to advance their interests based on their merits and what they had to offer society and not on what they inherited.

Most of Pinchot's convictions and actions can be readily viewed as a response to his Progressive philosophy, which viewed the land grabs of the nineteenth century and the cut-and-run operations of the fly-by-night timber operators as antithetical to his American idea of fairness. The "big men" were despoilers of the natural world. Pinchot believed in use of the forest, and he equally believed in long-term sustainability. Unlike the vast majority of western resource extractors who were solely takers, Pinchot both took and gave. He knew that taking for the short term was entirely dependent on giving back to the forest to ensure the long term.

Pinchot felt strongly that officers, hired based on their merits, not politicians, should decide how to manage the nation's forests. In his 1905 letter declaring the mission of the Forest Service, he refers to effective administration and management and makes clear his belief that sound science and sound administration would ensure a sustainable forestry. In his eyes, a primary function of the "greatest good" in the early 1900s was to ensure that people could build and own their own homes. This was a cornerstone of his Progressivism— that economic development of the country, a healthy democracy, and home ownership all benefited from the efficient and fair use of wood resources.

Especially in his early writings, Pinchot only infrequently referred to non-commodity uses of the forests, and that reflects both that he was a product of his times and his knowledge that many powerful forces were arrayed against his beloved Forest Service. Forests for recreation purposes, for aesthetic appreciation, for spiritual succor was simply not a priority for most of the public during the early years of the twentieth century; those values were not a reflection at the time of the "greatest good." Yet Pinchot did recognize that those values and beliefs could well change. He wrote in his 1920 book *The Fight for Conservation* that new policies may be needed to reflect changing public priorities and that the "Public welfare cannot be subserved merely by walking blindly in the old ruts. Times change, and the public needs change with them."

While Pinchot clearly believed that the dominant role his national forests played early on was to ensure a sustainable production of wood products, he also recognized that a different perspective and a new consensus could emerge. Charles Wilkinson in *Crossing the Next Meridian: Land, Water, and the Future of the West* stated that a new perspective could emerge as "long as the later generation would comply with the unwavering rules of Pinchotism—retention of public forest in federal ownership, conservation for yet more generations, and distribution to a broad range of people, not just large economic interests." Throughout his life, Pinchot acted on the basis of what was morally right. The Progressive movement was an enlightened approach to the more equitable distribution of natural resources. He fervently believed along with Theodore Roosevelt that without the intervention of government, ruthless monopolies would control the vast natural resources of the nation, especially timber. The end result of that control, he was convinced, would also result in colossal waste of those resources, and their destruction. Thus, those monopolies not only threatened the natural resource base of the country; they also threatened the foundation of a prosperous democracy.

5

The Custodial Role

Forests mend and shape themselves through subterranean synapses. And in shaping themselves, they shape, too, the tens of thousands of other, linked creatures that form it from within. Maybe it's useful to think of forests as enormous spreading, branching, underground super-trees.

—Richard Powers

For nearly four decades—although it was keen to show that active forestry could help the economy especially in rural communities—the Forest Service primarily took on a stewardship role in its management of Northwest forests. The seeds of change for the later radical transformation of the Northwest forests were planted in 1903, when Edward T. Allen, then an employee of the Bureau of Forestry, produced the first assessment of Douglas-firs, *Red Firs in the Northwest*. He observed that the Douglas-fir was not shade tolerant and thus grew most rapidly in areas that had been clear-cut; that growing Douglas-firs in clear-cuts would achieve the greatest production of wood; and that, given that their growth rate was greatest in their first hundred years of growth, he recommended that they be harvested on a ninety-year cycle in order to achieve the maximum yield from Northwest forests.

One of the first Forest Research Centers was established in the southern part of what later became Pinchot's namesake forest, then called the Columbia National Forest near Stabler, Washington. The focus at the outset was on Douglas-fir as this tree type was highly prized for building, whereas Western hemlock, another dominant species in the region, was considered weak in comparison to the straight-grained wood of Douglas-firs. Also, Western red cedar was considered inferior. As a result of being largely clear-grained and structurally superior, old-growth Douglas-fir soon established itself as the most valuable timber resource in the country, with Washington state as the number one producer because of its vast reserves.

Thornton Munger, as one of the first forestry researchers in the Pacific Northwest, built on the work begun by Edward T. Allen. He examined the regeneration of forests after massive forest fires. One of those fires, the Yacholt Burn occurred in 1902 in the Columbia national forest and burned nearly 100,000 acres. In *Forest of Time: A Century of Science at Wind River Experimental Forest*, Margaret Herring and Sarah Greene write that "The forest management Munger envisioned would mimic the way forest has established blocks of young trees that were all the same age and all the same size and that would eventually be harvested all at the same time." This view of forest management by Munger was based on his observations of how forests regenerated after forest fires.

Munger was convinced that this approach to management of timber in the Northwest would lead to more productive forests than the ones they replaced. Of course, this view rested entirely on the production of timber. Other known values, whether protection of water supply watersheds, habitat for wildlife, providing for recreation, species diversity, or aesthetics, received little consideration even though the 1897 Organic Act did emphasize protection of water resources. Munger's plan for management of national forests throughout the Pacific Northwest soon became the norm. This norm, which later resulted in massive clear-cuts and burning of the remaining vegetation and woody debris, was followed with little deviation for the next eighty years. Munger, however, failed to understand how fires and other major disturbances changed the forests. True, in some areas that experienced fire, trees of uniform size and age grew in those newly opened areas. However, most fires left a diverse mosaic of some patches of forest that were untouched, while other areas were only partially burned. The result was a landscape that was highly diverse in the ages, species, and spacing of trees. Munger focused primarily on the results of severe burns where almost all trees died and left large openings. However, for most forest fires in the Northwest this kind of severe burn typically affected only 30–40 percent of forests. Thus, this heavy emphasis on clear-cutting was based on a misunderstanding of the true impact of fires and forest regeneration.

Herring and Greene write that Munger's disdain for old-growth trees and his advocacy of intensive forest management is clear: "There is little satisfaction in working with a decadent old forest that is past redemption and calls for nothing but removal." Perhaps no other word shaped foresters' views of Northwest forests for almost a century than this idea of old-growth trees as "decadent." Decadent primarily refers to that which is in a state of decay. How ironic, then, that these massive trees, many of which were 8 to 12 feet in diameter and often 250 feet in height or taller, were viewed as decadent. Another meaning of decadence is to fall from grace. From the foresters' perspective, these old-growth firs, which had fallen from grace, need to be literally fallen and cut down across the landscape to achieve more productive growth.

These early foresters seemed unable to see the forest for the trees. The forests in the Northwest were among the most majestic and impressive in the world. For many, especially Native Americans, they evoked feelings of the sacred, feelings of respect for their grandeur, of beings reaching high into the firmament, closer, yes, to God. Almost all societies have great respect for their elders. These old-growth forests were our elders, yet foresters like Munger did not view them that way. During this early period of the Forest Service, most foresters saw only the utilitarian value of these extraordinary forests. Emotional connection seemed to be missing.

Another way to view this failure is to recognize the primacy of the utilitarian philosophy—*use* above all other values. Many of these early foresters seemed to feel little wonder in the presence of these astonishing old-growth forests. Rather than cherish these elders of the woods for their fortitude, for their strength, for the ability to withstand hundreds of years of wildfires, raging storms, terrible droughts, many felt scorn. Munger's disdain for anything in nature other than productive stands of timber can most readily be seen in his depiction of snags, standing dead trees: "They stand, fringing the skyline like the teeth of a broken comb in mute defiance of wind and decay, the dreams of the former forest, useless to civilization and menace to life of man and of forests . . . snags serve outlawry, yet they continue to practice murder and incendiarism on millions of acres of fertile Douglas-fir land. The day will come when snags are banished altogether from Douglas-fir logged off land." So disdainful of snags was Munger that he directed research dollars to discover the most effective way to remove them from the forests. He quickly settled on the use of dynamite to eliminate this "nuisance" of the forests.

During the first nearly forty years of the Forest Service's existence, the federal forested lands under its control were, in essence, a custodial forest, with the agency acting as the chief custodian. The forests were essentially treated as a protected reserve. This virtually passive management resulted from both the long-standing concern that a forest famine was imminent and a covert agreement with commercial forestry not to compete so that prices for timber coming off private lands would remain high. At the beginning of the twentieth century, the total production of timber products nationally was about 7.2 billion cubic feet and reached 9.2 billion cubic feet a decade later. In 1920, when national timber harvest reached an all-time historic peak of 40 billion board feet, the national forest contributed only 480 million board feet—a little over 1 percent of national production. After the Roaring Twenties, the Great Depression ensured a much lower level of production as demand for timber products dropped precipitously.

For most of this custodial period, timber harvested by the Forest Service averaged around 1 billion board feet annually. This annual harvest represented only 2 percent of the total timber supply nationally. The intention of most foresters working for the Forest Service during this period was to begin the transformation of the national forest from a natural forest to a managed forest. Little change in fact resulted, due primarily to two causes: private timber companies seeking to minimize competition with the USFS and the Great Depression.

6

The Struggle to Make Conservation Work

Among the Douglas Firs

Why is it
that one tree dances
while another,
mere feet away,
stands still?

Is it something more
than the vagaries of wind,
the differing shapes
of their branches?

Is it the way
their spray of needles,
like outstretched palms
cup the breeze?

Or is it just
that just like us
some have
at one time
or another
more of
an inclination
to move
To a rhythm
all their own?

—Joseph Bruchac

Early in Pinchot's years as a forester, he witnessed significant corruption within the federal government, especially in those agencies charged with protection of federal lands, and was determined to create an agency that possessed the highest level of integrity. He wanted an agency that worked to benefit the common people, not the elite. As a Progressive, Pinchot was focused not only on how to manage our national forests as a resource that would help rural communities prosper but also on a wider range of public concerns, including "the regulation of public power, the management of water resources, the prohibition of alcohol, the development of farm to market roads, and the improvement of rural life." Each of these concerns was a significant element in the Progressive movement.

Pinchot had witnessed the plight of rural communities that suffered as a result of cut-and-run forestry: homeless men, ghost towns, devastated landscapes. He wanted an agency that would achieve the opposite: healthy, long-lived communities surrounded by ever productive forests. He thus saw the Forest Service as a tool for social reform, one that would combat the evils of monopolies. Pinchot wrote: "Monopoly on the loose is a source of many of the economic, political, and social evils which afflict the sons of men. Its abolition or regulation is an inseparable part of the Conservation policy." Pinchot was strongly driven by that which he considered to be morally right—that the Progressive movement was an enlightened approach to achieve a more equitable distribution of natural resources. Nothing less than a prosperous and well-functioning democracy was at stake.

This intention to use the Forest Service as an instrument for social reform placed Pinchot and the Forest Service in the crosshairs of numerous groups who saw their own interests in jeopardy: cattle and sheep grazers who wanted unlimited access to public lands for their stock animals; prospectors who wanted unregulated access to mining opportunities; loggers who wanted to cut wherever and whenever they wanted; and, finally, many who were opposed to the entire concept of conservation. In their eyes, conservation was simply a cover for the federal government to control this hitherto wide-open resource, and thus restrict what private citizens could do with the land. Under Pinchot's leadership, the Forest Service viewed itself as the most effective arbiter in determining the public good.

One of the chief characteristics of the various federal agencies created during the Progressive Era was that in contrast to the politicians and industrialists who had influenced the federal government and its agencies in the nineteenth century to meet their own selfish needs, many of this new breed of executives, were, like Pinchot, technically trained and guided by reason and science as opposed to politics. Of course, Pinchot understood the role of power and politics. As a counterbalance, he strongly believed that as trained experts his agency would place a primacy on serving the public good. Pinchot also championed the values of efficiency and productivity that were gaining popularity in the industrial realm. Success was thus dependent on the training and employment of highly dedicated public servants like himself, who understood both the management and ecology of natural resources. While scientific management was the means for Pinchot, the result he was striving for was a healthy democracy with a more equitable distribution of wealth.

Pinchot made a strategic choice that came naturally to him given his utilitarian perspective. While he appreciated the diverse ecological values of the forests and their subtle aesthetic and sacred qualities, he recognized that these values were not shared by many of his peers or the public, especially in those early years of the Forest Service's life. Thus, he championed *use* as a primary means of assuring the survival of the agency he birthed. Use became the dominant focus of the newly trained foresters. Forest Service chiefs after Pinchot paid less attention to his guiding philosophy of sustainable forestry, giving much more attention to economic forces. They wanted to ensure that forestry paid its own way. For Pinchot's successors, economic forces were more powerful than ecological ones. These economic forces reinforced the technocratic training and scientific management approaches that the early Forest Service adopted.

Many of this first generation of foresters trained under Pinchot had every intention of righting the wrongs of those who came before them. These professionally trained foresters went into the woods and relied on scientifically informed management practices designed to achieve sustainable yields of timber. They were determined to do the right thing as they were inspired by Pinchot to provide the greatest good for the greatest number in the long run. In most cases, however, they lacked the science-based evidence that later researchers discovered about the ecological functioning of the forest.

Like Pinchot, many of the early foresters were trained based on European practices in which the ideal was a waste-free, well-regulated forest. European forests were more typically well-ordered and intensively managed with ongoing pruning and removal of fallen limbs from the forest floor. With this model of a healthy forest, early foresters viewed old growth as nonproductive, as decadent, and thus a forest that needed to be transformed. This transformation would surely lead to a well-managed, more productive, more vigorous forest.

Part of the blame for the production-oriented mindset of the Forest Service may be attributed to Pinchot and the influence of the *Use Book* on his followers. While he emphasized the need for a "perpetual supply of timber," a competing concern was that early foresters sought to maximize productivity, likely driven by their fear that supply would soon fail to meet demand. The solution—set harvest levels based on potential annual growth of a young and vigorously growing forest. To achieve this ideal required the liquidation of the old-growth forests.

At the turn of the twentieth century, over 70 percent of western forests were old-growth stands, which early foresters viewed as "decadent and over-mature." For them these forests were terribly wasteful and needed to be cut down so that the European model of an orderly, well-regulated forest could take its place. Nancy Langston in *Forest Dreams, Forest Nightmares: The Paradox of Old Growth in the Inland West* writes: "The best way to free up the land for timber production was to cut the old timber as quickly as possible, which meant pushing sales. This logic shaped a Forest Service that, in order to protect the forest, believed it necessary to first remove it."

A reliance on the seemingly clear rules of science, an unwarranted confidence in their knowledge and expertise, and the very enthusiasm and high energy that Pinchot viewed as key to success blinded these foresters to the untended consequences of their actions. They were intent on reproducing the kind of forestry that prevailed in Europe where old growth was practically non-existent. How ironic then that European foresters who visited the United States were some of the first to recognize that the prevalence of old growth in America made these forests unsuitable for the kind of forestry practiced in Europe. The result of this intent to adopt the European model was catastrophic: significant devastation of one of the most impressive, extraordinarily productive, and complex ecosystems on the planet and one that today we understand to store more carbon on a per-acre basis than any other ecosystem on the earth.

The early-twentieth-century practices of scientific management, which viewed waste and inefficiencies as abhorrent, led foresters to ignore the very qualities of old growth—complexity, messiness, disorder, decay—that are, in fact, integral to the healthy functioning of these forests in the West. Early foresters viewed old growth as an obstacle in the way of the needs of a healthy, productive forest, one that was young and vigorous. Langston captures well this fallacy: "Foresters' faith in competition theory was inextricably linked to their fear of waste and their desire for efficiency. These assumptions made it difficult for foresters to imagine that insects, waste, disease, and decay might be essential for forest communities; indeed, that the productive part of the forest might depend on the unproductive part of the forest."

The inherent complexity, messiness, and chaotic nature of old growth forest was ignored. The dominant narrative at work that shaped the practices of these early foresters was one that convinced them that they knew best how to redesign a more efficient and productive forest. Langston clarifies well how this narrative came to dominance: "Foresters were not, as many environmentalists claimed, greedy or stupid. Like everyone else, they needed to hold onto a story that made their lives make sense. Their work was based on the faith that they were making the forest better. If they let themselves see the evidence in front of them—that the forests were dying, not getting better—they would have to give up the vision that made sense of their lives. Instead, they blinded themselves to the consequences of their actions, ignored the doubts that crept in, and condescended to people who challenged their vision of the forest."

The move away from Pinchot's emphasis on sustaining yield for the long run began around 1925 when a new formula was developed for determining sustained yield. Langston identified this new formula, "which included a combination of annual growth increment plus orderly liquidation of a portion of the old growth. This represented the beginning of a shift in emphasis from regulating timber yield to regulation of the growing stock of the national forests; in other words, the Forest Service began thinking less about managing natural forest and more about converting natural forest into timber plantations." This was a momentous shift in how the Forest Service viewed its mission. Langston went on to note that: "Actual measurements of growth increment became less important than *theoretical calculation of the growing capacity of a fully regulated forest* (author's emphasis). Striving to achieve maximum potential yield became the new goal, and natural forests were accordingly seen as an impediment." Natural forests needed to give way to managed forests.

On the wetter west side of the Cascades, a fully regulated forest meant, over time, a forest dominated by plantations of even-aged trees, primarily Douglas-firs. This was counter, however, to what Pinchot advocated as he recognized that even-aged management created sterile, uniform-looking forests that had little aesthetic appeal for most Americans. Pinchot did not believe in clear-cutting as the primary harvesting tool. Rather, he called for selective cutting in which some trees ready for harvest are logged and others are left behind for regeneration purposes.

While many view Pinchot solely as one most interested in extraction, in logging, in use, this view is misguided. His recognition of the many attributes of the natural forest are clearly evident here:

> The forest is the most highly organized portion of the vegetable world. It takes its importance less for the individual trees which help to form it than from the qualities which belong to it as a whole. Although it is composed of trees, the forest is far more than a collection of trees standing in one place. It has a population of animals and plants peculiar to itself, a soil largely of its own making, and a climate different in many ways from that of the open country. Its influence upon the streams alone makes farming possible in many regions and everywhere it tends to prevent floods and drought. It supplies fuel, one of the first necessaries of life, and lumber, the raw material, without which cities, railroads, and all the great achievements of material progress would have been either long delayed or wholly impossible. . . . The forest is as beautiful as it is useful. The old fairy tales which spoke of it as a terrible place are wrong. No one can really know the forest without feeling its gentle influence as one of the most elemental parts of nature. From every point of view, it is one of the most helpful friends of man. Perhaps no other natural agent has done so much for the human race and has been so recklessly used and so little understood.

One of the great ironies of the Forest Service is that while Pinchot's disciples greatly revered him, the actual practices of the agency over time diverged significantly from his guiding philosophy.

The Forest Service developed quite quickly a strong, proud, cohesive, and effective culture that was largely a result of Gifford Pinchot's leadership. Even though Pinchot served for only five years as the chief forester from 1905 to 1910, the structures and practices he put in place along with his personal integrity, passion, care, presence, and even love for the agency continued to be felt for decades after his formal departure. Few, if any, leaders of federal agencies during this period achieved this kind of extraordinary legacy.

Organizational cultures are primarily a result of strong leadership, especially at the top. What leaders do, model, pay attention to, reinforce, and punish determines the nature of organizational culture. And strong, cohesive cultures will only form if leaders throughout the organization are likewise aligned on what they do, model, pay attention to, reinforce, and punish. That certainly was realized during the early years after the founding of the Forest Service.

The Forest Service was exceptionally effective in building strong identification with its mission and practices by its members. This was largely accomplished by a set of actions and practices that Pinchot put in place: clear employee selection criteria (selection especially was seen as critical; people had to pass civil service exams that determined cognitive and administrative capabilities, but also show physical capabilities such as horse riding and packing a horse, use of compass, skills with an ax, capability with pistols, setting up camps, and living in wilderness conditions) and promotion criteria, ongoing development as leaders and foresters, reliance almost solely on internal promotions, frequent transfers from one national forest to another, use of symbols and uniforms, and ongoing and frequent engagement of field staff by headquarters in the development of policies and procedures.

These early rangers were an odd mix of well-educated graduates from Yale School of Forestry and young, often idealistic frontiersmen looking for a stable job in the out-of-doors. In many ways these men (and they were all men) were a bureaucratic analogue of Roosevelt's Rough Riders. While they viewed Pinchot as their ultimate boss, they also were aware of the close relationship between Pinchot and Roosevelt and thus felt some connection through him with their president. While the historical Rough Riders experienced their popularity a decade earlier, like them, many of these early rangers felt a strong bond with their peers and commitment to an organization with a mission they strongly identified with. Gerald Williams in *The United States Forest Service in the Pacific Northwest* describes how the values of these rangers were a mix of "individualist spirit and progressive ethos, part nineteenth-century American and equally of the regulatory world that succeeded it. Often living as wilderness men on the fringes of established society, foresters embodied order, they determined the legality of land claims and uses, and they usually had the character to enforce their decisions. As such, foresters were an eclectic combination of scientists who understood the language of conservation and frontiersmen who could communicate with the most remote of homesteaders."

Gifford Pinchot put in place a highly decentralized organization that was a necessity given the highly dispersed geographic location of the national forests. Herbert Kaufman in *The Forest Ranger: A Study in Administrative Behavior* describes well the culture that emerged as one where people in the organization had "the capacity and willingness to adhere to a preformed decision announced by the leadership. Without realizing it, members of the Forest Service thus internalize the perception, values, and premises of action that prevail in the bureau; unconsciously, very often, they tend to act in the agency prescribed fashion, because that is the way that has become natural to them. Everywhere, they encounter men with similar interests, similar problems, similar objectives, similar aspirations, similar complaints. They find understanding and appreciation of their problems. Their ties with their fellow officials are multiplied and deepened. As they become part of the organization, the organization becomes part of them."

One of the early challenges that Pinchot recognized was that his staff would become overly identified with local people and their concerns. While he wanted his staff to be responsive to their concerns, first and foremost he wanted them to be responsive to the mission of the Forest Service and to understand that these are *national* forests, not local, state, or regional forests. The agency early on relied on rotation of personnel to address these competing needs of identifying with local interests while attending to national interests.

During these early years in which the Forest Service established its strong and cohesive culture, it continually and frequently referred to the mission of managing for the greatest good of the greatest number in the long run. Pinchot's guiding creed was inevitably referred to and highlighted in virtually every interview of people looking to join the service. Kaufman recognizes Pinchot's influence on the emerging culture: "One of the striking conclusions about the Forest Service is the degree of similarity among the men in it—their love of outdoor life, their pride in the Forest Service, their habit of taking the long view of things: their patience; their acknowledgment of their obligation to the local uses of the national forests; their enjoyment of the variety in Ranger district administration as compared with the narrower scope of industrial forests; their willingness to do more than is legally required of them in order to get their jobs done."

One direction the early Forest Service took directly countered the meaning of the forest as a place for rest. Centuries earlier in England, forests provided a refuge, a place for rest, not only for people but for many of the wild animals of the realm. The Forest Service took a diametrically opposite stance toward wildlife on federal lands, where many animals at the top of the food chain were exterminated. To a large extent, this was done to appease stockmen, who viewed coyotes and wolves as vermin that killed their sheep and cows. Data was always important to Pinchot as it enabled him to be accountable to the public he served. From the daily diaries the rangers maintained, Pinchot was able to boast about what 51 of them had accomplished over a total of 170 working days in 1909: they had "destroyed 108 bears, 96 mountain lions, 144 wolves, 62 wolf pups, 3,295 coyotes, 571 wildcats, and 81 lynx." As many of these predators threatened domestic sheep and cattle, probably most people in nearby communities, especially those dependent on grazers, viewed these "destroyed" animals as a positive outcome.

One of the administrative tools used to ensure integrity and account-ability and which was highly significant in ensuring adherence to cultural norms was the use of periodic, highly detailed, and thorough inspections of each unit of the national forests. These inspections were conducted to ensure conformance to Forest Service norms, policies, and procedures and more than any other tool or method had tremendous impact on the actual behavior of rangers in the field. Kaufman wrote that "taking the whole gamut of national forest administration tasks as its subjects, it reveals whether an organizational unit is administered in accord with policy, and whether everything that could be done is done." Pinchot was determined that the Forest Service as a government agency be viewed as a model for all other agencies as a result of its integrity, openness, transparency, and accountability. He especially was concerned during that first decade of the twentieth century to distinguish the honesty and efficacy of the Forest Service from its predecessor, the General Land Office in the Department of the Interior. His predecessor agency was rife with corruption, self-dealing, and dishonesty; the Forest Service was thus established to stand in stark contrast to that dishonorable reputation.

These periodic inspections identified some of the early challenges faced by the Forest Service as the agency worked to establish its authority over public lands, which, not surprisingly, was resisted by users of the forest who up to that period had largely unfettered access to its resources.

Regarding a request to build a summer camp on Spirit Lake near Mount St. Helens in Pinchot's namesake forest, an early inspection report notes, "No one person should be given absolute perpetual control of any specific tract on the lake." This statement strongly communicates the extent to which Pinchot's mission for the Forest Service—greatest good for the greatest number for the long run—had become embodied in the mindsets of its people. The forests are intended for the people, the communities, not for the benefit of individuals. And the notion of giving perpetual control of this resource was anathema as needs may change and the Forest Service needed the authority to respond in the long run to those changing needs.

Regarding a request to build a hotel at Government Mineral Springs in the southern part of Pinchot's namesake forest, another inspection report noted: "The property is becoming more and more popular each year because of the known medicinal properties of the Spring water. I believe that instead of being a menace to the Forest, the establishment of a hotel at the Soda Springs would really be a protection if we continue to allow the pubic to use the water at all." Again, the reality of providing for the greatest good as criteria for decision-making is clear. Here was a highly valued resource, mineral waters, which were thought to possess medicinal qualities. To provide ready access to that water the Forest Service agreed to allow a hotel to be built near the mineral springs. The inspector specifically mentions "protection" based on allowing public access. A reasonable question arises: what does he see being protected? The springs? The surrounding old-growth forest? The unintended outcome of his decision led to the protection of an extraordinary low-elevation old-growth forest.

Some years after the hotel was built, structures known as "recreation cabins" were built in this old-growth forest. For a short period of time beginning in the late teens, a number of these cabins, including my own, were built across the West to enable increased access to our national forests. This too was considered part of the greater good. This particular forest, much of it now protected from logging because of its status as the Trapper Creek Wilderness, would most assuredly have been logged had that hotel, and later the recreation cabins, not been built and the mineral springs not protected. Low-elevation drainages such as these were the first to be logged given their ease of access and the quality of wood within.

Regarding trail building, one inspection report describes in much detail an early trail located in the midsection of Pinchot's namesake forest: "The Morrison Creek Trail extends from the Deadhorse Ranger Station to the Gotchen Creek Ranger Station, distance of about fifteen miles. It is poorly blazed, and therefore very hard to follow. The grades, in places, are hard on both a man's nerves and a horse's endurance." Beyond dealing with grazing, much of the early focus of forest rangers was on building trails designed to enable access to the forest. This work was not done by the Forest Service employees but rather by temporary laborers. Here we see not only the attention to detail so characteristic of these early inspection reports but also the humor and forthrightness of the inspectors themselves. They had very high expectations and communicated them through these reports while also showing humility and a self-deprecating sense of humor. Later, the same author commented on the Trout Creek Trail: "In places the earth has worn away from the roots of the bordering trees. Many of these roots project from the trail for six or eight inches and are a menace to horse and rider. These should be removed. The trail should be brushed out and during the coming season, corduroy placed in four marshy holes. These holes are at present in very bad condition." Again, we see this considerable attention to detail and direct assertions on what needs to be done to correct the situation.

Illustrative of the inspector's attention to mission alignment, one inspection report noted, "Each man takes a thorough interest in his work and shows a particular loyalty of the Forest Service . . . most of the guards are thoroughly conversant with Forest Service regulations and the requirements of the Use Book." The inspection reports also contained detailed descriptions of each of the forest rangers and their staff. These assessments were derived from both on-the-ground observations and reviews of daily diaries the staff members were required to maintain. In the vast majority of cases, the inspections provided exemplary descriptions of rangers, although inspectors were quite willing to point out exceptions: "Diary of Dickerson seemed to show a lack of plan and thought in laying out his work . . . seems to go out on trail work in the morning and putter around headquarters in the afternoon . . . spends time chopping wood and inconsequential occupations." In another case, a forest guard was described as having "little knowledge of Forest affairs and seems to have done but a small amount of work to earn his salary. . . . I was not favorably impressed." With another guard the Inspector wrote: "He is very fond of the authority of his position and uses it to great excess . . . he is unpopular with his fellow employees and with the settlers in his district . . . he is very profane and is said to have an abnormal liking for intoxicants. . . . As for his capabilities as a drinker, I cannot vouch, however, his intense profanity was particular exasperating to me."

From a 1922 inspection report of Pinchot's namesake forest: "In the distribution of the Supervisor's time, the various activities appear well balanced. I was disappointed in the appearance of the immediate surroundings of the St. Helens Lookout Houses. . . . It looks as if the custom has been to simply open the door and throw things out. . . . The ranger's office does not present as business like an appearance as I should like to see. To be sure it is a combination of living room and office but that it seems to me there is too much litter on the tables and shelves." Here we see leaders being reprimanded for modeling carelessness in both how they dispose of waste and trash and how they maintain their office/living quarters. Neatness, thoroughness, care of one's place were all expected of these leaders, and inspectors were quite willing to communicate these expectations as they knew how important these leaders were to a culture that, while evolving, would meet the expectations of the man who created the Forest Service, Gifford Pinchot.

Conservation of resources at the turn of the twentieth century was not a well-understood concept by most of the public. Rather, use of resources and the view that resources, especially forest resources, were infinite was the dominant paradigm. Pinchot set out to change that viewpoint by creating an agency that championed sustainable use of the nation's natural resources, an agency that recognized limits, that recognized that forest resources were not infinite. To ensure the long-term health of rural communities in the West, to ensure the well-being of the "small man," he created an agency that he hoped would model and practice conservation over the long term.

7

Tensions: Stewardship or Production

Nature is not more complicated that you think, it is more complicated than you CAN think.

—Jack Ward Thomas

Three years after the US Forest Service was established, the Columbia National Forest was formed in 1908, largely from the southern portion of the Cascade Reserve, covering just under 1 million acres and bounded by the Columbia River to the south, Mount Adams to the east, Mount St. Helens to the west, and Rainier National Park to the north. Three people were responsible for the Columbia National Forest—a forest supervisor, his assistant, and a clerk. Virtually no roads passed through these lands north/south or east/west.

During these early years, public use of the Columbia National Forest was quite limited. Native Americans continued their traditional gathering of huckleberries west of Mount Adams. Some prospectors worked mining claims near Mount St. Helens, although with little success. The most significant use of the land at that time was by sheepherders who brought thousands of sheep from lower areas near the Columbia River to high mountain meadows for summer forage. Loggers, who had moved from the Midwest and lived in camps along the southern edge of the forest, cut timber for houses back east.

The rangers who came to work in the Columbia National Forest soon after the founding of the Forest Service were focused on basic tasks: building ranger stations, developing trails, establishing communication systems, determining boundaries of the forest, learning who had an interest in the national forest—for example, grazers, miners, and loggers—and beginning the on-going work of silvicultural assessments. During this first decade of the twentieth century, rangers on the ground, foresters in the supervisor's office, leaders in the district offices, and the senior leaders working under Pinchot, the chief, were almost all aligned on the few essential aims during these early years of the Forest Service's existence: clarifying how forestry should be practiced; establishing mutually respectful relationships with people in nearby communities and other stakeholders; and increasing and strengthening support with allies in Congress. A key element of Pinchot's strategy to build support in Congress relied on his highly effective public relations capabilities. He wrote in 1905, "we must make the necessity for forest preservation a household commonplace throughout the US."

The effect of Pinchot's declaration in 1905 to manage the national forests for the greatest good in the long run can readily be observed in a 1907 report by an early Forest Service leader in the Northwest: "It will be more desirable of the Service to be able to say that it has done its best to preserve the supply of timber than to say that it paid its expenses." This leader went on to write: "The final aim, even though its accomplishment may be a long way ahead, will be the placing of the forests on the basis of a sustained annual yield." One can almost hear the phrase "in the long run" as he later in the report stated: "Fifty years from now it seems to me that the question will be asked whether the Forest Service conducted its cuttings in a way which was best calculated to maintain the supply of timber, and not whether their return equaled the cost of maintaining the Service . . . the people are looking to the National Forests to preserve a perpetual supply of timber for home industries." Sustainability of the resource, in this forester's eyes, had primacy.

One of the early Forest Service supervisors in Pinchot's namesake forest, while leading a training session, referred to the classic story where several men building a wall were asked what they were doing. The first said he was laying bricks, the second said he was building a wall, while the third said he was building a cathedral. The supervisor then asked: "Has that any application to our jobs? Are we working for a dollar and a half a day or are we helping to grow timber to the best of our ability for the next generation, WHICH?" This conception, of working for the next generation, was prevalent among many of the early rangers and supervisors—they held to the founding ideal of serving with the long term clearly in mind. For the first forty years after its founding, the Forest Service did act first and foremost as stewards, as if they were guided by a preservationist ethic.

In a 1909 memo to a district ranger in the Northwest, Pinchot clearly declared his intention that national forests be managed in a sustainable fashion: "The removal of our mature timber in an amount approximately equal to the growth must not be had at the expense of future growth." In contrast to this principle was a competing need to demonstrate to Congress that the national forests were contributing to local economies if not the national economy. In his memo Pinchot also stated, "There must be immediate and material increase in receipts from the National Forests," and he noted: "At present much more timber is rotting in the woods each year than is being cut. We could cut, with entire safety to the forests, about eight times as much timber per year as we are cutting now . . . the Service has no task more urgent before it, from now on, than to get mature timber into use through timber sales." These competing needs in response to competing values and especially in response to a demanding Congress in many ways reflect an enduring dilemma faced by the Forest Service. Most often the agency viewed this situation as a zero-sum game with winners and losers. This was, perhaps, one of the most significant mistakes the Forest Service made during its early years that had tragic consequences much later. The results could have been much different had the agency approached the situation not as a problem to solve but as a dilemma to manage.

One of the most significant dilemmas faced by the Forest Service during this stewardship phase from 1905 was what to do with old growth. In 1914, the agency identified three classes of timber: immature, mature, over-mature. Terms like "old growth" or "ancient forest" as descriptions of what the Forest Service described as "over-mature" were not used at the time. During the stewardship phase until the end of WWII, the notion that old growth in the Northwest would ever be seen as threatened—that is, greatly reduced in size, because it was so extensive—was quite mistaken. Old-growth trees were the dominant trees throughout the Cascades; they appeared to be an infinite resource, especially to the vast majority of people living in the region. In such vast numbers, covering hundreds of square miles, how could these trees ever risk being greatly reduced in numbers?

The foundation, however, for transformation of a landscape dominated by old growth was laid in the first fifteen years of the Forest Service's life even though that transformation did not begin until much later. During the five years while Pinchot was chief of the Forest Service, and while forestry practices on the ground were still in development, the primary emphasis for the national forests in the Cascades and in Pinchot's namesake forest in particular was on a conservative approach, stressing conservation rather than exploitation of the resource. In a 1908 letter, the acting forester in the Columbia National Forest asked about his district ranger's thoughts on "the advisability of establishing a minimum limit of stand per acre below which no cutting, except of dead or insect infested wood be allowed." He wrote that he wanted to, from the best information available, "adopt a clear-cut, thoroughly practical policy in the management of timber on each National Forest or group of Forests." District Ranger Cox stated that because "the cut should never exceed the producing capacity of the Forests—a conservative policy is advisable." He went on to ask, "if timber is sold what percent of the estimated stand can be cut without detriment to the Forest?"

In an early 1909 letter, an assistant forester in Pinchot's namesake forest confirmed the primacy of sustainable forestry: "It is optional with us whether we make a sale or turn it down, but it is mandatory that we care for the forest to the best of our ability." Care for the forest—such a notion would have been considered absurd prior to the founding of the Forest Service, especially among the small numbers of people living in the Northwest who viewed the forest as boundless and as a resource that could be exploited endlessly to meet critical needs, whether building a cabin or providing heat. This assistant forester further noted, "Sales in excess of annual growth should be made only when necessary to prevent loss, as from insects, over maturity . . . unnecessary waste hastens a timber shortage," and finally, "The silvicultural needs of the forest must take precedence over the desire of the purchaser." This perspective, which dominated these early years, was representative of foresters who saw themselves as stewards, as the few who recognized how valuable this resource was and how quickly it could be exploited. For most of these foresters, protection of forest resources was the highest priority in contrast to many of the users of the resource who were mostly concerned with exploiting it. These early foresters were critical in establishing Pinchot's legacy, that production must always be achieved in the context of the long-term health of the forest.

Sustainable use of natural resources was viewed as essential to enabling economic development during this period, development that benefitted the common citizen and that would ensure future prosperity. While many leaders of the Progressive movement did not view Native American peoples in high regard, they unknowingly adopted a long-held belief among Native Americans, that current decisions should be made in light of their impact seven generations out, what was right in the long run. The effectiveness of the conservation movement resulted from both this new approach to forestry and the effectiveness of the public relations arm of the Forest Service. Roosevelt recognized this link in his autobiography: "The conservation movement was a direct outgrowth of the forest movement. It was nothing more than the application to our other natural resources of the principles which had been worked out in connection with the forests. Without the basis of public sentiment which had been built up for the protection of the forest, and without the example of public foresight in the protection of this, one of the great natural resources, the conservation movement would have been impossible."

What Pinchot accomplished in the early years of the twentieth century was breathtaking: an addition of nearly 150 million acres protected as national forest, about three-quarters of the current total. Rarely has one person had such influence on shaping the landscapes across wide swaths of a country. Charles Wilkinson in *Crossing the Next Meridian: Land, Water, and the Future of the West* captured well Pinchot's many facets: "One can string a bevy of adjectives, each accurate, to describe Pinchot—brilliant, patrician, knowledgeable, manipulating, charismatic, arrogant, and savvy all come to mind. . . . Pinchot's policies were so forceful that he managed to offend nearly every private group, from ranchers to timber companies to preservationists. But whether he had to go around or over his opponents, he achieved most of his goals."

After the founding of the Forest Service, lands were soon classified as either reserves or lands for timber production, grazing or wildlife. While recreation was acknowledged, it was far less important than commercial use of these public lands. What took precedence in Pinchot's mind and what he championed during his five years as chief were what he took away from his schooling in France as the United States' first forester: the importance of scientific, sustained yield and effective timber management. Little attention was given to aesthetics, to planting of trees along roads, to gardens that might highlight native species, or to creation of parks designed around preservation of a special landscape.

The relationship between the Forest Service and communities close to national forests, especially in the Northwest, was greatly influenced by the US Congress in the early twentieth century when it mandated that counties that had much of their land base taken over as national forest receive 25 percent of receipts for timber sales. This revenue could be used for development of roads, building of schools, and support of law enforcement agencies. This revenue-sharing policy fit well within the Progressive movement of economic development of rural communities so that the common citizen would benefit. Congress took this action in recognition of the loss of taxable lands. This policy in turn provided a powerful incentive for timber-dependent communities and their congressional representatives to encourage large timber sales. The larger the timber sale, the more revenue for the county and the less need to tax its citizens. This policy, enacted soon after the creation of the Forest Service, led to the development among forest-dependent communities of an implicit social contract between these communities and the Forest Service. This contract implied a never-ending flow of timber and thus a never-ending flow of revenue to these rural counties. A symbiosis emerged between the giver, the US government, and the taker, these small counties and communities.

One of the first forestry schools in the western United States was the School of Forestry at the University of Washington in Seattle, a school largely funded by monies from the timber industry. C. S. Judd, the assistant forester for the Northwest region, told the incoming class of forestry students in 1911 that a timber famine was on its way unless the Forest Service took quick action. Since the forest would soon be running out of trees, the fix was to enable trees on national forestlands to grow quicker. Judd declared, "The good of the forest demands that the ripe timber on the National Forest and above all, the dead, defective, and diseased timber, be removed"; and to accomplish this, the agency needed to "enter the timber sale business and heavily promote sales." Behind this drive to increase sales was the need to log the old growth and "free up the land for new crops of timber for future supply." This was a message that forestry schools preached for many decades and one that foresters accepted as gospel. From the perspective of adding more annual mean increment, this made perfect sense. From the perspective of maintaining a well-functioning ecosystem, it was a disaster.

A foundational concept that guided the actions of the Forest Service from its founding to the present day was that of the "allowable cut." Allowable cut answered the simple question, how much timber could be cut on the forest while enabling sustained yield harvests? David Clary in *Timber and the Forest Service* clarifies the concept: "Theoretically, allowable cut was determined by finding the maximum volume that could be harvested periodically in perpetuity. That required a knowledge of the total amount of timber on hand, the age at which a species reached its maximum growth, and the typical rate of replacement of a harvested tree by a seedling."

Because of the concern in the early decades of its existence for ensuring a perpetual supply, the Forest Service recognized that the private timber industry was cutting timber on their lands beyond what was sustainable. Knowing the importance of the industry to the economy, especially of the Pacific Northwest, the agency acknowledged and accepted the importance of stewarding the forest resources under their control. Early foresters' view was that someday the private timber products industry was going to realize that it had eaten its seed corn and would turn to the USFS to meet the nation's needs for wood products. The other driving force behind Forest Service policies was its view of what at the time was referred to as over-mature trees. In fact, old-growth trees represented about 70 percent of the forest on Pinchot's namesake forest at the time of the founding of the USFS and even higher percentages on other national forests in the Northwest. The percentage of old growth on the Columbia National Forest was lower than other national forests in the Cascades as the Columbia National Forest had experienced several catastrophic fires shortly before and after the founding of the USFS.

Foresters did not understand old growth as repositories of diversity. The focus of these early foresters was almost entirely on volume. David Clary in *Timber and the Forest Service* elaborates on this view: "If the national forests were to hold only 'over-mature' timber when the 'timber famine' struck, they could only stave off disaster until they also had been consumed. If, however, the national forests contained mostly fast-growing trees that were approaching maturity, sustained yield would see the nation through." With the best of intentions, Forest Service staff in the Pacific Northwest developed a conviction that, although it would not be acted on until after WWII, led to the transformation of one of the most wild and glorious habitats on earth, the ancient forests of the Pacific Northwest.

Simply put, the transformation was from a natural forest to a managed, highly regulated forest.

Webster's Dictionary defines decadence as a state of decay, decline, and deterioration. Decadence was more often used to describe societies or groups of people that had fallen from a state of grace. Fallen is the key word here. To transform such societies, those fallen from grace needed to be replaced by the virtuous to allow for renewal. Old trees needed to be logged and replaced by young, fast-growing trees. This view honed foresters' attitude toward the old-growth forests that dominated the landscapes of the Pacific Northwest.

The foresters of that early era were convinced that they had the requisite knowledge and skills to make the forest as productive as possible. This conviction was strongly reinforced by forestry schools. Likewise, early foresters were convinced that they knew how to make the Northwest forests grow faster, better, smarter: remove the old growth from the landscape as quickly as possible as those forests represented inefficient systems. These early foresters assumed that older trees had stopped growing and were convinced they could engineer much more productive forests that would produce wood fiber for lumber and pulp like the most finely tuned factory. Henry Graves, who succeeded Pinchot and served as Forest Service chief until 1920, gave this perspective a solid footing as emerging policy. He wrote in his annual report: "Virgin forests are merely reservoirs of wood . . . production can be secured only by converting (old-growth forests) into thrifty, growing stands through cutting . . . the timber sales policy aims, therefore, as the first requirement of good management, to work over the old stand on the National Forests, utilizing mature timber . . . and putting the ground in such condition that forest production will be renewed at a much faster rate." "Work over the old stand," which meant eliminate all the old growth, became the operative policy for most of the twentieth century.

The chaotic, messy, ugly, snag-filled ancient forests would be replaced by neat, virile, hardy, young forests. And, assumed the Forest Service, the timber famine would be avoided. Home industries would be saved from want. Forest Service leaders believed an admiring public would come to appreciate this foresight. Chief Forester Graves sought the transformation of an ecosystem that in its way was as significant as the transformation from feudal societies to industrialized societies. What was missing from this sought-after transformation was an appreciation of ecological, cultural, recreational, or spiritual values. This mindset that championed a wholesale transformation of the dominant landscape throughout the central Cascades was not acted on during the first forty years of the custodial phase of the Forest Service's existence. Those prevailing beliefs about the decadence of the forests, which were taught at forestry schools and professed as policies by the Forest Service, were not put into operation until after WWII.

The hotel at Government Mineral Springs, early 1900s. The presence of the hotel was likely key in protecting the old growth in the Trapper Creek Wilderness. *GPNF image.*

A log drive in the Gifford Pinchot National Forest, Wind River. In the early years of logging this was an easy way to move logs to the mills. *GPNF image.*

Breaking up a logjam in Trout Creek, Gifford Pinchot National Forest. In describing the effect of these when Gifford Pinchot first practiced forestry in North Carolina, Carl Schenck noted that they typically resulted in significant damage to the streambed. *GPNF image.*

A lookout tree in the Gifford Pinchot National Forest. *GPNF image.*

A huge old-growth ponderosa pine in the Gifford Pinchot National Forest. *GPNF image.*

The very early days of logging: two loggers on springboards some 10 feet above the ground are cutting a notch in a massive old-growth tree. *GPNF image.*

In 1937, Gifford Pinchot toured many of the western national forests and expressed his view (as noted by Char Miller in his biography of Pinchot) that "clear-cutting of some western forests was neither scientifically justified not politically acceptable." *USFS, Grey Towers, NHS. Courtesy of the US Forest Service.*

Gifford Pinchot: his trademark hat and a full mustache were part of his public persona. *USFS, Grey Towers, NHS. Courtesy of the US Forest Service.*

8

Setting the Stage for Liquidation of Old Growth

Trees with trunks three feet in diameter generated three times as much biomass as trees that were only half as wide. So, in the case of trees, being old doesn't mean being weak, bowed, and fragile. Quite the opposite, it means being full of energy and highly productive. This means elders are markedly more productive than young whippersnappers, and when it comes to climate change, they are important allies for human beings.

—Peter Wohlleben

Reliable records on the amount of logging in Pinchot's namesake forest begin in the early 1920s. For the first half of that decade, 17–18 million board feet came off the Columbia National Forest annually. That number dropped into the low teens in the second half of the 1920s and remained at that level into the early years of the Great Depression. After Franklin Roosevelt came into office in 1933, the numbers dropped even further and reached their nadir in 1934 at the height of the Great Depression when under 100,000 board feet were removed from the Columbia National Forest. The numbers did not exceed the highest level of production in the 1920s until midway through WWII when 29 million board feet were removed. Much of what little timber did come off Pinchot's namesake forest was a result of clear-cutting.

Based on the early studies conducted by Edward T. Allen, one of the early Forest Service researchers, the Forest Service understood that Douglas-firs were shade intolerant, and thus concluded clear-cutting was needed for effective propagation. Because hemlock, a less merchantable tree, seeded itself in the rich humus forest floor, Allen recommended as well that all slash and debris be burned after logging. The Forest Service assumed that the greatest volume of timber from the forest could be obtained by clear-cutting roughly on a ninety-year cycle. The old needed to be eliminated to make way for the new. Decadence needed to be replaced with vigor. Through death would come a faster-growing forest. However, a complex, diverse forest would be transformed into a simple monoculture, a crop.

Research conducted as early as the 1920s, however, began to raise alarms about the impact of clear-cutting on the reproduction of Douglas-firs. Natural regeneration was not as successful as hoped. By the 1930s, researchers discovered that a "reforestation crisis loomed in the most heavily logged areas of the Douglas-fir region . . . these finding pointed to one conclusion: unregulated clearcutting with modern over-head logging systems posed a threat to the perpetuation of the forest and the timber economy." In 1938, J. V. Hoffman's earlier theory of natural regeneration, which stated that clear-cuts and burning of leftover slash would lead to quick regeneration of Douglas-firs, was thoroughly repu-diated with the publication of Leo Isaac's "Life of the Douglas Fir Seed in the Forest Floor" in the *Journal of Forestry*. His research confirmed that clear-cuts depended on seed trees to reestablish the forest. Foresters also discovered that the practice of leaving several seed trees per acre was ineffective as those trees were often blown down in windstorms and their production of seeds was highly variable from year to year. To achieve effective reforestation, groups or strips of trees were needed to optimize their ability to withstand strong winds and reduce damage from logging or slash fires. In addition, the traditional practice of slash burning, which foresters had assumed was effective to seed generation, was discovered to be actually counterproductive. Slash burning, in fact, damaged the soil and reduced its capacity to promote the growth of seedlings.

One of the Pacific Northwest foresters during this period, Walt Lund, participated in an oral history project and personally observed the dilem-mas faced by the Forest Service in trying to determine how best to manage the forest. He stated: "During the late 1930s we went from clear cutting to the tree selection method of cutting, but that did not pan out well as many of the remaining trees died—some blew over and it was a slow and expensive process. We had to go out and map the area, locate trees that were going to be cut on the map. So, we began patch cutting—clear cut-ting, using the cable system, whatever we could reach within that system. So, you would have a patch of clear-cut areas. Earlier whole drainages were cut, and we wanted to avoid that. We tried to use seed trees—two trees per acre but they often blew down, so we abandoned that method." Trial and error were the methods of the day. At the time no one was certain what was the optimal method for timber management in the Pacific Northwest. Clear-cutting, though, was emerging as the easiest and most efficient way of maximizing cut of timber off the forest.

Pinchot was never a fan of clear-cutting. Decades after he left the Forest Service, when he returned to the Pacific Northwest, he was shocked by the devastation he observed and wrote in his diary, "The Forest Service should absolutely declare against clear-cutting in Washington and Oregon as a defensive measure." He also believed that even-aged management created sterile, uniform-looking forests that held little aesthetic appeal for most Americans. Rather, he advocated for a selective approach to logging—later called "uneven-aged management"—in which some trees are harvested and others left behind either for future harvests or for purposes of regeneration. This method was distinct from "high-grading," which led to taking only the most valuable trees out of the forest, leaving only poorer specimens for regeneration. This latter approach was one that foresters frequently encountered in the early years of forestry.

Clear-cutting of our national forests was not suddenly terminated in response to the Forest Service's own research. As often happens, research results are ignored, buried, or simply become "pine riders," unread and gathering dust on a bookshelf in a back office. During the stewardship phase, which lasted until WWII, clear-cutting, although it did lead to some objections among motorists who began to tour around the forests in greater numbers in the 1920s, was applied over many hundreds of miles. For the first forty years of its existence, Forest Service harvest level rarely exceeded 1.5 billion board feet of timber and averaged less than 1 billion board feet annually. About 125,000 acres were cut yearly during the stewardship phase—less than one-fifth of one percent of the 75 million acres of the national forest's commercial timberland.

While they were a small minority within the ranks for the Forest Service, some rangers began advocating that some parts of the country's national forests be protected forever as wilderness. These rangers recognized that while these special landscapes may not warrant protection as a national park, they did contain attributes that made them special and worthy of protection from the chainsaw. To the majority of Forest Service personnel, this idea was anathema as the ethic of use gained stronger and stronger credence. Inventory of roadless areas larger than a quarter-million acres began in 1926. Whether this resulted from the advocacy of those few calling for wilderness protection of some lands or was simply a matter of classification is unclear. The predominant view, however, was that wilderness designation would be unfair to those rural communities dependent on national forests for timber and grazing resources.

In the 1920s, as the automobile became more accessible and affordable, sightseeing became popular. A Sunday drive out of town became a prized leisure activity. For the first time, families could drive several hours from their town or city and visit national forests. Motorists thus became increasingly alarmed and dismayed at encountering vast clear-cuts rather than scenic landscapes—regardless of whether these were private or public lands. Cut-over forests did not appeal to those seeking recreation opportunities, whether they were sightseeing, birding, hiking, hunting, or fishing. For an agency that placed the greatest emphasis on use and paying its own way, this presented a real dilemma.

The solution soon developed by the Forest Service was to hide their clear-cuts. The agency not only resolved to leave linear strips of uncut trees along roadways, but they were also determined to make the linear strip itself even more aesthetically pleasing. In a 1921 letter, an assistant forester wrote, "It is seldom, if ever, the case in the virgin forest that the landscape architectural value of the strip cannot be improved by the removal of unsightly trees or trees which will become unsightly (snags, broken topped or badly diseased trees, hopelessly over-mature trees) before there is much probability of securing their removal after the present cutting." The values for many in the Forest Service are clear in this assessment. Snags and broken-topped trees serve no purpose. Old growth, which is "hopelessly over-mature," serves no purpose. What does serve the prevailing purpose are young, fast-growing, straight trees with no imperfections. These early foresters were unaware of the many critical functions that snags and broken, rotting trees and, especially, old growth play in a well-functioning forest ecosystem.

Given this objection to seeing large swaths of the landscape as clear-cuts, the ready solution was the adoption of a policy of leaving uncut strips of land along public highways and Forest Service roads. These linear uncut parcels of land were initially called "leave strips." That term was later changed to "beauty strips," and finally the agency settled on the term "visual buffers."

Burned-over forests also upset the sightseeing public. Unlike clear-cuts, which could be hidden by visual buffers, thousands and thousands of acres of burned-over public lands could not be readily hidden. Uncontrolled fires represented not only a danger to households and communities close to national forests but also an existential threat to the Forest Service itself. What the agency lacked was the scientific understanding that fires were integral to the health of the ecosystems of the Pacific Northwest. This was simply part of the natural cycle.

For over twelve thousand years, Native Americans had lived in the Pacific Northwest. Native Americans were not threatened by fires; they understood not only that fires were part of the natural cycle, but that they could use fires to their benefit. Low-level fires helped create a mosaic of grasslands and forests and the kind of habitats that sustained Native American economies, traditions, and livelihoods. Fires were also used to maintain berry patches and camas fields in western Oregon and Washington. The Division of Forestry and then the Forest Service, however, only saw fires as a threat. One result was what became known as the 10 A.M. policy. Any fire that was identified on day one should be extinguished by 10 A.M. on day two.

Pinchot recognized fires as a well-wrapped Christmas gift. Fighting fires served as a highly visible vehicle for building public support for his agency. He proclaimed to the public that no one in their right mind would ever view and treat passively a fire burning in their city. No, they would fight it with every available resource. Why, then, should we treat our national forests differently? These valuable resources, critical to the well-being of the home builder and rural communities dependent on forest resources, needed protection as well. And, Pinchot argued, the Forest Service was the only agency prepared to take on that mission.

Two years after the agency's founding, Pinchot declared: "I recall very well indeed, how, in the early days, forest fires were considered simply and solely as acts of God, against which any opposition was hopeless and any attempt to control them merely hopeless and childish. It was assumed that they came in the natural order of things, as inevitably as the season or the rising and setting of the sun. Today we understand that forest fires are wholly within the control of men." His rangers were up to the challenge; they had the will. But they would need the resources, the tools, the capability to get the job done.

This need for forest resources provided Pinchot a highly effective vehicle for countering the naysayers in Congress. What congressman, who hoped to stay in Congress, especially in the West, would tell his constituents, Let it burn! Practically, none. To fight fires effectively required the building of infrastructure including trails and roads for access, telegraph and telephone lines for communication, lookout towers for early detection, and rangers and people on the ground able to act quickly and decisively before the fires grew out of control. Timothy Egan in his book *The Big Burn* captured well this newly developing purpose of the Forest Service, that catastrophic fires "gave the foresters exactly what they needed and what their critics lacked: a magnificent story, folk heroes, a drama so elemental it became its own morality play. The emerging story of dedicated fighters battling for the nation's interest made for a vivid conservation message."

This approach, which made so much political sense during the first several decades of the twentieth century, became entrenched Forest Service policy. Smokey the Bear became the Forest Service's symbol for the importance of preventing forest fires, "Only YOU can prevent forest fires." This view of putting all fires out as quickly as possible served an important public relations purpose. The Forest Service was greatly rewarded for putting the fires out, and that policy gained tremendous public and political support. Fighting fires was heroic. Only much later, as with so many aspects of forest management, would the agency recognize that fires serve a vital role in well-functioning forest.

From its founding in 1905 until the Great Depression, the Forest Service engaged in extensive analysis of its holdings of millions of acres of largely old-growth forest in the Northwest and how to shape policy regarding treatment of this extraordinary resource. In 1914, Chief Graves recommended that "In order to maintain the Forests producing timber perpetually . . . is to hold the limitation (of cut) at their present figure except when revisions are necessary." At this early date, debates were already occurring on what to do with old growth. The higher value that provided the guiding light on what to do on the ground, at that time, was "producing timber perpetually." In Pinchot's namesake forest, soon after the establishment of the Forest Service in 1905, the limitation of annual cut was described as no more than .5 percent of the total acreage. Later, in 1911, the limitation of cut was set at 40 million board feet and then in 1914 at 118 million board feet. In 1924, the limitation of cut increased to 196 million board feet, and by 1939, that number became 325 million board feet. One can reasonably ask the question, how did Pinchot's namesake forest, over that twenty-eight-year period, become so much more productive? By greatly increasing the potential level of cut, the seeds were being planted for a transformative future.

In 1914, when Gifford Pinchot was still a symbolic presence in the agency, the guiding policy was a conservationist one: ensure this resource continues to provide good for the long term. Twenty-five years later, Pinchot's legacy was more like that of a ghost. He hovered above the agency, was still revered as its founder, but he was no longer the presence he was in 1914 but rather a revered founder who could be readily ignored. The times had changed and so did the Forest Service. Pinchot's vision of sustainable forestry, while still inscribed in pamphlets and on the agency's walls, was increasingly becoming a historical artifact—something to be preserved, like an insect in amber, but kept on a shelf in the backroom and ignored.

Pinchot's strong early influence even after his departure from the agency he created can be seen in a letter, written in 1911 by a Forest Service leader in the Northwest, George Cecil. In discussing how to ensure the agency achieved Pinchot's vision of providing for the long run, Cecil wrote: "We must look into the needs of the future and exercise the greatest care in adopting a method at the start which we believe will produce the best result. Communities will depend upon the National Forests for a steady supply of timber, and if we cannot meet this demand, we shall have failed in our mission . . . the ideal management should aim to establish small mills in various parts of a National Forest, to each of which is tributary, enough timber to supply it indefinitely." Cecil made clear that conserving for the future was the most important aim. By doing so, the Forest Service could meet the Progressives' goal of ensuring a healthy economy for the common citizens as mills in rural areas would forever have a steady supply of timber. At this point in time, no thought is given to either old growth or forest productivity. Rather the guiding force is still Pinchot's mission of the greatest good for the greatest number in the long run.

Something changed for forester Cecil over the following ten years. Old growth came into his sight, although not as something to be preserved. In 1924, he wrote, "It should be remembered, however, that after the surplus is removed the sustained cut must come down to the normal annual increment . . . that so long as there exists a large acreage of surplus stock in old mature timber the normal increment could not be realized in full. In other words, for some of our forest, it is an overestimation to state that we can realize all the potential normal increment annually now and at the same time realize annually a large cut of surplus growing stock." A non-forester may be forgiven for having difficulty making sense of Cecil's declaration. Yet making sense of this statement is critical, as it, along with others, set the stage for the elimination of most of the old-growth forests in the Northwest. Cecil is still concerned about the long term, the "perpetual supply," which he makes clear when he refers to the need to realize the "normal increment" annually. This future need to realize the normal increment will only be realized by removing the surplus. Surplus in Cecil's declaration equates with old growth. Removing the old growth translates into a higher level of annual cut, which, he is acknowledging, cannot be sustained. Implicit in his note is the belief that by removing the "old mature timber," the stage will be set for a more productive forests as the surplus will have been eliminated. Surplus is wasteful. Surplus was anathema to an agency that prided itself on efficiency. To do what is right for the forest, the agency concluded that it must first cut down the old-growth forest.

The Forest Service, however, faced significant obstacles to doing so during the stewardship phase, as acknowledged in a 1910 letter from Cecil Park to a Northwest ranger regarding management of the Columbia National Forest: "The present annual cut is very much lower than it should be, in fact amounts to almost nothing. There are two factors: the present market conditions and the inaccessibility of practically all of the timber in this forest." These two realities mitigated against higher levels of annual cut in Pinchot's namesake forest for the next three decades. Market demands were being addressed by logging from private timberlands, and private landowners did not want that reality to change. Also, access to much of the national forests was extremely poor. Roads into the interior of remote forests like the Columbia National Forest were almost nonexistent.

Leaders in the early Forest Service expressed both awe and frustration about the extent of old growth. In 1926, E. A. Sherman wrote: "The aged veterans go down and young ones spring up and, in the long run, it holds its own. If it is not touched for 100 years, there will be still 35.5 billion board feet of timber, but gentlemen, we could sell 500 million feet of timber every year and as long as the sun shines and the rain falls, and during the next 100 years, that we could have 50 billion board feet and, at the end of that time still have the equivalent of the original stand untouched. It is like your corn field. You can have a crop each year, but if you don't use your field every year, you have not gained anything." The stands of old growth that early Forest Service leaders assessed seemed to them almost limitless. Even though they were foresters and not farmers, some adopted the mindset of farmers. Of course, a farmer who planted corn and then let it go unharvested at the end of the season would be thought either mad or foolish. Some of these early Forest Service leaders viewed their early failure to harvest much old growth as similarly foolish. They ignored the ecological services provided by these rich, complex, multilayered, towering old-growth forests. Lack of access and poor market conditions ensured during the stewardship phase that the many diverse and important ecological services provided by old-growth forest such as watershed and stream protection, which safeguarded habitats for species ranging from salmon to spotted owls and marbled murrelets, were not significantly degraded prior to WWII.

Market conditions for wood products were healthy throughout the 1920s and were met primarily by private interests. Market conditions changed significantly with the onset of the Great Depression. The difficult economic conditions faced by the country were the primary reason little timber was cut on national forestlands throughout the 1930s. In 1931, less than 5 percent of the total timber cut in Washington and Oregon originated in the national forests.

The desire to cut old growth became stronger and stronger throughout the 1920s as Forest Service leaders became ever more convinced that their duty was to ensure ever more volume to meet what they were sure would be increasing needs, needs that could not be met in the future by private interests. One agency leader from the Northwest noted in 1931: "It is the business and duty of the Forest Service to grow timber to provide for the future needs of the country . . . that few will deny there is now a vast amount of forest land covered with forest which is stagnated and either making no growth or actually losing in volume . . . that decay is in excess of 30 percent of the total volume . . . that it would be good business to salvage such stands so that those areas may be restocked with young and thrifty growing timber." This forester's frustration is evident.

He wanted to get the cut out. As a "scientific forester," he was appalled at the "waste" his forest was experiencing. This forester, however, lacked a true understanding of forest ecology, which would not be realized until many decades later.

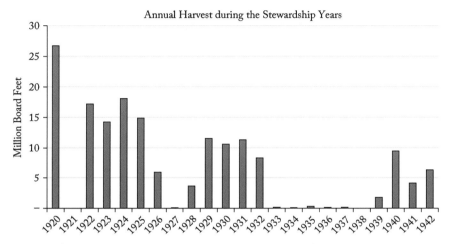

Figure 1. Annual harvest during the stewardship years on the Columbia National Forest (later renamed the Gifford Pinchot National Forest). From USFS, Region 6. (Note: no data reported for 1921 or 1938)

Part II

High Production:
The Death of the Forest

9

The Beginning of Production

Any fool can destroy trees. They cannot run away; and if they could, they still would be destroyed—chased and hunted down as long as fun or a dollar could be got out of their bark hides, branching horns, or magnificent bole backbones. . . . God has cared for these trees, saved them from drought, disease, avalanches, and a thousand straining, leveling tempests and floods; but he cannot save them from fools—only Uncle Sam can do that.

—John Muir

By the late 1950s, general inspection reports for the Gifford Pinchot National Forest, which were often forty to fifty pages in length, had transformed into a "Summary of Information" put out by the supervisor of each national forest. Outside audits were a thing of the past. Now high-level summaries, typically one-third the length of the general inspections, with pictures of people recreating in the forest and of changing timber practices, took the place of outside audits. These summaries, which emerged out of the general inspections in the later 1950s, continued to provide data regarding allowable cut and actual cut, miles of road constructed, and miles of trails constructed; but rather than serving as a tool for ensuring accountability, they now served primarily as a public relations document. The summaries for the Gifford Pinchot National Forest stopped reporting one critical piece of data by the late 1960s, allowable cut, the level of cut beyond which even the Forest Service acknowledged was beyond what was sustainable. For the first time in the history of Pinchot's namesake forest, the actual cut began to exceed the allowable cut.

The 1947 general inspection of what was then the Columbia National Forest was conducted by L. K. Mays. In the opening paragraph of his summary, he extolls the Columbia as "one of the most fortunately located national forest in the region. It covers both sides of the Cascade Range from the foothills of Mount Rainier south to the Columbia Gorge. It has west-side Douglas-fir, alpine, and east-side pine types. Manufacturing facilities for its timber products are close to the forest boundaries on the west and south. The Columbia River . . . provides two shipping ports. . . . Rail transportation north and south parallels the western side of the forest, and a water-grade rail route up the Columbia Gorge permits a rate differential east that no other large Douglas-fir area has." What is especially notable in this first paragraph of his summary is that Mays is emphasizing the commercial potential of this forest, not the extensive old growth, not the aesthetics of mountain ranges and volcanoes, not the extent of wildlife. He goes on to write, "The value of forest resources is always increased by nearby agricultural lands" and that "abundant hydro-electric power, favorable climate, suitable topography, and good transportation all point toward rapid industrial development of southwestern Washington. Demands on forest resources will increase tremendously. The Columbia National Forest's timber, water, recreation, and other values can contribute much to local, regional and national wealth."

General inspection reports for the Columbia National Forest had been generated by outside auditors for nearly forty years. This was one of the first to connect the Columbia National Forest (soon to be called the Gifford Pinchot National Forest) with the wealth of the country. We can see here the shift that was occurring within the Forest Service from valuing conservation as a first priority to valuing production and economic development as a first priority. Mays makes this transformation clear in his next paragraph: "The job of managing the Columbia National Forest is rapidly changing from protection of an inaccessible virgin backwoods to the intensive management of forest lands adjacent to a heavily populated industrial zone" and that "Timber management planning, administration of timber harvesting, access road planning and supervision, and fire protection of cut-over areas are in the 'spotlight' on the Columbia." He further noted that "most rangers are well aware of the new trends" and that they are "constantly improving logging practices and utilization."

Rarely does one encounter such an explicit description in the transformation of the culture of a federal agency. Two key phrases are distinctive in this general inspection: "inaccessible virgin backwoods" and "intensive management." The first phrase was the on-the-ground reality that had existed not only for the first forty years of the Forest Service's existence but also since time immemorial. The second phrase, "intensive management," was not an on-the-ground reality but rather an aspiration if not a measurable objective. One reflected the past, the other the future. The practices of the past, such as "diary analysis," however, still continued for the time being. Cultural transformation is messy—some practices are held onto while new ones emerge. Why change what has always worked; diary analysis was a primary tool for ensuring staff were carrying out and meeting their duties and responsibilities as expected.

In Mays's general inspection, he identified excessive travel by rangers, as reported in their diaries, as an area of concern. He writes, "This is a difficult problem to solve, but careful planning should combine trips of two or more officers, reduce the number of trips necessary and provide for efficient travel to the Mount Adams and Wind River district whenever possible." Further on, he notes: "Over-the-weekend trips or stops on the forest by regular forest officers are practically non-existent. It would seem good practice for staff officers and rangers to occasionally spend Saturday and Sunday out in the campgrounds, huckleberry fields, logging areas, and with the guards and take time off some other days in the week if they prefer." Again, we see the old attention to detail, to the value of connecting with the public, the real customers of the forest, and with other national forest staff, the guards. These audits were highly unusual and exceptional for an agency of the federal government. They were not in the nature of reports from government agencies, which most often were simply about data; these reports reflected the kinds of assessments that were later conducted by for-profit organizations intent on addressing not only revenues and profit but also employee engagement and fulfillment and the power of the brand. The general inspection reports that had been generated for Pinchot's namesake forest and all other national forests for many decades, and which were far ahead of the best practices later adopted by Fortune 500 companies, sadly, were being discontinued. By the latter half of the 1950s, they had disappeared. And with their demise, so too did the old culture die.

In his 1947 general inspection report, Mays analyzed extensively the silvicultural practices on Pinchot's namesake forest. One of the ongoing concerns was the extent to which regeneration of the forest occurred naturally after clear-cuts. Mays reported: "There is some sentiment on the forest here as on other districts visited to discount the theory that natural regeneration inevitably follows clear-cutting where a seed source is readily available. Some of the men on the Columbia are inclined to believe that immediate and positive regeneration would be established by planting without waiting for several years to see if nature will do the job." Many Forest Service personnel who spent years in the forest relied on their observations and experiences, and one of the realities becoming increasingly apparent was that some clear-cuts were not naturally regenerating. In some cases, seed trees were left to increase the likelihood of natural regeneration, but often those seed trees, which were lone sentinels in the clear-cuts, were blown down in storms. The workers on the ground had a clearer picture of those results than professionals like Mays. They recognized that in many cases tree planting was key to regeneration after clear-cuts.

Mays reported that because much of the forest in the Columbia National Forest was found in large isolated units, extensive and expensive development work was required, that is, roads and bridges to access those isolated stands of timber. He noted that big decisions needed to be made regarding the when and where of construction of roads, bridges, and culverts. These kinds of decisions were largely absent from earlier general inspections, but now they were seen as critical to developing the forest so that the amount of timber cut on the forest could increase significantly. Toward the end of his report he writes, "Close attention is being paid to raising the cut on each working circle to its sustained yield capacity and in maintaining that level of production indefinitely." During the stewardship phase of the national forest, the allowable cut was viewed as a maximum that the Forest Service should never exceed as higher levels of cut would not assure an ongoing supply of timber for the long run. The allowable cut was not viewed during the stewardship phase as a goal to be reached but rather as a ceiling never to be exceeded. Now, with the focus on production, the goal became to achieve a level of logging that equaled the allowable cut. Significant obstacles in the way of achieving that goal were the lack of roads to access the timber and the number of people on the ground needed to ramp up logging to fill the logging trucks for the mills. Engineering, road and bridge building, and hiring of increasing numbers of employees were now the top priorities of the Forest Service. All else was secondary.

Gifford Pinchot, first chief of the US Forest Service, died in October 1946. After his death, many within the Service felt that he should be honored by naming a national forest after him. The most logical choice was Pisgah National Forest in North Carolina. Pinchot was born and raised in Pennsylvania, and he had served as the nation's first forester in the 1890s on what was then land owned by Cornelius Vanderbilt; much of this land later became part of what is now the Pisgah National Forest. According to the 1947 annual inspection report, when local residents in western North Carolina were approached about changing the name of their forest from the Pisgah to the Gifford Pinchot National Forest, "They were mostly violently opposed, and their Congressman sided with them. Pisgah is, of course, a biblical name so this probably was a large factor." While the account of this opposition from an outsider's perspective is believable, a more likely reason for the strong opposition is that the Pisgah National Forest is located entirely in western North Carolina, in the southern Appalachian Mountains, which were originally settled by highly independent minded Scotch-Irish, many of whom had migrated to these mountains from Pennsylvania or from the United Kingdom. They viewed outsiders with a wary eye and were even known to refer to people from eastern North Carolina visiting their region in the early 1900s as "furreneers." A much more likely explanation is that they were highly conservative, significantly isolated, resistant to change, extremely independent, and not at all inclined for someone from outside their region telling them that Gifford Pinchot was a better name for their forest. As a native of southern Appalachia might have replied, "the hell with that."

The Forest Service was forced to find another forest to rename and after much consideration settled on the Columbia National Forest. Pinchot had spent some time exploring and hiking in what became his namesake forest during the inspection trip conducted by the National Forest Commission in 1896. Little opposition was expressed locally when the proposal was made, and so the change was made official. Gifford Pinchot's grandson, Gifford Pinchot III, described to me in an interview one of his earliest memories being that of sitting on President Truman's lap when he signed the legislation changing the name of Columbia National Forest to Gifford Pinchot National Forest.

What is unstated in this account about the name change is that other forests that Pinchot visited could just as easily be chosen but were not. One reason may have been that other logical choices such as Mount Hood National Forest in Oregon and Mount Baker-Snoqualmie National Forest in Washington had much larger constituencies that cared about those forests and may well have opposed any name changes. Portlanders prized Mount Hood, and Seattleites prized Mount Rainier and Mount Baker. In each case, people from Portland and Seattle acted as guardians for what occurred on those forests they most cared about. The Columbia National Forest, because it was on the other side of the Columbia River from Portland and infrequently visited by Portlanders, and because it was a far drive from Seattle, was mostly ignored. A characterization that evolved over time was that the Columbia was the "forgotten forest."

At the dedication ceremony for the renamed Gifford Pinchot National Forest in 1949, Pinchot's widow, Cornelia Pinchot, spoke eloquently about her husband and his conservation legacy, "He insisted that conservation be reinvigorated, revived, re-manned, revitalized by each successive generation, its implications, its urgencies, its logistics translated in terms of the present of each of them." She knew her husband better than anyone else and had witnessed his evolution as a conservationist. Cornelia Pinchot was a lifelong Progressive, and, throughout the years of their marriage, she strongly encouraged her husband to champion Progressive initiatives.

One can well imagine Pinchot nodding approvingly were he standing nearby as his wife spoke about the necessity of reinvigorating conservation. In his later years, he expressed much greater appreciation for the forest not only as a refuge for wild animals and a landscape that should be appreciated for its aesthetic qualities, but also as a place that offered spiritual sustenance. Pinchot, however, would not have nodded approvingly at the cultural transformation of his cherished Forest Service, which accelerated, ironically, at the time of his death in 1946.

A press release at the time of the dedication ceremony renaming the forest spoke glowingly of the area's scenic resources, wildlife, watershed, and recreation resources; at the same time the press release stated that "its greatest resource is some 16 billion board feet of commercial timber" and further noted that "managed for sustained yield, the timber growth is estimated to be sufficient to yield perpetually an annual cut of 200 million board feet." This statement reflected the already ambitious plans for timber in the Northwest, but with increased pressure and willingness on the part of the Forest Service, those numbers soon morphed into even higher numbers. The factors that drove these numbers skyward included massive levels of road construction, assumptions based on intensive forest management, and intense political pressures.

In twelve years, the changes that Mays had prophesied in 1947 had become a reality in the Gifford Pinchot National Forest. The "allowable cut" had increased from 190 million board feet in 1947 to 397 million board feet in 1959. This level of harvest represents almost doubling in ten years the allowable cut of 200 million board feet that was identified in 1949 as the level of cut that could be maintained perpetually. The timber cut on the GPNF increased from 101 million board feet in 1947 to just over 332 million board feet in 1959, a greater than tripling increase. Road mileage in 1947 was 634 miles and by 1959 had reached 1,142 miles, almost a doubling. The mileage of trails went from 1,442 miles to 1,505, a negligible increase. The number of permanent and seasonal employees went from about 170 in 1947 to over 400. The Forest Service as represented on the GPNF in 1959 had utterly transformed from what it looked like prior to WWII. Just as FDR ramped up production of military weaponry and sent millions of men to the United Kingdom in preparation for the D-Day Invasion and transformed a country from the poverty of the Great Depression to one that could fairly be characterized by its robustness, vitality, and strength, so too had Forest Service leaders transformed an agency that previously was small, quiet, and modest to one that was large and growing, active and dominant, bold and questing.

This transformation from one where stewardship prevailed to one where production dominated was propelled by the demands of WWII; the patriotic duty was clear, and foresters throughout the country responded. Just as automobile plants transformed into tank-producing manufacturers, foresters ramped up output to support the war effort. These efforts ranged from the mundane, such as building bridges, to the esoteric, such as lightweight aircraft dependent on spruce. Timber sales on national forests increased from just over 1 billion board feet in 1939 to over 3 billion board feet in 1945, an increase of over 200 percent. More significantly, the proportion of national forest contribution to the total national timber production economy in that same period doubled from 5 percent to 10 percent. WWII set the stage for the Forest Service to transition from the custodian of forest resources to production of forest resources, from a largely passive, caretaking role to one of intensive management. The increases were quite extraordinary given how little wood had come out of the national forests in the preceding decades. Cut levels in national forests more than doubled from the end of WWII in 1945 to 1955 when it reached 6.3 billion board feet. Five years later, in 1960, the cut level reached 9.4 billion board feet, and almost all of that was coming from the Pacific Northwest.

Pinchot, who early and consistently called for regulation of the private timber industry, was seen as a radical and viewed by that industry with loathing. That was not the case with the leaders of the Forest Service who followed in his footsteps. They understood that prior to WWII, private timber interests did not want competition from logging on public lands, and they were quite willing to practice patience and act as stewards of this resource. The relationship with the timber industry slowly evolved from one of covert support to overt alliance.

These changes in cut levels and with the timber industry were spurred to a great extent by the return of hundreds of thousands of GIs who wanted to quickly catch up on a life that had been on hold during the war years. They married, they had children, and they wanted a home of their own. A significant demand for forest products materialized—one that private industry was not prepared to answer. In addition, leaders in Congress called for increased output on national forests as that enabled them to discuss the increased employment and dollars they were bringing to their districts. For the previous four decades, the Forest Service had been preparing for just this opportunity. One of Pinchot's unsung legacies was that of establishing an agency whose practices and systems ensured transparency, accountability, and honesty. Now the agency was prepared to act forcefully.

Organizational cultures almost inevitably change over time, and the Forest Service culture changed radically over the two decades after WWII. At the time of its creation and during the succeeding several decades, the Forest Service culture that emerged from Pinchot's agency was one that developed in opposition to cut-and-run loggers. Pinchot and his followers successfully challenged that paradigm beginning in the Pacific Northwest woods. Cut-and-run logging would not happen on national forests. The culture established by Pinchot, who, no matter what role he took on over the years after he left the Forest Service, and who always identified himself first and foremost as a forester, had endured for forty years. One of the great ironies for Gifford Pinchot was that this legacy of conservation—of always keeping the long run in the forefront, about which he felt much pride, and which he pointed to as his most significant accomplishment during his long life, more important even than serving as governor of Pennsylvania for two terms—came unraveled after his death in 1946.

Prior to WWII, in what was known as the "Stetson Hat Period," the Forest Service was seen as a reliable guardian, a respected steward, of the nation's public lands. This public image slowly changed over the following three decades from that of an agency that protected the forest from rapacious cut-and-run loggers to one that was seen primarily as focused on getting the cut out.

Gifford Pinchot was both a forester and a steward. He knew that without the promise offered by a sustainable approach to forestry, rural communities would suffer. One of the most prominent foresters following in his footsteps, Chief Forester William Greeley, warned as early as 1946 that western states were "rapidly approaching the end of their virgin forests, and that the region faced the same sort of migratory forest industries and ghost towns" that had occurred on the East Coast and Midwest. Shortly after Pinchot's death, Chief Forester Lyle Watts reaffirmed his belief that the Forest Service needed to continue practices on the ground that would sustain timber-dependent communities for the long term: "We hope to have milling or logging communities so located with respect to the merchantable timber . . . that wood workers will have an opportunity to live at home in permanent communities and to commute to and from work." The key word is "permanent." Watts, like Pinchot, wanted policies that promoted the well-being of families and their communities over the long term.

As the first half of the twentieth century ended, many of Pinchot's spiritual descendants, who had absorbed his values and beliefs of conservation and what constituted a healthy, functioning forest, were retiring. They were being replaced by graduates of forestry schools, well-funded by the timber industry, who had a very different set of values and beliefs about what constituted a healthy, functioning forest. They became champions of what they called "intensive management," and over the next two decades, they moved from entry roles into leadership roles. And the culture of the Forest Service changed from one that prized stewardship to one that extolled production. Active, intensive, focused, disciplined, energetic, scientific management of the forest, in these emerging leaders' eyes, would prove to the world that forests, like factories, could be made to be more efficient, and more productive. As the culture of the Forest Service adopted this mindset after WWII, so began the transformation of an agency and, ultimately, the forest itself.

Few conflicts arose among the various stakeholders of national forests, whether hunters, fishermen, hikers, or sightseers, and the Forest Service during the custodial years, the three decades after its founding. Over the three decades after WWII, however, the agency, rather than being seen as a watchdog of the timber industry, began to be viewed as its lapdog. With the dramatic increase in logging that accelerated tremendously in the 1950s, new interest groups emerged that grew both in numbers and in strength, and the Forest Service found itself, increasingly, under attack. Chris Maser in *Forest Primeval: The Natural History of an Ancient Forest* describes well how Pinchot early on professed his faith in government scientists because he felt that it was the morally, scientifically, and economically right thing to do. "But in so doing, he isolated the agency from the public and Congress. Forest Service leaders would slowly lose touch with the constituents they served, leaving the agency vulnerable to increasing criticism after the 1950s." For the first time, the Forest Service's ability to make decisions regarding policy toward land uses on the forest without interference from outsiders was threatened. Whereas Pinchot had nurtured a culture that relied on relating to and connecting with its stakeholders, of winning them over to his conception of conservation, the Forest Service culture that developed after WWII placed a premium first on preserving its well-established privilege of power over resource management, which increasingly, in turn, was focused on intensive management.

Foresters began arguing forcefully against preservation and for logging in the 1950s by emphasizing that single use—that is, preservation—was unpatriotic. Logging was needed to enable a strong economy, and a strong economy was needed to demonstrate to the citizens of the United States that capitalism was a much more effective economic system than communism. With the growing threat of communism and the cold war during this period, even wilderness designation could be seen as a threat to "our way of life." A senior Weyerhaeuser executive captured this world view succinctly: "With this economic cold war in mind I am sure Mr. Khrushchev would like to see the entire Cascades range plus the Sierras put into one huge wilderness area."

Pinchot was both a forester and a conservationist. He would have recognized wilderness designation as one of the reasonable multiple uses for his national forests. The culture of the Forest Service of the 1950s, however, had changed. The value of production overtook the value of conservation of the forest. These views were fully rewarded and promoted across the agency. Kevin Marsh in *Drawing Lines in the Forest: Creating Wilderness*

Areas in the Pacific Northwest describes how "the culture of the Forest Service fostered a righteous sense of loyalty to the agency and to the expertise of its professionals . . . in their idealized vision of the agency and its mission, they believed that they made their decisions based on professional judgment and long-term public interest, and above the political fray of interest groups."

The cohesive culture that Pinchot had so effectively established now became the means for overturning so much that he cared about— sustainable forestry. With the primacy of production driving Forest Service decision and policies, many other needs of the forest were reduced in value and focus. The agency's culture was united in believing that it acted in the best interest of the country. Throughout the nearly half century following WWII, it acted as a unified organization. As humans we tend to shape truth based on our limited subjective experience and to ignore other people's views based on their own limited subjective experience. The foresters who were focused on the trees had little sympathy for those embracing other values like preservation of beautiful places and as refuges for wildlife.

10

Culture Change

The forest canopies of the earth are realms of unfathomable nature, and they are vanishing. The earth's forests are being logged off, burned away, turned into patches, and reduced to small fragments.

—Richard Preston

The 1950s was a decade of transformation for the Forest Service and its culture. Cultures, however, do not transform effortlessly. While new leaders may model, promote, and reward the behaviors and practices they want the new culture to take on, inevitably resistance emerges from the old guard. They want to hold onto past practices and past values. The last gasp of the old guard can be most clearly seen in the general inspection of the Gifford Pinchot National Forest by A. R. Standing in 1950. This was the first inspection after the forest was renamed and is especially poignant in that Standing's lyrical report is reflective of a past approach that was rapidly disappearing, one that was being replaced by a hard-edged, mechanical realism. In Standing's summary of August 1950, he captures well his personal appreciation of this wild and treasured landscape, Pinchot's namesake forest:

> Late one afternoon, I dismounted from my horse on the crest of a rocky ridge that divides the Upper Lake Creek and Cispus River drainage. Though it was the sixth of August, the Snowgrass Flat behind me was still largely covered with snow. Goat Lake, nestled in a high barren basin on the side of Hawkeye Peak a mile to the west, was still encased in emerald colored ice. For the last mile I had been riding, the snow was so deep it still covered the rock cairns marking the trail. . . . I was ahead of the rest of the party and this gave me time to look around and to reflect on what I saw.
>
> The view to the east was cut off by massive Old Snowy Mountain which towered above me, and by the jagged castellated pinnacles of the Goat Rocks. Southward and westward there was an unobstructed view for

40 miles airline, though high up hung the heavy cloud of an impending storm. Immediately in front of me a mass of fog swirling skyward from the Upper Lake Creek basin was so dense I could barely see the edge of Packwood Glacier only 20 feet away. Shortly the fog bank thinned out, and spread before me was a view unexcelled in grandeur. There lay the glacier, the crossing of which had frequently been the topic of conversation throughout the day. For fully a mile it clung to the steep sides of Old Snowy. At its low end, precipitous cliffs formed an almost vertical wall to the floor of the deep gorge of Upper Lake Creek. North of the glacier, in a little basin carpeted with green fescue and early spring flowers was a timber-studded hill which I knew by its shape must be Egg Butte. Twenty-five miles northwesterly, I could see the glaciated sides of Mount Rainier, but its crest was shrouded in storm clouds. I was amazed that a country so primitive and spectacular could be found so near to the byways of men. I fervently hoped this area can always be kept as wilderness.

Gradually some of the details of the vast expanse of mountainous terrain came to my awareness. Between me and majestic Mount Adams and Mount St. Helens was the solid green of forest, broken only by old burns and the rocky bareness of Twin Sisters Mountain, Castle Butte, Sunrise Peak, Jumbo, Craggy, Badger, and dozens of other stony protrusions above the blue green of the distant trees. I know that beyond the horizon of the hazy far-away hills, the forest stretched on to the banks of the Columbia, to the cutover lands that fringe the forest to the west. Within that space was the 1,263,342 acres of the national forest land, and 156,220 acres of private land inside the exterior boundaries. I thought of the 190 million board feet of timber that can be harvested annually by us and our progeny—of the logging operations, mills, commerce, products, payrolls, taxes, and careers stemming from that timber. I thought, too, of the 177,769 visitors to the forest last year (and a like number every year) to the retreats and attractions of the forest—of 6,500 winter sports fans, hikers, campers, fishermen, hunters and countless others who find personal satisfaction in their own way somewhere in that sweep of mountains, lakes and forests. . . . Talk about continuity of livestock operation, the stockmen have it on the national forests within the reasonable limits that must be imposed to protect the invaluable watersheds and provide for the greatest good to the greatest number in the long run. I could see portions of the 600,000 acres covered inside and outside the forest by the Cispus and Yacholt burns, and was proud of the men who have kept most of the fires small through the years, especially the past ten, and also of the people who have been taught to be careful with fire.

The tiny trickle near my feet, joined by a million more, was forming the Cispus River whose valley soon became broad and deep as it dropped rapidly away to the southwest. Down there . . . is Indian Heaven country. . . . There some 15,000 people, both Indians and Whites, would soon be gathering some 20,000 gallons of huckleberries.

Northwest of me, a mist hung over the valley of the Cowlitz River. Somewhere down there was the La Wis Wis campground. . . . Many no doubt would be looking at the plaque embedded in a granite stone besides two giant Douglas-firs, informing them and generations to follow that this great forest is named for and dedicated to the memory of a great man—Gifford Pinchot. I thought of the leadership and inspiration he gave to Conservation in our nation and felt that he must be proud of this honor. I was grateful for the wisdom of those who selected this forest to bear his name.

Past and present were linked for a moment, and I couldn't help but feel that in these men, and their associates throughout the forest, is the same zeal that stirred Gifford Pinchot. . . . I thought then, as I do now, that the general inspection is completed, the Gifford Pinchot personnel are doing a commendable job, and the work on the forest as well as its resources are worthy of the name it bears.

This general inspection report is remarkable in so many ways. First is the love, awe, inspiration, and spiritual feeling that Standing has for the landscape he is surveying. Such lofty statements are rarely found today in official government documents. He speaks of a wilderness landscape and his desire that that part of the world always be preserved as wilderness fourteen years before the passage of the Wilderness Act and at a time when many in the Forest Service were loath to designate any lands as wilderness. He undoubtedly recognized how unique and distinct this report was compared to the many that had been written before him. He skillfully included the data that every inspection is expected to report on while also emphasizing the agency's mission of providing for the "greatest good." And, most poignantly of all, he refers to the plaque honoring Pinchot, which had been dedicated one year earlier, and how proud Pinchot would be of his namesake forest were he in Standing's shoes, surveying the scene as Standing was doing.

Standing represents the old guard looking back unwilling yet to acknowledge the transition that was already under way. He was the rare romantic who was being eclipsed by the hard-edged realist. One of the last general inspections conducted on the GPNF was in 1954; the old guard was still inspecting diaries. The inspector in 1954 noted: "Diaries showed rather wide variation in quality and completeness. The principal fault lies in a failure to summarize for each day's entry the time spent to the nearest full hour for functional accounts." This report summarized that "in reporting on performance, two words suffice, Well Done," while also stating, "The greatest single weakness is inadequacy of long-range planning." These inspections had been a part of the Forest Service culture for almost fifty years and along with them the keeping of diaries by rangers and other personnel. They were very soon a thing of the past. No more diaries; no more general inspections. These changes in practices accelerated the cultural transition of the agency. An agency that was rapidly transforming from stewardship to high production no longer had need for that particular form of accountability, which seemed to emphasize penny-pinching and counting of pencils. The money was rolling in like it had never done before. Accountability became much simpler: How many roads did you build? How much timber did you sell and cut? The new guard was all about business, and the business of the transformed Forest Service and for the forest supervisors on the Gifford Pinchot National Forest was all about getting the cut out.

In 1958, the cut was 206 million board feet; in 1959, it was 332 million board feet; and in 1960, it had increased to 440 million board feet, over a 100 percent increase in three years. The value as well of that cut went from $5.5 million to close to $11 million. These are remarkable increases. During WWII, such numbers for the increase in production of tanks and aircrafts was not unheard of due to the war effort. In the post-WWII period from 1950 to 1954, automobile and truck production actually declined. In contrast, the increases in the amount of timber coming off the GPNF (and other Pacific Northwest national forests) were not from the demands of a wartime economy; rather they resulted from a transformed agency, a reformulated culture that would not have been recognizable in the preceding decade. A new term had recently come into use to describe the United States: "superpower." This superpower was fueled by can-do people in a can-do culture, and the Forest Service adopted that mantra with a vengeance; they were determined to exemplify that attitude. They were absolutely sure that the clearest way to demonstrate to the world that can-do capability was to have an endless line of logging trucks streaming out of the national forests and into the mills. Michael Frome described this new attitude in his book *The Forest Service*: "Man could do things better. This might require a level of destruction that could upset some by its unsightliness, but clear-cuts were a necessary tool to create a more productive forest in the long term."

One of the threats to that unending stream of logging trucks flowing out of the national forests was any attempt to set aside forests as wilderness. Beginning in the 1950s, as cut levels of timber coming out of national forests significantly increased, advocates for change were coming not from inside the government but from outside. These advocates were driven by one overriding need: to preserve public lands in their primitive state. While not large in numbers, they were highly vocal and effective in capturing public attention. Perhaps the most notable example was when David Brower, then executive director of the Sierra Club, placed a full-page ad in the *New York Times* comparing building dams in the Grand Canyon to flooding the Sistine Chapel in order to gain a closer view of its magnificent ceiling. Just as environmentalists were outraged at the plan by the Bureau of Reclamation to build several dams within the Grand Canyon, so too were wildland advocates disturbed by the accelerating destruction of old-growth forests.

Wildlands advocates' stance that some percentage of public land be protected rather than logged was anathema to an agency that had been waiting fifty years to fulfill its mission of supplying wood to the nation. For an agency that had transformed itself during the 1950s into one whose highest value now was maximizing timber production, preservation of wildlands made no sense. Wildland advocates saw as their only recourse transfer of national forestlands into the Department of the Interior. One area, however, in which wildland advocates and the Forest Service were aligned was in their view of those wildlands that could be categorized as "ice and rock." These high-elevation lands in the Northwest, found almost exclusively around the iconic volcanoes up and down the Cascade Range, simply had no value to the Forest Service as they did not contain old growth. Kevin Marsh in *Drawing Lines in the Forest: Creating Wilderness Areas in the Pacific Northwest* writes, "Preserving the high elevation alpine and subalpine regions for recreation was rarely challenged." Thus, little controversy happened on the Pinchot's namesake forest after the Wilderness Act was passed when much of the high country of Mount Adams was declared wilderness.

One of the early outcomes of this alignment between the Forest Service and environmentalists was the emergence of what some described as "wilderness starfish." This description was apt as the agency drew its lines on the maps designating the areas above tree line as wilderness. Of course, the icy volcanic mountaintops had no value for the Forest Service, along with the many high ridges that, like bicycle spokes, radiated from the central peak. These ridges were like the arms of a starfish. Only on lower-elevation forested public lands did conflicts increasingly develop between the Forest Service and the growing environmental communities. In the Pacific Northwest, this became for the agency an almost existential issue as they viewed the preservation of old growth as antithetical not only to common sense but to a more productive forestry. At the time of this paradigm shift from custodial care to production, almost 75 percent of the old-growth forest on public lands in the Northwest was still standing.

What became more and more apparent to those calling for preservation of wildlands was the very real strategy of the Forest Service to minimize future designation of lands as wilderness by building roads into roadless areas. Early on, the agency adopted a "purity" concept toward wilderness—that only those areas never logged and never roaded should be designated wilderness. Building roads into roadless areas and logging those lands became the key strategy for ensuring they would serve what the Forest Service saw as the "greater good"—hauling logs, especially old-growth logs, off public lands. Increasingly, the Forest Service held the view that the highest and best use of the land was to manage the forest as a crop.

During the stewardship phase, 230,000 acres was the minimum to merit listing an area as "roadless." At that time, the Forest Service was reluctant to designate any lands as wilderness as they viewed that designation as unfair to timber-dependent communities that relied more and more on the national forests for timber and range resources. The strikingly large size of roadless areas during the stewardship era reflected the paucity of roads and logging in the national forests at that time. Much later, roadless areas to be inventoried required a minimum of just five thousand acres, clear evidence of the effectiveness of the Forest Services' success in building thousands of miles of roads throughout Northwest national forests.

As early as the 1950s, some observers of the Forest Service recognized that logging in the Pacific Northwest was far beyond what was sustainable. Charles McKinley in *Uncle Sam in the Pacific Northwest: Federal*

Management of Natural Resources in the Columbia River Valley wrote: "In addition to the reduction of the timber supply by cutting, there are losses from fire, insect, fungus, and other diseases, which brought the total drain from all sources in 1944 to an estimated 16.3 billion board feet. The significance of this to the perpetuation of the timber industries, and their dependent communities, is clear when that drain is compared with annual timber growth, now calculated at 5.5 billion feet. Briefly put, the timber is being used and destroyed three times as rapidly as it is being produced."

McKinley identified two options: to continue the current practices until the logs ran out or to begin a planned reduction that would lead to a sustainable level of harvest and keep timber-dependent communities healthy for the long term. With the hindsight of over sixty years, we now recognize that the first option was vigorously pursued, leading beginning in the 1990s to the economic collapse of many rural communities across the Northwest. McKinley was extraordinarily prescient when he wrote some forty years before this collapse: "A community with only a few years' supply of raw materials for its mills may remain complacent because the shriek of the saws and the roar of the planers may continue unabated until the last log is cut. Only silence breaks the illusion and awakens, belatedly, community awareness." This passage brings to mind the kind of events that Jared Diamond describes so well in *Collapse*, that led to the destruction of societies. Easter Island is a particularly poignant example.

The rulers of distinct districts on Easter Island competed to place monuments—the well-known stone heads—along the coast. These heads were in fact monuments to the rulers' egos that blinded them to the consequences of their actions, which led to the deforestation, impoverishment, and subsequent decline of their island. Up to the last moment, stone carvers and sculptors were at work in the quarries busily cutting and shaping stone when their work came to a sudden halt. Jared Diamond posits the theory that their work had suddenly become worthless as there were no longer enough logs to roll the immense stone heads out of the quarry to the coast. The last trees had been cut. How, one may ask, could they be so short-sighted? How can a society act in ways that bring about its collapse? How can we not have learned from these past examples of exploiting natural resources beyond what is sustainable? And yet, like Easter Island, we too failed to plan for the long term. The result was the virtual collapse of numerous timber-dependent communities throughout the Pacific

Northwest and heartrending dislocation and hardship for thousands of families who lived in those communities.

In the very early years of increased logging on public lands, Earle Clapp, the acting chief of the Forest Service in 1942, expressed concern that sustained yield was being jeopardized. In just a few years, with increased demand as a result of WWII, harvest of timber off national forests had increased sevenfold, and most of those sales were coming from the Pacific Northwest. While Clapp expressed concerns about aggressive logging, he also recognized an upside. His views epitomized the view of the new generation of timber cruisers (those hired to walk, or cruise, in the forest to determine the rate of growth of trees in that forest and other relevant information) and engineers. The upside for Clapp was that aggressive logging would quickly eliminate old growth, which as "decadent" forest was slow-growing and impeding the formation of vigorous and fast-growing younger forests, which would rise up in their place. These younger trees could then be harvested on a shorter rotation and thus serve as a much better "crop" for eager loggers. This view became the rallying cry in the postwar years for converting old growth into plantation forests. Little thought was given to the loss of biodiversity, to the ecological health of an extremely complex system, which inevitably resulted from replacing ancient forests with same-aged plantations of uniform species of trees that more closely resembled crops of corn than the miracle of old-growth forest.

Paul Hirt in *A Conspiracy of Optimism* noted that "The heavy timber orientation is built in by legislative action and control, by executive direction and budgetary restriction" and that "the major emphasis on timber production continues." Maximum production became the primary objective of the Forest Service as it entered its fifth decade. Old growth stood as a barrier to the practice of modern scientific forestry, which championed intensive management. The most effective way to meet the country's growing needs for wood products was to replace the ancient forests with faster-growing, second-growth trees. Other needs, whether for clean water, wildlife, salmon, plant and animal diversity, were secondary.

Several changes in the technology and political realms abetted this paradigm shift. The technology change that most aided this attack on old-growth forest was the emergence of the chainsaw. The chainsaw, along with a logging system comprised of a yarder, or logging equipment, and cables that either pull or lift logs from where they were cut to a landing where they are then loaded for transport to mills, transformed logging practices. The political change was the emergence of the cold war between the United States and Russia, which birthed an anti-planning bias, as centralized planning was viewed as akin to socialism or communism. This bias also led to a negative view within the Forest Service of conservation and stewardship of resources as they were seen as obstacles to the need for unfettered development. In a letter by Forest Service chief Lyle Watts, he wrote of the need to make adjustments to harvest levels in response to defense needs and that "national emergency" required a "program to intensify management" and that the "national defense justifies a more rapid depletion of mature timber resources." A free market economy and unregulated capitalism were the leading sirens of the day. These two changes were vital to what became a dominant Forest Service practice in the Pacific Northwest during the 1950s and beyond: clear-cuts.

One other factor heavily influenced the transformation of the Forest Service into a production-oriented agency: budgets. From the outset, it was dependent on timber sales for revenue, and the one certain way to increase revenues was to increase timber sales. Like many for-profit organizations, the Forest Service viewed growth highly positively. Growth meant increasing its revenues so that it could hire more employees, build more roads, log ever-increasing amounts of timber. Rural counties in which national forests were found also benefitted greatly as they received 25 percent of receipts from timber sales in their counties. The county in Pinchot's namesake forest with the most Forest Service land within its borders was Skamania County, which received $1.6 million from federal timber sales in 1960. By 1970, this figure more than doubled to $3.7 million. Little wonder, then, that members of Congress throughout the Pacific Northwest and their rural constituents became among the most vocal advocates for increasing the logging of old growth on national forests.

Of course, there were others inside and outside of the Forest Service who did not favor intensive management of the forest. One of the most forceful advocates for viewing the forests other than as a commodity was Aldo Leopold. Leopold became interested in forestry after learning about Pinchot's efforts to establish the nation's first forestry school in Yale in the early 1900s. He attended Yale and soon thereafter joined the Forest Service, where he remained for almost two decades. During that time, he developed a view of the forest that was quite distinct from most of his peers. He was one of the first foresters to recognize the complexity of old-growth forests and to understand that much about the forest was unknown. Leopold in his journals counseled: "If the biota, in the course of eons, has built something we like but do not understand, then who but a fool would discard seemingly useless parts? To keep every cog and wheel is the first precaution of intelligent tinkering."

Leopold died in 1948, two years after Pinchot's death, and so did not live to see the transformation of the Forest Service into a production-oriented agency. He viewed a production-oriented ideology as a form of violence on the landscape. It seems logical to presume that he would have been appalled by the violence let loose on the wild landscapes he prized. In his seminal work *A Sand County Almanac: And Sketches Here and There*, Leopold declared: "A thing is right when it tends to preserve the integrity, stability and beauty of the biotic community. It is wrong when it tends otherwise." During the stewardship phase, the Forest Service to a great extent did preserve the integrity of the biotic community. After WWII, it very consciously "tended otherwise."

11

Intensive Management

Clear-Cut

Humans love the sun on a cold morning,
so do young Doug-firs,
insects in song,
and little winter wrens.

The men in the machines have given us sun,
but have taken away
liverworts, magic,
and most of the mushrooms.

A woodpecker flies by
with no place to land.
The pale stumps he sees
are dead as rocks.

Healing can be imagined,
but I will not witness it.
Only at this place do I want time to hurry,
only here the years do not go fast enough for me—
no matter how old I may be.

—Joan Maloof

The GPNF supervisor from 1976 to 1983 was Bob Tokarczyk. When I interviewed him some thirty years after he served as supervisor, his response to the question, "What did Gifford Pinchot mean when he said the mission of the Forest Service was to provide the greatest good to the greatest number in the long run?" was that "multiple use was important" and that included "protection of water sheds and providing habitat for all wildlife of all kinds; provide fiber for communities to build houses; and protect the soil and environment so that it is there forever." Tokarczyk described in our interview how, after WWII, demand for "fiber" increased. He noted that on the GPNF stood a "tremendous amount of over-mature timber" and on several occasions during the interview referred to the "decadent timber" on the forest. Tokarczyk spoke with pride of getting the cut up to 400 million board feet on the GPNF and noted, "We erred on the side of never cutting more than we were growing to ensure our base was already there," and this approach "allowed us to provide jobs for rural communities without hurting watersheds or the soil."

My interview with Tokarczyk took place long after the production phase was over, after cuts on the GPNF had dropped from the high 400 million-plus of board feet to 20 million board feet. He continued to feel strongly and positively about the role he and his staff played in removing old growth from the GPNF. He declared, "Through our activity we reduced the old growth as we focused on fiber. We don't have the same make-up of decadent trees as we took a lot of those out during the high cut days . . . probably 60 percent that was cut had never been cut before. We had our plans that focused on taking timber out when it reached maturity and was not going to grow any more—that is when you want to take it out."

Tokarczyk's beliefs and values were congruent with the vast majority of people he worked with in the Forest Service. References to "fiber" and "over-mature" and "decadent" are representative of the language used to describe forest during the high-production phase. That language disappeared from agency's usage, which began to adopt, recognize, and accept the best available science. But that acceptance only happened after decades of fierce resistance on the part of the agency and only after the courts intervened.

Probably the most poignant statement by Tokarczyk during our interview was, "But you can go back and look at those lands, and I don't know that I did anything that was wrong." Bob Tokarczyk—even with several decades of hindsight during which logging of timber crashed, thousands of jobs in mills were lost, rural communities were hollowed out, and drug and alcohol addictions soared in those communities—did not feel that he had done anything wrong. And as outside observers we cannot blame him. He was part of a complex system and a cohesive culture that rewarded and reinforced all of the actions that ultimately did lead to the collapse.

The long-retired Tokarczyk continued to profess the values and beliefs of the old culture: "We use to have the 10 A.M. rule—put out the fire by 10 the next day"; "Wherever there is salvage because of bugs, then you should go in and take those trees out." "They were telling me not to cut on the ridges because the soil was thin and fragile, but that did not stop me from cutting on those ridges." These statements reflect just how difficult change is for most people and the challenge of acknowledging the adverse results of one's actions. Tokarczyk continued to believe that harvesting 400 million-plus board feet was sustainable for the long term. Most Forest Service scientists disagreed.

John Todd, one of the foresters in the region interviewed as part of an oral history project on timber management in the Pacific Northwest, reflected on the almost sole focus on timber of that era, "I don't think there is any question but what that's been true. I don't think there's been anything sinister about it. Foresters, historically, in my era and before, have thought that. That's what forestry was about, producing timber. Nobody was taught to ignore other resources in the process, but that may be the result of perhaps putting so much emphasis on timber. And to some extent, I think we did make our own problems, by not looking hard enough, at some of the results of what was going on." Todd acknowledged the simple truth that foresters were trained to cut down forests—that is what they knew best and what they were trained to do. It was not sinister. It was not Machiavellian. While not stating explicitly what those "problems" were or what adverse "results" occurred, Todd had the courage to acknowledge them. He, at least, was not exempting himself as a contributor to the collapse of logging in the early 1990s.

Jack Usher, another long-term employee of the Forest Service during this high-production phase, confirmed the practices on the ground: "Up until the late 1960s, all we were doing in the region was cutting old growth. There was so much over-mature timber and so much of it was decadent, realizing little net growth—and suffering heavy volume and value losses in mortality—that high priority had to be given to harvesting those stands and using much of the capital value in those stands to build the access roads needed for current and future management." What is especially noticeable about his statement is that "capital value" was key to future harvesting. Harvesting of old growth generated needed revenue to build even more roads and harvest even more old growth as if this cycle would never end.

One of the more intriguing factors influencing intensive management and allowable-cut definitions was based simply on how much money was flowing into the national forest in the Pacific Northwest. Glen Jorgensen, who was the supervisor of the GPNF in the late 1950s and early 1960s and who was interviewed as well as part of the oral history project, confirmed the influence of financial investments on Forest Service policy. He reflected that agency leaders "could not accurately determine what the allowable cut would be without knowing future investments needed to support intensive management: pre-commercial thinning, genetics, improved utilization" and took those concerns to the chief, who expressed a more flexible view of allowable cut. According to Jorgensen, the chief emphasized, "The objective is to maintain or increase harvest levels and that we are not against increasing allowable cut, we do object to decreasing it," and that the chief then changed the policy to one of "non-declining even flow in which it can go up but cannot go down." Jorgensen thought that was a "very good decision," and noted that the plan for the GPNF helped shape national policy and that the chief decided to make the GPNF a "test case" for the nation. The chief agreed to provide the GPNF with "intensive financing" so that the forest could prove the value of intensive management. With this increase in funding, the GPNF changed its allowable-cut level from 293 million board feet to 404 million board feet. One other anecdote shared by Jorgensen again emphasizes the influence of money. He stated that Congressman John Duncan visited the GPNF and asked how many more board feet could be produced with more money and that as a result "the plan became 443 million board feet." Money mattered during the high-production phase, not ecology. To this congressman, increased timber production mattered more than ensuring a sustainable resource. Higher levels of timber production would see to it that even more old growth would be logged even quicker. What it would not result in was a sustainable level of harvest.

One can reasonably ask the question, why did foresters like Jorgensen argue decade after decade for increasing the allowable cut off their national forests? They made a series of assumptions about the prospects of intensive management:

- Fire suppression would eliminate almost all natural forest loss due to fires,
- Pesticide use would virtually eliminate all insect and disease losses,

- Genetically engineered (and faster-growing) trees would quickly populate all cutover areas,
- With new harvesting capability, trees could be cut at sixty years rather than a harvest cycle of one hundred years,
- Careful logging would increase utilization, and
- Negative effects of timber cutting on other uses of the forest could be readily mitigated.

Not just one or two of these assumptions would need to be true to meet the timber objectives that flowed from intensive management; they all would need to be true. The founding purpose of the Forest Service—to ensure a sustained yield in perpetuity—was increasingly placed at risk with the focus on more timber production. In the Gifford Pinchot National Forest, which was picked to demonstrate the impacts of intensive management, the leaders relied on all these assumptions to shape the allowable cut determinations and then increased their percentages by 10 percent or 20 percent or greater. Efficiency was the driver. They did not face the constraints faced by private foresters, who were unwilling to make the kind of needed investments based on such risky assumptions. Forests in private industry had to be much more accountable than those of federal foresters who often acted as if they had a bottomless bank account.

The production-oriented leaders in the Forest Service after WWII were clearly exhorting the agency to move forcefully into high production. In 1950, the assistant chief of the agency, C. M. Granger, made clear his expectations to intensively manage the public forested lands: "Maximum production of forest crops is one of the objectives of national forest timber management . . . more and more intensive management must be applied to them if they are to continue to furnish practical examples of leadership in applied forest management." He also noted, "Development of additional timber hauling roads is urgently needed to harvest the full sustained yield cutting capacity of the national forest. More roads and permanent roads are the key to more intensive timber management."

The political environment in the early 1950s with the advent of the Korean War also played a role in the emergence of intensive management of our national forests. In early 1951, Chief Lyle Watts emphasized the importance of ramping up production in response to the defense needs of the country: "The present policy is to build up our working circles to full sustained yield cutting capacity . . . we have requested additional funds for timber use and access road construction . . . that the present national emergency will be of lengthy but indefinite duration" and that the Forest Service needed a program that would "intensify management and develop inaccessible areas so as to be in a better position to meet the emergency demands of a full-scale war." Although the phrase "no crisis should go to waste" was not in usage at the time, the concept does seem to apply here. At the outset of the 1950s, the Forest Service recognized that it was poised to double or perhaps triple the amount of logging on its lands over the coming decade and needed to provide a rationale for that dramatic increase. The war "crisis" became a means for rallying a patriotic public behind ensuring a steady flow of logging trucks coming off public lands.

In 1960, Robert McArdle, the chief of the Forest Service, pointedly noted that if the national forests were to meet the nation's need for wood products, the Pacific Northwest would need to produce the lion's share. He stated that the Pacific Northwest would need to produce around 7.5 billion board feet by the year 2000. To enable that volume of logs coming off the forest, he noted that some 77,000 miles of roads were needed and that to date 27,500 miles of roads had been completed. His projection would amount to almost tripling the road system in the region.

As occurs in almost all bureaucracies, these pressures for increased logging and roadbuilding were passed down from headquarters in DC to the Pacific Northwest regional office and finally to the Gifford Pinchot National Forest's supervisor. The GPNF Management Plan for 1953 identified the amount of Douglas-firs in the GPNF at over 22 billion board feet. The supervisor noted that lack of access was the primary reason the forest was not producing up to the annual allowable cut. Providing for the long run, which was the primary distinction between private and national forestry, was becoming a relic of the past. The confidence that Pinchot cultivated in his agency served him and his successors well. That confidence had, however, after WWII, transformed into arrogance. Any strength can become a weakness. Strong leaders are able to act with both confidence and humility. To a great extent, the Forest Service culture throughout the high-production phase lacked humility. The confidence of its leaders that they were doing the right thing with their focus on logging blinded them to the many diverse ecological benefits provided by the forest.

In many ways, the outlook of the Forest Service that emerged in the 1950s matched the name of a popular television program of the same time period, *Father Knows Best*—that when it comes to how best to manage the multiple uses of the forest, the Forest Service, with its trusted father-like sages, knows best. The agency's leaders believed that the disagreements they faced from the public were largely a matter of perception. They thought they could quell public objections to ever-increasing levels of logging by providing more information and education. In their view, the public was simply ill-informed. David Clary in *Timber and the Forest Service* captures well this perception: "A posture that relied on explanations instead of corrective action reinforced charges that the Forest Service was devoted to timber production above all else. The failure to listen to others or to appreciate that other people might have valid objectives for forest land different from timber production appeared to deny multiple use." The Forest Service launched an extensive public relations campaign at the same time that clear-cutting continued unabated. While some narrow strips of land were left along roads, those strips could not hide the vast swaths of clear-cuts behind them, and public sentiment against those barren fields of stumps only increased. The wizard behind the curtain was increasingly exposed, and with that exposure, objections to Forest Service policy only grew.

In 1954, the GPNF supervisor noted that current timber access roads were 316 miles in length and that 612 miles were identified as needed in the next five years. By 1964, the supervisor forecast the need for roads totaling 3,000 miles in length, an astounding increase of nearly 400 percent in just ten years. Growth was the mantra of the day.

The GPNF supervisor in the 1950s also noted, "Since the forest is predominantly mature or over-mature, net growth on a large part of the area is zero, or of a negligible quantity. To minimize loss, cutting during the current rotation will be confined mostly to the oldest and most decadent stands." He later wrote, "Program will be planned in each unit to aid the industry in converting from an old growth to a young growth economy." Leaders at all levels—from supervisor to regional head to chief—were aligned. Intensive timber management demands first cutting the old-growth virgin forests, which were viewed as not contributing to the productivity of the forest because they were considered to be adding no "net growth." This belief—that old growth had ceased growing—was viewed by the GPNF supervisor in the 1950s as a loss of potential revenue. While the sustained yield cut was identified in 1953 as 278 million board feet, the actual cut was about 150 million board feet. The supervisor bemoaned the fact that the "difference between the sustained yield and actual cut is lost forever whenever it is not harvested." He then translated that loss into a lost revenue of $1 million per year and used that figure to advocate for more personnel "in order to get up to the allowable cut." The Gifford Pinchot National Forest was intent on growth.

In 1960, Pacific Northwest national forests were estimated to contain 400 billion board feet of timber—nearly one-fifth of all the timber in the United States. Some 3.5 billion board feet were harvested in the Pacific Northwest that year, a phenomenal level of production compared to a decade earlier. Yet Forest Service leaders projected that even that amount was inadequate, given that the Timber Resource Review, which they had conducted earlier, predicted that the nation would need about twice as much wood by the year 2000. Given these projections, Forest Service leaders stated that the allowable annual cut of 4 billion board feet needed to be doubled within the next forty years to 8 billion board feet in the Pacific Northwest by the year 2000. These numbers are astonishing. How could the Pacific Northwest double its allowable cut? Foresters recognized that, for a forest to produce for the long run, one could not continuously cut annually more than the forest was producing annually. Foresters also understood that timber-dependent rural communities needed a long-term sustainable supply if they were to survive. One simple statement in the Timber Resource Review captures the can-do attitude of the Forest Service: "Standards of management must be intensified." A doubling of the allowable cut was a simple matter of increased intensity.

One can reasonably ask how the level of allowable cut could be so easily manipulated. Although in some few cases the allowable-cut level fell, most of the time, especially during the high production phase, the level of allowable cut rose inexorably. This steady increase was driven by the emergence, beginning in the 1950s and accelerating in the 1960s, of the "iron triangle"— the US Forest Service, Congress, and the timber products industry. All were aligned on getting the cut up and out. Timber sales goals, rather than technical determinations, became the driver for allowable cut.

Hirt describes how these forces conspired to change the industry: "With these powerful institutional, economic, and political incentives in place, the Forest Service, from the 1950s through the 1970s, dedicated itself to market-oriented production and the conversion of natural forest ecosystems into timber plantations." One of the clearest examples of the iron triangle at work can be seen in an exchange between Chief Max Peterson (head of the Forest Service during most of the Reagan presidency) and Les AuCoin, Oregon congressman. While giving testimony to Congress early in Reagan's first term, Peterson stated that continuing the high level of cuts risked running out of wood to cut by the year 2000. AuCoin responded, "But Chief, neither you nor I are going to be here in the year 2000." The strength of the iron triangle was such that concerns with sustaining the resource for the long term were not seriously considered.

Just as tax policies shape the behavior of citizens paying taxes—for example, deductions, which promote home ownership—so too were Forest Service policies shaped by economic realities: 10 percent of receipts from logging sales were automatically returned to the agency for road construction; 25 percent of receipts were distributed to local counties in lieu of taxes; and significant amounts were retained by the agency for "timber sale betterment," or site preparation and planting after logging to foster even-aged, single-species-dominated forest plantations. With these economic incentives, it is unsurprising that the Forest Service greatly emphasized roadbuilding and responded enthusiastically to local counties advocating for increased cutting knowing that this translated into fattening their budgets. Like most organizations, of course, the agency's desire to maximize its budget was viewed as highly desirable. The addiction to growth is alluring and powerful.

In June 1960, President Eisenhower signed into law the Multiple-Use Sustained-Yield Act (MUSY). For the first time, our national forests were identified as important for purposes beyond timber supply and water needs. Provision of outdoor recreation and protection of habitat for wildlife and fish were also identified as additional purposes for national forests. All of these multiple uses—timber, water, range, recreation, and wildlife and fish—were to be treated as equals. Up until 1960, the Forest Service had operated with broad authority; now for the first time the agency had a congressional directive that communicated that no one of the five multiple uses was to be viewed as greater than any other. From the perspective of this legislation, timber was no longer king—rather, it was a co-equal with the other uses. This change in Forest Service policy came about as some in

Congress began to feel pressure from their constituents, especially conservationists, who were becoming increasingly alarmed at the rate of logging on federal forestlands. Clearly, if Pinchot's philosophy of managing the forests for the long term was still being followed, then legislation focused on sustained yield would not have been needed. Because the Forest Service had become consumed with getting the cut out, with the elimination of old growth as quickly as possible, Congress felt the need to act. MUSY stated explicitly that the "renewable resources of the national forests" should be managed "without impairment of the productivity of the land." Congress realized that the Forest Service needed to be restrained.

Although protection of water resources was identified as one of the driving forces behind the creation of the Forest Service, this was not reflected in its budget, with the vast majority of funds going to timber sales and roadbuilding. Hirt captures well the disjunction between the practices of forestry and the drivers behind politics: "Because forestry is a long-term affair requiring consistency, and politics is a short-term affair requiring compromises, the two make terrible business partners." Congress consistently applied pressure on the Forest Service to maximize revenues, and the agency responded by building more and more roads and increasing the level of cut. At the time of the passage of MUSY, less than two-tenths of 1 percent of budgets were aimed at soil and water protection. Like an addict hooked on heroin who ignores the other needs of the body for healthy foods and nutrition, the Forest Service had become hooked on logging and roadbuilding.

One of the often-overlooked requirements of MUSY was the creation of multiple-use planning. An agency dominated by people focused on getting the cut out and building roads was now required to hire a wide range of specialists including soil scientists and wildlife biologists to help in the preparation of individual forest plans and to participate in land management decisions. Land managers at the time had little understanding of the long-term impact of this requirement. In fact, this requirement would lead to another transformation of the Forest Service. Just as some cactuses require thirty years of growth before they are ready to flower, the new resource specialists—or, as they were derisively known within the agency, "ologists," which included wildlife biologists, hydrologists, archaeologists, and soil scientists—being hired by the Forest Service in the 1960s would also require nearly thirty years of presence and research and advocacy before they would flower into a force the agency could no longer ignore and one that would eventually bring its high-production phase to a close.

In the GPNF, Forest Supervisor Glen Jorgenson reflected on multiple use in his 1959 annual summary: "Multiple use is a concept rather than a system or method of land use," and the "first need in applying the concept is to define management objectives." He then stated, "The harmonious combination of uses to arrive at the maximum over-all service from the forest requires some concessions in individual use." What Jorgenson was covertly recognizing was that, even with the impending adoption of a multiple-use philosophy, individual use would dominate. That individual use was timber production. In discussing the pressure from recreation users for recreation facilities, Jorgenson makes clear his priorities: "The demands on funds for timber access roads and engineering surveys limit the amount available for campground roads." He went on to state, "Road mileage in the ultimate system when the forest is fully developed is 5,091 miles," and that "a big job lies ahead in the location, survey, and construction of 3,949 miles of non-existing roads." This represents an expected 346 percent increase in roads in the GPNF. Boom times were on and the Forest Service as represented by the GPNF was quite giddy about the future. In their eyes, they represented an unstoppable juggernaut. Booms are inevitably followed by busts, but those who are in the midst of boom times are almost always blinded to the future busts. And such was the case with the Forest Service, especially during the high-production phase.

Gifford Pinchot would no doubt have been shocked to learn how the secretary of agriculture viewed conservation during the Eisenhower administration. Secretary Ezra Taft Benson drew a strong distinction between preservation and conservation, stating, "Conservation means management," and emphasized his view of timber as a crop. The pressure to get the cut out is well reflected in what the Forest Service identified as the allowable cut for all national forests, which increased from 6.5 billion board feet in 1953 to 8.3 billion board feet in 1961. The incredibly accelerated production of timber begun in the 1950s continued unabated into the 1980s. In 1962, however, the timber planners felt that it was necessary to revise the allowable cut in the GPNF down to 381 million board feet, reflecting their awareness that the existing rate of cut was not sustainable. Even with these concerns that the GPNF was logging at a rate that could not be sustained for the long term, logging continued to increase until it reached almost 560 million board feet on the GPNF in 1968.

In 1960, in his annual report on timber management, GPNF supervisor Glen Jorgenson noted that the GPNF intended to begin an "extensive inventory of its timber resources." The intent of this inventory was to determine the "total volume by species and size classes, of available timber, about the growth of the entire timber stand, and about natural mortality occurring in the stand." The data from this project, which was to be revisited, and remeasured every ten years, was to be used to establish an allowable cut that would ensure "continuous optimum production of the timber crops." What is most notable is the reference to timber as a crop. Virtually no reference is given to the other values of the forests that were acknowledged in the MUSY Act. While this inventory of timber resources was supposedly initiated in 1960, and clearly was intended to address concerns about the sustainability of the high levels of cut on the forest, no mention is made of this inventory in the annual reports put out by the GPNF supervisor over the succeeding ten years. One wonders why not: was this omission an error or possibly a smokescreen to placate production concerns while cutting continued unabated?

In 1961, supervisor Jorgenson again emphasized that ensuring a sustained yield "permits harvesting only as much timber each year as is grown, thus insuring a continuous flow of raw materials to the mills adjacent to the forest." In noting that the "crop rotation" was an average of 120 years, Jorgenson went on to recognize, "Much of the present standing timber is beyond the age of best utilization" and that "harvesting to prevent further deterioration and at the same time observing the principles of multiple use and sustained yield and coming out with an economically feasible program is the job of our professional foresters." Again, what is clearly evident is the primacy of economics over ecology. His view, which was entirely consistent with his peers throughout the Pacific Northwest, was that most of the timber on his forest was no longer productive because it was old growth. Little concern was given to the requirements of MUSY, that foresters also must attend to the needs of wildlife and their habitats and recreation. The fact that old growth met the needs of many species especially adapted to old-growth habitats was simply irrelevant. What was most important was to assure "survival of the fittest trees and maximum rate of growth." A Darwinian view of the forest prevailed—that by eliminating old growth and supplanting them with even-aged trees in plantations, the fittest trees would inevitably prevail. Only time would prove this view wrong—dense and crowded plantations did not lead to the emergence of the fittest. Single-aged, single-species plantations were more susceptible to insect infestations and catastrophic fires. While hoping for maximum growth, they were engineering unhealthy forest—which led to both increasingly poor habitats for diverse species and slower-growing trees competing for sunlight and nutrients in their overcrowded thickets.

By 1963, GPNF supervisor Ross Williams recognized MUSY by titling his annual report "Progress in Multiple Use." The first paragraph, however, makes clear how misleading the title was: "Harvesting of the full allowable cut of timber from the forest each year is of vital importance to the local economy. It is also the only practical way to keep the forest in a healthy, growing condition." A bold illustration shows a heavily loaded logging truck with a few large logs—clearly old growth—barreling down a logging road. In the background is a yarder, in which a large spar tree has a medusa of cables flowing from its top toward the ground with logs ready to be hauled to a landing. Cutting the full amount of the designated allowable cut had now become an imperative, a necessity, to ensure a healthy forest. Williams further stated: "Yields of young timber stands are increased by thinning which removes the smaller suppressed trees and favors the vigorous ones remaining. Quality of stands is improved by removing poorly formed trees and pruning those that will eventually be 'crop' trees." In previous reports, Williams had simply referred to the forest of trees as crops without quotation marks. Now in 1963, he felt the need to put "crop" in quotes. What compelled that change? Perhaps Williams was responding with growing sensitivity to the idea that some in the public might object to only viewing these towering behemoths, these old-growth forests hundreds of years old, as simply a crop. Crops are corn and wheat that are harvested annually. Are these ancient trees, which on a per-acre basis represent the highest level of biomass per acre (weight and density of living organisms) on the planet, to be regarded as one would consider a farmer's crop of corn?

Old-growth forests in the Pacific Northwest are unique for their combination of size and longevity. While California's redwoods are bigger than old-growth Douglas-firs, several species of big trees grow to enormous sizes in the Pacific Northwest, including cedars. Perhaps the GPNF supervisor putting the word "crops" in quotes was recognizing, although not acknowledging, that these forests were much more than a crop, that they were complex ecosystems. Ecosystems are much more than trees; they include diverse organisms as well as the climate, soil, water, and air where those organisms live and interact in that diverse panoply of life. Like the those in Pinchot's namesake forest, forest supervisors across the Pacific Northwest failed to recognize their forests as ecosystems and continued to view this rich diversity of growth in their forests as crops, as fiber, as wood products. This failure continued through the 1960s and into the 1980s as acknowledging the value of ecosystems would jeopardize getting the cut out, and no need was greater than that.

Edward Cliff, chief of the USFS in the early 1960s, compared forestry to farming by noting, "A new forest, man-planned and managed and coming up sturdily where century-old giants formerly stood, also has its brand of beauty—similar in its way to the terraced contours and the orderly vegetative growth upon well managed farmland." This comparison of forest with "well managed farmland" was probably the impetus in the late 1960s for an entirely new approach to intensive management by the Forest Service: terracing. Replacing haphazard stands of old growth would be orderly rows of newer forest that represented humankind's control over nature.

To showcase this new approach to the public, the Forest Service chose the Bitterroot National Forest in Montana. One of the drivers for this choice was that regeneration of trees had failed in some of the cutover areas. The agency began bulldozing mountain sides to create terraces that would allow for easier planting and, they hoped, regeneration and harvesting of timber "crops." Most leaders within the agency were convinced that they could demonstrate to the public the efficacy and wisdom of making the forest more productive. Some Forest Service leaders did object to this level of utter transformation of a natural forest—for them, it was a step too far—but they were a small minority, and their concerns did not stop the terracing. Looking back, one wonders how the agency was able to ignore the changing values of the American public and the increasing importance that the public was placing on environmental issues. From the Forest Service perspective, they were showcasing the triumph of science over nature.

Many in the public were dumbfounded on first seeing the wild forested landscapes clear-cut and then bulldozed to create uniform terraces across a steep hillside in a forest that once had trails and wildlife. Human arrogance and the power of the iron triangle—the tacit agreement among the Forest Service, the timber industry, and Congress to act in concert—prevailed over the ecosystem. The view that the forest was a crop prevailed over any aesthetic sensibilities that the public might have. Gifford Pinchot's only son, Bryce, when he saw what the Forest Service had done to the Bitterroots, exclaimed, "If my father had seen this, he would have cried."

The terracing of mountainsides to ease the planting of trees as crops marked both the apotheosis of intensive forest management and the nadir of treating the forest as a vibrant, complex, diverse ecosystem. Production had seemingly become the Forest Service's sole goal. The terraces were designed to have contoured benches on which tree planting machines could be operated. The agency began to conceive of itself as a farmer harvesting wheat with a combine harvester, which combined three functions—reaping, threshing, and winnowing—into a single process. Likewise, the agency sought to create the conditions for using complicated machinery to plant, thin, and then harvest its trees. Even old-time loggers were disturbed by what they saw. One logger explained: "They're ruining our timber stands for the next three generations. They're taking out all the timber and pretty soon there won't be any more to log." Farmers and ranchers complained that watersheds were being ruined. Fisheries were negatively impacted. And the many people who cared about aesthetics were simply appalled at what they saw when they looked at the mountains—bare terraces. The forested mountains had been transformed into cultivated hills ready for the next crop of trees. Natural beauty was gone. In its place was a mountain that had been brutally scalped.

The conservation community viewed terracing as quite misguided. Gifford Pinchot, had he suddenly resurfaced, would not have recognized the agency he founded. No doubt he would have viewed vast clear-cuts and terracing of mountainsides not only with disdain but also with disbelief. How could a Forest Service that had been so loyal to his original vision for forty years then take actions diametrically opposed to it? The agency's leaders ignored the many clues and evidence around them, indicated by the passage of key environmental bills under President Nixon and the first Earth Day that demonstrated that they were increasingly out of touch with the values of mainstream Americans.

While the terracing of the Bitterroot forest received extensive attention as a desecration, the same kind of terracing occurred in the GPNF on what had been the Yacolt Burn and was publicized in the 1964 annual report by Supervisor Ross Williams. Just as in the Bitterroot case, significant regrowth of trees was not occurring as hoped, especially on the high ridges of the Yacolt Burn. Williams placed a photograph of terraced slopes on the Yacolt Burn prominently in his annual report on the GPNF and noted the terracing of slopes was done prior to seeding. This terracing of slopes and the little attention it received in contrast to the terracing that took place in the Bitterroot forest is another example of the extent to which the GPNF was the "forgotten forest." Just a little over 50 miles from Portland but on the other side of the Columbia River, the GPNF lacked a natural constituency. In considering the situation, who in the Forest Service developed the idea of terracing mountainsides? Perhaps knowing that such an approach might spark controversy, the proponent of terracing decided to use it on a pilot or trial basis, largely out of the public eye. The remote and not easily accessed Yacolt Burn may have provided an ideal location to test out this new approach to intensive management.

In his 1967 annual report, GPNF supervisor Ross Williams stated that, while 381 million board feet was the allowable sustained yield volume, the actual cut for that year was 510 million board feet. The actual cut exceeded what had been determined as the allowable cut by some 33 percent. Perhaps he was responding to internal pressures for increased production while knowing that such numbers were not sustainable. A photograph in that report features a 79-inch-diameter log on a logging truck. The supervisor noted that these logs were "one-log loads" out of Morton, Washington. That size log was not uncommon coming off the old-growth forest in the GPNF. By the 1968 annual report, Williams stated that 627 million board feet was harvested and that "this record cut is one which the timber industry and the Forest Service share with pride." This extraordinary level of cut exceeded what was stipulated to be "allowable" by 65 percent. The idea of allowable cut, in essence, had become a hollowed-out concept that hid from the environmental community a highly undesirable reality: the rapid elimination of old-growth forests.

The reality on the ground in the GPNF was a yawning gap between what had been identified as "allowable" and the actual cut. How, then, could Ross Williams justify this disparity? Simple: approve a higher allowable-cut level. In 1971, Williams determined that the allowable-cut level was now determined to be 416 million board feet and would be achieved by an unprecedented level of intensive forest management. Over the next two decades, harvest levels in the GPNF were in the 450–500 million board feet range annually. Over a nearly thirty-year period in the GPNF, the Forest Service clear-cut 10 to 20 square miles of forestland every year. By the late 1980s, old-growth forest with trees over two hundred years of age remained in only 9–14 percent of the forest. All but 2 percent of that old growth, which was mostly in protected wilderness areas, was ecologically fragmented into numerous blocks scattered throughout the forest.

Williams went on to write: "Timber harvest also enabled us to manipulate our forest landscape. The creation of new forests adds a pattern of natural beauty." It may strike many as ironic that Williams found more beauty in the new plantings than in the lost forest, but he clearly saw production as the most desirable outcome. The natural forest was rapidly disappearing as old-growth logs were being carted off as "one-log loads," and in its place, absurdly, was the "natural beauty" of clear-cuts. By 1970, Williams began to address some environmental concerns regarding the size and shape of clear-cuts by acknowledging, "Timber harvesting has created many rectangular shaped openings in the Forest landscape" and stated his intent to place more emphasis on "making harvest units blend into the scene as much as possible . . . by using irregular or curved cutting lines to create openings which blend with natural shapes already in the forest." Over several years, Williams shifted his stance from proclaiming that clear-cuts provided a "pattern of natural beauty" to agreeing to shape clear-cuts so that they blended in. His move was likely more about public reactions than concern for aesthetics.

In 1965, Forest Service chief Edward Cliff spoke to a group of his leaders at a meeting in Portland, Oregon, and it is likely that GPNF supervisor Williams was in attendance. Cliff confirmed, unambiguously, that the Forest Service was thoroughly wedded to a high-production vision. He compared aspects of clear-cutting to urban renewal, as "a necessary violence prelude to a new housing development. When we harvest over-mature, defective timber that would otherwise be wasted, there is bound to be a temporary loss of natural beauty. But there is also the promise of what is to come: a thrifty new forest replacing the old. The point is that there often must be a drastic, even violent, upheaval to create a new forest." Perhaps Williams was in the audience taking notes and decided later to use that reference to "natural beauty" when he wrote his annual report. Seemingly many forest supervisors took to heart the notion that to grow a new forest, they must cut down the old forest. In its place, a thrifty new forest would grow. And an old-growth ecosystem would largely disappear.

Looking back on these remarkable comments by Edward Cliff, his views are notable for both their acknowledgment of the actual violence taking place in the forests and their lack of awareness of how the public might respond to this violence. Humankind could make things better. This might require a level of destruction that could upset some by its unsightliness, but clear-cuts were viewed as a necessary tool to create a more productive forest in the long term. Foresters were convinced that they knew best what was needed to make a forest more productive. Nature simply had to be manipulated, and it would yield to humankind's superior knowledge. Eventually, the Forest Service did learn to acknowledge the complexity of the forest and the important role that old growth played in ensuring vital habitat for a variety of forest plants and animals, including many endangered species. By the time the tide finally turned, though, most of the old growth in the Pacific Northwest was gone.

The local counties with land in the GPNF were quite content to see the liquidation of old growth and were overjoyed by the increasing scale of timber harvests. Steadily increasing revenues translated into robust funding of schools and public services and low taxes. And while Pinchot designed an agency that would ensure a sustainable supply of wood to rural communities and counties, the transformed agency during the high-production phase was quickly running out of "one-log loads" and fast running into a wall that would later cripple those same rural communities and counties that, in the high-production heyday, assumed the good times would last forever.

The practices of the Forest Service during this high-production phase were, in many ways, like a Greek tragedy in which the actual tragic event—for example, a brutal murder—takes place out of sight of the audience. Likewise, the Forest Service believed it could hide the vast clear-cuts expanding across the landscapes with forested screens alongside roadways. However, just as with Greek tragedies, in which the characters eventually must face up to the effects of their actions, so too did the effects of clear-cuts slowly begin to register on the consciousness of an increasingly conservation-oriented and aware American public. As the tragedy of the increasingly degraded forest "commons" became more and more evident, the public with stronger fervor began to question these supposed guardians of the public trust. How had things gone so wrong? How had the Forest Service allowed wild landscapes dominated by majestic old-growth trees to be mowed down like the grass in someone's front yard? Paul Hirt in *A Conspiracy of Optimism: Management of the National Forest since World War Two* answers this question persuasively: "The intensive management program that cloaked the high harvest levels with a façade of rationality simply became irrational and unacceptable. The result is a rather sudden collapse of timber production, a sudden rise in local and regional unemployment, a lot of contention and bitterness, and a sense that the Forest Service has failed in its fundamental mission to produce commodities sustainably while protecting the nonmarket values of the forest."

Less than 13 percent of all the original old growth in the Pacific Northwest remained in 1990. The ending, though, did not come about because of some internal awareness and insights; rather, it was solely a result of actions by the judiciary. Forest plans as of 1990 projected that virtually all unprotected old growth was to be logged by 2023. Only 6 percent of all the original old growth was to remain, and that would be found almost entirely in designated wilderness and other protected lands.

The high-production phase was greatly aided by the fact that private timber industry had cut most of the existing old growth on its lands by the end of the 1940s. Demand for national forest timber increased greatly during the 1950s, and the national forests in the Pacific Northwest retained the vast majority of old-growth forest left in the United States. While private timber industry had some supplies of second-growth timber, that did not satisfy those who sought high-quality, virgin timber with its clear, tight grains, its superior strength, and its superior aesthetic quality. The Forest Service, in the interest of timber management and supply, was happy to meet the needs of private industry. This need for high-quality wood dovetailed with the new emphasis of the Forest Service on replacing "over-mature" or "decadent" trees with faster-growing young trees. This new paradigm transformed the relationship between the Forest Service and the timber industry: two groups that had often been adversaries during the stewardship phase now became allies.

This alliance can be most clearly seen in examining how both the Forest Service and the timber industry now defined the greatest good for the greatest number: maximizing production by maximizing the logging of old-growth forests and replacing them with even-aged plantations. Timber management translated into intensive management. Paul Hirt captures well the dynamics behind this new approach to forestry: "When facing conflict among users or situations that called for a choice between production and preservation, managers adopted instead the optimistic view that choices did not really have to be made if foresters simply applied more intensive management. Intensive management was a special phrase adopted by foresters in the agency and in the timber industry that signified the lavish application of capital, labor, and technology to increase the commercial productivity of forests." A timber plan for one Pacific Northwest forest very similar in size to the GPNF well illustrates the extent to which timber management became almost the sole focus of staff for that forest. Explicitly stated in that plan was that good timber management was the "most useful tool for enhancing other uses." Examples include:

- Timber management and scenery: "Clear-cuts break the monotony of the scene, and deciduous brush in these areas furnish fall color and spring flowers for at least ten to fifteen years."
- Timber management and roads: "The roads built in connection with timber harvesting furnish access for more people to enjoy the use of other resources."
- Timber management and soils: "The orderly harvest of old-growth timber can reduce soil impact from roots."
- Timber management and recreation: "Openings also improve berry picking and are highly favorable to the development of large herds of elk. This increases the potential for hunting."
- Timber management and multiple use: "The timber manager should direct his management of timber toward the use of timber harvesting as a tool in attaining true multiple-use management."

The single-mindedness of the Forest Service during this period of intensive forest management was quite extraordinary. Agency personnel selectively and enthusiastically touted the benefits of logging and clear-cuts: cutover lands provided more deer browse; increasing miles of roads simply provide more roads for tourists to drive on; and increased water flows off clear-cuts provided more water for downstream users. Some of the Forest Service's justifications bordered on the absurd, such as claims that a patchy landscape of clear-cuts in various stages of regeneration would offer a more pleasing view to visitors than a landscape of unbroken ancient forests with its trees of breathtaking size and height.

As noted in the timber plan, the Forest Service viewed timber management as key to meeting a whole range of other needs. Whether the agency truly believed those claims for timber management is not clear. What is clear is the necessity it felt to convince the public that the greatest good was still being addressed.

The dominant focus of the Forest Service throughout the high-production phase was on production and timber management. That the agency had a dismissive attitude to all other uses of the forest is perhaps not too surprising given that around two-thirds of professional staff in the agency were silviculturists and road engineers and that they dominated in the leadership ranks. Their education and training, their rewards, their promotions, their recognition were almost entirely dependent on the ultimate aim of doing whatever it took to get the cut out.

Pinchot would almost certainly have been greatly saddened by the resulting unsustainable level of harvest. The father would no longer recognize what had become of the prodigal son.

Old growth being loaded onto a logging truck in the Gifford Pinchot National Forest. *GPNF image.*

Old-growth Douglas-fir recently logged in the Gifford Pinchot National Forest. *GPNF image.*

An old-growth Douglas-fir stand in the Gifford Pinchot National Forest. *GPNF image.*

Gifford Pinchot III, Gifford Pinchot's grandson, in 1949 stands alongside President Harry S. Truman as the president signs the bill that changed the name of the Columbia National Forest to the Gifford Pinchot National Forest. *GPNF image.*

A log train crossing the Cowlitz River in the Gifford Pinchot National Forest during the early high-production years. 1949. *GPNF image.*

A pre-eruption classic view of Mount St. Helens with Spirit Lake in the foreground. *GPNF image.*

Mount St. Helens erupting.
May 18, 1980. *GPNF image.*

Clear-cuts near Mt. Adams in the
Gifford Pinchot National Forest.
Image courtesy of Susan Saul.

Clear-cut area near Mt. Adams
in the Gifford Pinchot National
Forest. *Image courtesy of Susan
Saul.*

A parade of one-log logging trucks from the Gifford Pinchot National Forest in the early days of the high-production phase. *Forest History Society, Forest History Society Photograph Collection.*

Clear-cuts with Mt. Adams, Gifford Pinchot National Forest, in the background. *Forest History Society, Forest History Society Photograph Collection.*

12

New Environmental Policies

NEPA (the National Environmental Policy Act), a brilliantly articulated, concise, visionary, bendable statute, would be the foundation of US federal sustainability efforts well into the twenty-first century.

—Douglas Brinkley

Early in the high-production phase of forestry, the Forest Service, with the help of more sophisticated computer technology, realized that harvest levels could not be sustained after the old growth had been harvested in the Northwest and that harvest levels would need to be reduced by 45 percent. In *Managing Multiple Uses on National Forests, 1905–1995,* John Fedkiw recognized the extent to which the Forest Service's own findings "shattered the traditional basis for determining sustainable harvest levels in western old-growth forest—estimating the annual allowable cut by dividing the total old-growth inventory by rotation age and adding the net annual growth of immature timber to it." Because the timber industry objected, based on their concerns that harvest levels would decrease, the agency chose to apply a more intensive timber management approach to the problem: increased reforestation, thinning, timber stand improvement, and other intensive practices intended to accelerate growth of young stands of timber. Initially, this led to the designation of "allowable-cut effect," which later came to be called "earned harvest effect." Through intensive management "today," the Forest Service was going to earn the right "tomorrow" to cut higher levels because of assumed greater growth levels in the future. Hoping for the best—and that is what these assumptions were, merely hopes—they were gambling with the healthy functioning of national forests throughout the Pacific Northwest and the economic well-being of the many rural communities that depended on them.

As the Gifford Pinchot National Forest was the first national forest as part of a pilot program to assess the effectiveness of intensive management, in 1975 it became the first national forest in the country to be permitted to account for what the agency called "earned harvest effect" in its allowable-cut determinations. Based on those many assumptions, the GPNF was able to pursue extremely high harvest levels well into the 1980s. In the GPNF Timber Management Plan, 1975–1984, Environmental Impact Statement, the plan identified a potential yield of 5.3 billion board feet of "sawtimber" for the next ten-year period based on intensive forestry practices. Although the plan suggested some reduction in the allowable cut from previous years, it also stated that "more intensive management could reduce the amount of the reduction." It makes clear that the assumptions of the pilot were baked into the new plan: "Allowable harvest benefits are included in the potential yield to show the results of more intensive management. Allowable harvest benefit is the resulting increase in yearly harvests indicated by the results of a silvicultural practice." To translate these rather arcane sentences, the meaning is that ongoing high levels of harvest were dependent on the results of planned silvicultural practices designed to make future forest even more productive.

For the first time, the Forest Service in the GPNF was required to identify adverse impacts on the environment. Acknowledgment is made that on the GPNF, air quality will be degraded, soil erosion will increase, water quality will be affected, "change in fish and wildlife habitat will result," along with "alterations in the appearance of the landscape." The GPNF plan goes on to identify a potential annual sustained yield under fully intensive management of 527 million board feet a year and specifies that this is based on "implementation of each intensive practice now technologically feasible to each qualifying acre." The plan acknowledges that the present level of harvest is not sustainable, but that "ample opportunity" exists to increase allowable harvest level through "increasing the level of management intensity." Such a declaration in the plan indicates a level of optimism that was not warranted if sustaining the resource was a priority. To achieve this extraordinary level of output, each intensive practice needed to be implemented on each and every "qualifying acre."

With the growth of the environmental movement came Earth Day in 1970 and soon after an assessment of Forest Service practices, the Bolle Report. This report found the agency's timber bias "led to 'timber mining' not sustained yield." The US Congress during the first half of the 1970s was the most environmentally-friendly Congress of the twentieth century and was determined to ensure that the nation's forests were treated as a renewable resource, one that met Pinchot's vision of providing for the long run.

Enveloped in its own bubble, little did the Forest Service realize at the time that its focus on intensive management, along with its expanding clear-cutting and bulldozing and terracing of mountainsides, would lead to changes in policy that eventually would force the agency to radically transform its practices. The public gave much greater attention to the environment in the 1960s and 1970s. This increased attention was likely in response to public campaigns led by groups like the Sierra Club that drew attention to a host of environmental harms. The public and many environmental groups began to pressure Congress to act to better protect the environment. This pressure led to landmark laws including the National Environmental Policy Act (1970), which established requirements for environmental reviews of any federal actions, including logging in roadless areas, that could have significant environmental impacts; and the Endangered Species Act of 1973, which required conservation of species that were endangered or threatened in all or some part of their range. A critical aspect of that act was the requirement that the ecosystems, on which those species depended, also be conserved. This act more than any other environmental act of the latter half of the twentieth century would have far-reaching impacts on the practices of the Forest Service, far beyond what anyone at the time could have imagined.

The other act that most directly and immediately impacted the agency was the National Forest Management Act (NFMA), which was passed in 1976. Congress believed that the Forest Service needed to be restrained. Some members of Congress were concerned that the high level of cut in the Pacific Northwest was not sustainable. They viewed the agency as more influenced by the desires of the forest products industry than the wishes of the public. Although some guidance had been provided in 1960 with the passage of the Multiple-Use Sustained-Yield Act, Congress recognized that timber remained the almost sole focus of the agency. Many in Congress were no longer convinced that the greatest good was defined by the amount of timber coming off the forest. The NFMA mandated extensive planning and public participation in the planning process. For the first time since the creation of the Forest Service in 1905, the public had a real seat at the table and an opportunity to influence policy in a way that had been missing in the past. The most significant change beyond that of public participation was the requirement for each national forest to prepare long-term, integrated plans. These plans needed to address a wide range of issues previously largely ignored by the Forest Service: suitability of various uses of lands under their management; hazards to riparian areas; unstable lands or endangered species; providing for a diversity of plant and animal communities; and, importantly, identification of alternative resource management systems. Once a particular alternative was chosen, the agency was required to monitor and assess the results. The statute also directed the agency to establish standards and guidelines for timber management and protection of "other resources." This reference to "other resources" opened the door to environmental organizations to ensure that "habitat shall be managed to maintain viable populations of existing native and desired non-native vertebrate species in the planning area." The addition of a few words—"viable populations of existing native . . . species"—in a long and wordy federal statute had a far-reaching impact on an entire region, the central Cascades, and led, ultimately, to the end of old-growth logging in the GPNF and throughout the Pacific Northwest.

While the NFMA mandated increased public participation in the development of forest plans, the reality was that national forest managers still retained exclusive decision authority, authority that had been delegated by the Organic Act of 1897. Although public participation increased, few managerial decisions changed as a result. Listen and ignore was essentially their response. This lack of influence by outside forces caused environmental groups to turn to the courts.

The growing disconnect between the public and the leaders of the Forest Service became starkly evident in 1970 with the agency's release of "The Forest Service Environment Program for the Future." This document was likely a response to the public's increasing concern with a wide variety of environmental harms ranging from oil spills off the California coast to endangered species such as eagles and peregrine falcons to water pollution as exemplified by Ohio's Cuyahoga River catching on fire in 1969. Among those environmental harms was an ever-expanding landscape of clear-cuts, especially in, but not limited to, the Pacific Northwest. In response to these concerns, the first Earth Day was held in April 1970 with the intent of building on the emerging consciousness of environmental degradation and the need to make addressing it a priority.

While the Forest Service's document professed to address the public's concerns for non-timber values such as wilderness protection, recreation, habitat and watershed protection, the reality, in a closer reading of the document, was that the agency was looking to log even more timber off the national forests. To achieve this aim, they identified the need to dedicate nearly 100 million acres of forestlands solely to timber production. These forests would thus be off-limits for watershed protection or wilderness designation. The document called for spending vast sums of money to accomplish ever more intensive management of the forest. By the early 1980s they wanted to increase the allowable cut for all of the national forest from 13.6 to 21 billion board feet, an increase of 54 percent. While the title of this document, "The Forest Service Environment Program for the Future," sounded promising, its contents essentially promised more of the same: more clear-cuts and logging of old-growth trees. Perhaps some agency leaders felt they were at least acknowledging environmental concerns, but those who looked closely realized that true substance in terms of attendance to environmental values was missing.

Opposition to clear-cutting grew significantly in the 1960s and into the 1970s and was a direct response to the adverse impacts on wildlife habitat, fisheries, plant and animal diversity, water supplies, recreational experiences, and aesthetics. The Forest Service had lost sight of Pinchot's guidance in which he made clear the "National Forests exist today because the people want them. To make them accomplish the 'most good,' the people themselves must make clear how they want them run." Unfortunately, the agency had, to a great extent, stopped listening to the public. Some within the Forest Service were beginning to acknowledge by the 1980s a need to apply an ecosystem approach to multiple-use management; at least one agency leader did acknowledge that "our ecology conscience could stand improving."

The reality on the ground, however, was business as usual. The ecological conscience of the Forest Service showed little improvement. Clear-cutting continued unabated. Targeting of old growth for logging continued unabated. Roadbuilding continued unabated.

The National Forest Management Act set the stage for a much greater involvement of the federal judiciary. New regulations were identified that enabled outside groups to challenge the Forest Service if they were not abiding by those regulations. To help with the creation of these required forest plans, the agency had to hire even more specialists: biologists, hydrologists, archaeologists, geologists. These scientists played a critical role in developing a scientific knowledge base underlying forest policy. The Forest Service, however, continued to be dominated by foresters and engineers who continued to put a priority on timber. They largely ignored the advice of their specialists. Clary captures well this nearly obsessive focus on timber and how the centers of power in Washington, DC, influenced the agency: "Talk of balanced programs, interdisciplinary planning, and multiple use could not alter the Forest Service's focus on timber. It was, after all, a federal bureaucracy, and, accordingly, it was affected by the flow of power in the government. By its nature as a revenue producing activity, timber management figured in the national economic calculation. Congress and successive presidents reinforced the Service's timber orientation by calling for expanded national forest sales to support economic growth or to provide federal revenues. The latter became especially important during the administration of Ronald Reagan, whose materialistic attitude toward natural resources exceeded that of the federal foresters."

Although the NFMA passed in 1976, it was not until the beginning of the Reagan administration that regulations were defined, and by that time, the administration made clear its view on cutting of old growth. John Crowell, the chief national forest policymaker during Reagan's first term, stated in 1982: "One of my major initiatives has been to speed up harvest of the slow-growing or decadent, over-mature timber stands in the Pacific Northwest." In addition, Crowell wanted Forest Service planners not to place too much emphasis on protecting wildlife and scenery. Crowell was a classic example of the fox guarding the henhouse. Prior to taking on responsibility for the USFS, he had spent his entire professional career as an attorney and advocate for Louisiana Pacific and other timber companies. He was a leader for those companies in fighting limits on the size of clear-cuts and restrictions on the use of herbicides. While researchers on the ground were increasingly aware of the many ecological services that old growth provided, among them critical habitat for endangered species like the spotted owl and marbled murrelets, many policymakers in DC retained the perspective of early foresters who viewed old growth as an obstacle in the way of productive forests. After Crowell was appointed as chief of the Forest Service by President Reagan, he soon put out memoranda that timber harvest levels should be doubled.

In his oral history included in *Timber Management in the Pacific Northwest, 1927–1965*, Jack Usher acknowledged that, even with the shrinking of the land base as a result of roadless area designation, the allowable cut did not slow down the rate of cutting old growth. "We were cutting the full allowable cut off about two-thirds of the land base used to calculate it. It's all right if you did that for one or two years or even five but if you do it for a decade, which we did, you begin to run into trouble. . . . It was just poor business all the way round. Sooner or later you're going to have to pay the piper for such concentrated cutting." In the midst of the almost manic cutting of old growth, few foresters anticipated that the high level of cutting would come to a sudden end. As with many bubbles, those in the midst of it typically have lost all perspective and believe the good times will roll on forever. Only looking back did many of the old-timers in the forest industry acknowledge that truth—eventually they would have to "pay the piper."

Paying the piper was one of the least concerns for the foresters in the GPNF at the beginning of the 1980s. The experiences of the three previous decades reinforced the sense that the past predicts the future and that the Forest Service was on the right track. A culture that prided itself on its competence, confidence, and capability was surprised and shocked, like the rest of the public, when one of the iconic peaks on the west side of the GPNF, Mount St. Helens, literally disappeared.

13

The Eruption

The concept of disturbance regimes—the frequency, severity, and spatial pattern of disturbance across a landscape and over time—provided multiscale views of forest dynamics. Understanding the roles of disturbance and death complements the centuries-scale change of living parts of the ecosystem viewed through the lens of forest succession. Life and death, order and chaos, continuity and change, all intertwine in the ongoing procession of an old-growth forest.

—Nathaniel Brodie, Charles Goodrich,
Frederick J. Swanson

Early on a clear sky Sunday morning, May 18, 1980, Mount St. Helens erupted. The eruption was far beyond what anyone expected, including the many experts who had been studying the mountain closely for over two months, following a swarm of earthquakes that served as a warning that the mountain was once again coming to life. In *Eruption: The Untold Story of Mount St. Helens*, Steve Olson described what occurred that day as the "single most powerful disaster in US history, more powerful than Hurricane Katrina in 2005 . . . and generated one of the largest landslides in recorded human history." Mount St. Helens, along with Mount Adams, is one of the two perpetually snow-covered volcanic peaks found in the Gifford Pinchot National Forest. Mount St. Helens, located on the western border of the GPNF, and highly prized before the eruption for its lovely symmetrical cone and for the beauty and recreational opportunities offered by places like Spirit Lake, was a favorite summer haunt of thousands of recreationists. All that changed radically when over 1,000 feet of the mountaintop disappeared in a few minutes, and Spirt Lake was transformed into a barren, virtually lifeless, log-filled body of water. Fifty-seven people who were too close to the mountain at the time of the eruption died that Sunday morning. One of the legacies of that eruption would be a vastly changed understanding of the life, death, and rebirth of old-growth forests in the Pacific Northwest.

After the rescues of the survivors, after the repair of bridges and roads destroyed or damaged, after the mountain began its slow rebuilding process, a strenuous debate began among the many competing interest groups on what to do with this western half of Pinchot's namesake forest. The conservation community wanted to establish a national monument that would protect not only the blast zone but surrounding impacted areas as well. On the other side of the debate were the Forest Service and logging companies that opposed any additional protection. Susan Saul, one of the leaders among the conservation community, recognized that the Forest Service had no real vision for Mount St. Helens beyond doing what they had always been doing, getting the cut out. In an interview with the author, Saul related how the Forest Service leaders in Pinchot's namesake forest "did not get it because they were the old-time timber guys. They had plans for an interpretive area and then wanted to do extensive salvage so that everything would go back to what it was before. They just wanted to go back and make it look like it did before the eruption. They lacked vision." The Forest Service showed no interest in viewing Mount St. Helens as this extraordinary opportunity to examine the ecological processes that take place after a catastrophic eruption and to allow the natural restorative processes to take place over time. They did not recognize the importance of protecting the landscape for science. As far as these Pinchot heirs were concerned, all they needed to do was to salvage the thousands of acres of blown-down trees, plant grass across the barren blast zone, and pretend nothing significant had happened.

The Mount St. Helens eruption and its aftermath, however, were an epiphany for many of the researchers and scientists working for the Forest Service. In the interview with the author, Susan Saul captured the essence of the need to protect undisturbed the landscapes around the mountain after the eruption, "As we saw with Mount St. Helens, it's not what you take away but what you leave behind that is important." Many of the early predictions after the eruption were that the blast zone would be barren for many years if not decades. But because the Mount St. Helens National Monument was created in 1982 and 110,000 acres were protected, the landscape was allowed to undergo whatever processes would naturally occur. Most assumed that a moonlike terrain would long dominate the landscape. The recovery, however, was much more rapid than expected. Many small mammals like pocket gophers, deer mice, shrews, and voles survived underground and were quick to emerge. Their underground actions enabled the soil to be much more receptive to seeds. Lupine was one of the early colonizers, and soon vast fields of purple flowers flowed over the countryside. An entirely different landscape evolved from what many expected. Saul represented well the views of the environmental community: "Mount St. Helens now is the most biologically diverse landscape in the entire Cascade Range. No one predicted that. Only because the Monument was designated as a Research Area do we continue to have these important discoveries. There are still many questions on what is going on ecologically and biologically. What we are seeing on Mount St. Helens helps us understand the whole Cascade Range—this is much more than understanding volcanoes and eruptions, but also the creation of this whole mountain range."

The reality on the ground was that those areas that were left undisturbed in the chaotic conditions left by the blast were in fact the quickest to recover. Where salvage logging did occur, biological diversity was reduced. However, where the natural decay process was allowed to unfold, the soil more quickly gained needed nutrients, seeds were more readily able to take root, and as a result, plants and animals began to flourish in an astonishingly short time. Several species that had previously not lived in the area such as western meadowlarks found a home there. Ecologists began to speak not of the recovery of the mountain but rather the renewal of Mount St. Helens.

Jerry Franklin, the preeminent old-growth guru, was one of the researchers who experienced an epiphany after the Mount St. Helens eruption. A new term came into play—biological legacy—that would reshape how many came to understand the role of catastrophic disturbances in shaping landscapes not only in the GPNF but across the Pacific Northwest. Scientists were truly stunned by how quickly life returned to the seemingly sterile, bleak landscape post eruption. Rather than an inhospitable environment, a biological legacy ensued in which a wide variety of living organisms, spores, seeds and fungi, and plants and animals emerged. And one of the most important requirements for this emergence was leaving the landscape undisturbed; dead trees and snags and downed logs were left alone, which provided just the habitat needed to propagate new life. According to Franklin, these emerging insights stimulated a "re-examination of the recovery processes following other natural catastrophes, including wildfire and windstorm, and a comparison with recovery following human disturbances, particularly clearcutting."

A key lesson from post-eruption studies was the importance of leaving all remaining organic material as it was found after the natural disturbance, whether wildfire, windstorm, or catastrophic eruption. Ecosystems recover much more rapidly and with greater diversity when left alone after natural disturbances; what may appear as a chaotic landscape is, in fact, a legacy of living and organic materials, a legacy of plants of diverse composition and structure. In stark contrast are the legacies that result from most clear-cuts in which snags and downed logs are removed and leftover slash and woody materials are burned. The result according to Franklin "is that the young forests that develop following traditional clear-cut practices are typically much simpler in composition and structure than those which develop following natural disturbances." One of the clearest examples of that was just east of the Mount St. Helens blast zone where thousands of acres had been clear-cut in the GPNF. Within the blast zone could be found, surprisingly, an emerging landscape with much greater biodiversity and complexity than the forests that were growing from clear-cuts. On the east side of the blast zone were monocultures of single-species, same-aged plantations, the "crops" desired by Pinchot's heirs in his namesake forest.

Franklin and his fellow scientists learned the importance of allowing the seeming chaos and mess after a major disturbance—whether eruption, wildfire, or windstorm—alone. Downed logs, snags, islands of green trees aid recovery and are vital to wildlife and genetic and structural diversity. We can best assure the long-term healthy functioning of the forest after a major disturbance simply by letting it be.

One of the places where the distinctive approaches and practices between those determined to eliminate all old-growth forests and those wanting to protect them played out was the H. J. Andrews Experimental Forest in the central Cascade Mountains of Oregon. Even though the Andrews Forest, as it was known, was established as a research forest, the early scientists in the Andrews were also pressured to contribute their share of logs to the overall cut. The Andrews Forest staff effectively resisted these demands; key to this resistance were findings from their research on the Andrews Forest that would over time prove pivotal in changing silvicultural practices throughout the Pacific Northwest. One of the alarming discoveries documented by Max Geier in *Necessary Work: Discovering Old Forests, New Outlooks, and Community on the H.J. Experimental Forest* was that, as timber harvests advanced southward from the Columbia River into the higher elevations of the Cascade Range, there was a "dramatic increase in the percentage of logged land that did not naturally regenerate." At the time of this discovery, the concept of biological legacies and their importance to recovery was many years in the future. Discoveries on the Andrews, however, did lead to greater understanding of some of the reasons behind those failures of forests to regenerate. For decades, foresters required loggers to keep the rivers clean of debris (no mess!). Researchers on the Andrews Forest conclusively demonstrated that rivers and riparian ecosystems benefited from woody debris being left behind: mess is important. Aquatic insects and other invertebrates thrive; streambanks and stream channels are stabilized, resulting in less erosion; and the deeper pools of water that result provide much better habitat for fish, especially endangered and important species like salmon. This initial insight into the importance of woody debris in streams led to another conceptual breakthrough, that large woody debris was needed also for the well-being of forests.

While Franklin's conception of biological legacies was fully fleshed out by the early 1990s, the work at the Andrews Forest prior to that time led directly to changes in practices on the ground after clear-cuts: that leaving a "mess" was in fact a means to ensuring improved regeneration of forests. Snags, downed trees, standing green trees, woody materials of all sizes and shapes, which were the hallmarks of a biological legacy, were critical to the regeneration of forests.

14

Old Growth

Before it dies, a Douglas-fir, half a millennium old, will send its storehouse
of chemicals back down into its roots and out through its fungal partners,
donating its riches to the community pool in a last will and testament.
We might well call these ancient benefactors giving trees.

—Richard Powers

O ne of the clearest indicators for what leaders in the GPNF wanted to
do about the little remaining old growth is found in the 1987 Environment Impact Statement (EIS) for the GPNF. The EIS projects what
the annual demand for timber in the GPNF would be in the following
three decades (all numbers represent millions of board feet):

1986–1995: a range of 480–567
1996–2005: a range of 676–1,196
2006–2015: a range of 999–1,519

Almost all the assertions in the report are supportive of continued cutting of old growth. The astronomically high projected future demands and
this succinct statement in the plan, "Since the Forest is the primary source
of large diameter logs, any amount of Forest timber offered for sale will
probably be purchased," clearly make the case for continuing on the same
course as the previous three decades. Old growth on private lands disappeared many years earlier, and now the national forest was the last preserve
for the remaining old growth, and the Forest Service in the GPNF had
every intention to do what private foresters had done over the previous
hundred years: harvest virtually all remaining old growth. And building
roads was key to accessing that old growth.

As late as the mid-1980s, Forest Service leaders in the GPNF
were calling for even more roads, primarily "to accommodate timber
management." The Forest Service was highly consistent during the

high-production phase of its existence: any action that could reduce the acreage available for logging needed to be fought, and fought aggressively. Potential wilderness areas in heavily wooded landscapes especially were viewed as a threat. While forest supervisors throughout the Pacific Northwest refused to acknowledge that they were building roads strategically into areas that had the potential to later become wilderness, they did make those choices. One example of that in Pinchot's namesake forest was the area around Mount St. Helens prior to the eruption; the Forest Service recognized a significantly sized roadless area close to the mountain and divided those lands into four different roadless areas that then made them more susceptible to punching roads into them.

By the mid-1980s, the GPNF road mileage had reached 4,300 miles, an increase of 700 percent over the previous forty years. One of the rationales that Forest Service leaders used to a great extent was the support for high levels of cut that came from local communities. The EIS noted that, "While many local residents use the forest for recreation, they relate to it primarily as a source of employment and financial support for local schools and roads." Nowhere does the EIS mention that a little over 60 miles away was a population of nearly a million people who had little concern for sales receipts and great concern for recreation. One of the questions the plan initially addressed related directly to this divergence of interest among these two very distinct groups: "How much timber and where should timber be harvested?" While noting the economic dependence of the local communities, the report also acknowledged that the harvest level "is also of concern to people visiting the Forest for recreation . . . and impacts of timber harvest on scenic quality, fish, wildlife, and natural ecosystems." While acknowledging that increased demands for primitive forms of recreation could put additional pressures on roadless areas, the plan again stressed that "valuable stands of timber in some of these areas are economically important to adjacent communities." One of the most tragic statements addressed the question of what to do with the small remaining amount of old growth: "Old-growth forests are dwindling in the region. Standing, they have significant social and biological value. They also have high economic value when harvested." No mention was made of the fact that old growth was dwindling because of the practices on the GPNF over the previous forty years to eliminate old growth as quickly as possible to make way for plantations of same-aged conifers. What is highlighted is their economic value and the need for revenue by local communities.

The GPNF plan did acknowledge many of the discoveries made by Jerry Franklin of the roles and importance of old-growth forests, especially for at-risk species like the northern spotted owl. One of the most alarming statements in the plan, given the recognition of the value of old-growth forest to a healthy functioning ecosystem, addressed "Anticipated Conditions": "It is anticipated that a major portion of the timber harvest on the Forest will continue to come from older stands. If the current rate of harvest (an average of 6,200 acres annually) were to continue, the existing old-growth inventory outside of the withdrawn areas could be gone in 35 years." The end of old growth was in sight. This stark reality catalyzed the formation of environmental groups like the Gifford Pinchot Task Force (now Cascade Forest Conservancy), which mobilized in the 1980s and then sought to protect the remaining old growth.

Bob Williams was GPNF supervisor for most of the 1980s, taking over from Bob Tokarczyk in 1983. He viewed the move as a lucky one as he wanted a "big forest," and the GPNF certainly represented one of the biggest in the lower forty-eight states. When I asked about his proudest accomplishments, he spoke about the quality of the planning process at the GPNF. He then talked about his work accomplishments and the high level of output from the forest. "We for a while had the biggest budget in the entire system. Willamette (National Forest) had been the Big Granddaddy, but we exceeded them." At the same time, Williams viewed himself as a loyal disciple of Gifford Pinchot and believed that he was always guided by his vision of providing the greatest good for the greatest number for the long run. "To me it was never a difficult concept to understand—think long term, think about everybody, think about the resources. Just a common-sense approach to what we were doing. It was always in place and fit my wise view of conservation. This idea of taking care of what you got and you take care of it forever—just fit with my values." His view took people into account—you got to take care of water and the soil. His view brought people more into account as he came out of the robber baron area—people who had had their own way for a long time, and he recognized the need to do more for the "common people." Williams clearly acknowledged important Progressive Era values and principles.

Bob Williams had a strong land use ethic that revolved around doing what was right for the forest. At the same time he was part of a strong and cohesive culture, one that he had been a part of at that time for over thirty years. Most of the foresters and engineers that he worked with had similar backgrounds and perspectives and values. Little disagreement occurred as they planned and worked together. The leadership team was largely of one mind. When I asked about any regrets he had, he mentioned having "heated discussions around such things as whether to have wider strips along roads." This cohesive culture was of one mind when it came to managing the forest. Williams spoke cogently in a way that represented that culture and also spoke to the pressures he faced in Pinchot's namesake forest, pressures that led him to ignore fundamental Pinchot principles:

> There was a backlog of available material on the national forest that we should be moving quickly to convert unthrifty stands to thrifty stands. Stands not growing—that were stagnated we wanted to convert those to stands that were growing, superior trees, higher-quality trees. We recognized that eventually that would taper off and the private forest would be ready to provide more supply. Key was getting the road system in. Would have been better if we could have had much more dispersed cutting across the GP's 1.3 million acres but you can't do it that way as you have to cut where your roads are. The calculations acknowledged that we were cutting faster than we wanted to, but we were trying to get roads back in there so we could relax the level of cuts in other areas and then let that stuff grow faster. . . . We had a one-hundred-year rotation and, you just do your math, and it is pretty darn simple—take one hundredth every year. But then you have this other stuff as you don't have roads everywhere you need to go but you had a plan assuming you were going to get into all these areas and some of those had been taken off the table. This is where you get into political conflicts. I talked to the assistant secretary [of agriculture] and told him we needed to reduce harvest levels because of lack of access or roadless designation, and his response was that we will have that solved in a few years. You can keep this thing going, he said, because we don't want to shut down a bunch of mills. It came from all levels—all the way to Congress—they did not want to see reductions. Everyone wanted to keep a stable flow. . . . Between the administration and Congress—they were very clear about this—that is how the system works.

"Cutting faster than we wanted to." Perhaps no words better capture how Pinchot's legacy was being abandoned on his namesake forest. Williams captured well the many dynamics and dilemmas and tensions that existed for Forest Service supervisors. The "backlog" and "unthrifty stands" he mentions were old growth. The term old growth was not used by Forest Service managers like Williams; that term was anathema to them, as it represented a value they were reluctant to acknowledge. The conversion to more thrifty stands was a call for even-aged plantations of uniform stands of conifers. In the past, the most common term, as used by his predecessor Bob Tokarczyk, was "crops"; now, with greater sensitivity to the public, Forest Service leaders instead referred to "thrifty stands." The "superior and higher-quality trees" he referred to are a direct result of the planned intensive management of the forest. A key variable was how quickly roads could be built and pushed into watersheds so that more and more of the remaining old growth far up in the drainages could be accessed. One of the more telling statements made by Williams, and reflective of Forest Service leadership broadly, was that they "had a plan assuming that you were going to get into all these areas." Plans were made; assumptions were made that provided the rationale for maintaining high levels of cut, for not reducing the allowable-cut level. Time and time again those assumptions were proven wrong. Charles McKinley, writing in *Uncle Sam in the Pacific Northwest*, made clear how these assumptions were incorrect: "Briefly put, the timber is being used and destroyed three times as rapidly as it is being produced."

In 1990, the GPNF issued its first comprehensive, integrated "Land and Resource Management Plan," which replaced land management plans for nine units within the GPNF. For the first time, the GPNF acknowledged the large metropolitan areas of Portland and Seattle, "The Forest contributes to the quality of life for over 3 million people who live within a two-hour drive of the forest." Three years after the draft EIS, the plan continued to acknowledge the competing perspectives on old growth. On the one hand, old growth has "intrinsic value," and because its role in forest ecosystems is "imperfectly understood," enough should be "retained to perpetuate the elements of biological diversity it contains." The key word is "elements." Rather than call for retaining large intact tracts of old growth across the GPNF, the report called for a much weaker retention of the "elements" that old growth represents. The last statement about old growth reads, "The high volume of wood per acre and large log sizes makes old growth stands more economical to log." Not surprisingly given the rigid Forest Service culture, little had changed since the draft report from three years earlier. The implicit message is that the agency intends to log old growth as that is the most "economical" action. For the Forest Service as an agency and the GPNF in particular, economics ruled, not the needs of the ecosystem. This becomes even more clear as one examines what was planned for key wildlife species that depend on a healthy ecosystem.

The GPNF plan proposed selling 334 million board feet annually, beginning in the 1990s, which was described as somewhat lower than the average of around 400 million board feet for the previous ten years. Later in the report, the plan reviewed what the forest looks like "today" (1990) and fifty years in the future with respect to age classes of trees in the forest. Two sets of numbers stand out: for the age class of zero to fifty, the numbers go from almost 200,000 acres to 362,000 acres; for the age class of two hundred-plus years, the numbers go from 104,000 to 68,000. These are probably the most illustrative numbers in the entire inch-thick report that illustrate the aim of Pinchot's heirs on his namesake forest backed by their superiors in the Pacific Northwest and the chief in DC: liquidate almost all of the remaining old-growth stands and replace them with young, "thrifty stands."

One of the statements in the GPNF plan, which makes clear the extent to which Pinchot's heirs ignored the wealth of science that had emerged, reads, "The conversion of old growth stands to young, thriving stands, and the maintenance of stands through cultural treatments, including thinning and fertilization, have the greatest potential for displaying productivity potential or improving the health of a site." The plan in essence declared that the actual health of the forest would be improved by eliminating old growth. One can only wonder about this definition of health. Eliminating a habitat that had developed in many cases over a period of thousands of years resulted in increased health of the forest? Replacing those habitats with even-aged, uniform rows of trees that resembled a field of corn more than it did a natural forest improved the health of a forest? With this plan, the long-term aspirations of the Forest Service for the previous forty-five years would be finally realized. Old growth would virtually disappear from the landscape. Even though Jerry Franklin had published ten years earlier within the Forest Service a groundbreaking report on the vital role played by old growth to numerous species and to healthy forest ecosystems, his findings were essentially ignored. Rather, Pinchot's heirs proclaimed that they would continue full speed ahead deploying the same strategies and practices they had deployed for the previous forty-five years.

Nothing would stop them. Not public opinion. Not court cases. Not vital research truths.

Vital truths, however, continued to emerge based on research that called into question the viability of the liquidation of old growth. One of the many unexpected discoveries about old-growth forests was the importance of what took place high in the canopy. Production-oriented foresters had little care for what happened 200 to 300 feet above the ground in Douglas-fir canopies. Yet what happened up there was critical to the health of Douglas-firs, the health of the forests. A particular lichen, *Lobaria oregano*, played a vital role in nitrogen fixing in old-growth forests. With the help of cranes in the Wind River Experimental Forests (the southern end of the GPNF) and tree climbers, researchers learned that *Lobaria* is the major contributor of nitrogen in old-growth forest. *Lobaria* lichen only appear in old growth after about one hundred years. Shrubs such as snow-bush and alder trees provide much of the needed nitrogen during the early succession period, but then *Lobaria* takes over that role. Conventional logging practices often relied on controlled burns to suppress brush growth after logging to reduce competition with recently planted tree seedlings. One researcher described this intensive leave-no-wood-behind approach as "anal retentive forestry."

One of the Forest Service researchers, William Dennison, recognized that a rotation of sixty to eighty years risked exposing the forest they hoped to nurture to a "long, slow, silent nutrient disaster." The removing or burning of the early colonizing but nitrogen-fixing shrubs and alders and cutting trees before they are old enough to nurture *Lobaria* rather than contribute to a healthy functioning forest would, in fact, result in harming the forest.

Another fundamental understanding that came out of the Forest Service's research was how old-growth forests functioned. Jerry Franklin was the key researcher in developing that understanding. What compelled him to begin that research was his realization beginning in the 1960s and accelerating into the 1970s that old-growth forests throughout the Pacific Northwest were rapidly disappearing. He viewed old growth as others viewed bald eagles and osprey during that period, as a threatened and endangered species, and he wanted to at least understand it better before it was all gone. Because the Forest Service refused to fund research into old-growth forest, Franklin was able to acquire funding through the

International Biological Program funded by the National Science Foundation. He then began to examine old growth in the Andrews Forest. The improved understanding of our ancient forests, which had covered many millions of acres across the Cascades, began on an isolated twenty-five-acre tract within the Andrews Forest. In an interview I conducted with Franklin, he described what motivated him: "If you came to someone, a scientist in 1965, and asked them to tell you something about old-growth forest, natural forest, basically, they could not tell you a thing, except for how much merchantable timber there was."

Old-line foresters within the Forest Service were not interested in the research Franklin and his peers were conducting. That lack of interest evolved into competing narratives about the forest. The tensions between Forest Service leaders focused on outputs and researchers like Jerry Franklin focused on the ecosystem, which began in the 1960s, continued for several decades. Those tensions continued until the high-production phase of the Forest Service came to a close in the early 1990s when the need for stewardship of the ecosystem finally prevailed over the narrative that demanded achieving the highest level of cut possible. Of course, the National Forest Management Act, which required systematic and comprehensive forest management plans with wide-ranging participation from the public, was one of the contributors to that change. The key contributor, however, was the research on the ground, in the forest. Decades of research and fundamental findings about how the forest functioned were like a slowly building tsunami that suddenly hits land. The truth could no longer be ignored by leaders of the Forest Service and, as Franklin stated in our interview, led to a "complete change in the philosophy of the agency—in the character and gestalt and ultimately in the practices on the ground—from an agency focused on timber production led by foresters and engineers to an organization that is multidisciplinary and based on an incredible body of knowledge of forests as ecosystems."

While the iron triangle of the Forest Service, timber industry, and Congress reigned supreme from the 1950s into the1980s, the reputation and image of the Forest Service as a trusted government agency slowly eroded, and like a streamside tree whose roots are increasingly exposed until it suddenly collapses into the river, the agency too lost credibility until its old-growth-cutting mania came to a sudden end in the early 1990s. Science was an unstoppable force aiding that change. For many years, the Forest Service was blind to its loss of credibility and was unreceptive to findings coming from scientists in the woods. The many "ologists" the agency had been forced to hire as a result of the NFMA had been largely marginalized, as the foresters and engineers did their best to keep those groups' conclusions under wraps. The word was out among agency leaders that they needed to "get these researchers under control" and their work ignored. But animosities and distrust between line staff and agency scientists had not stopped the scientists' important work and had led them to push even more strongly for acknowledging this new understanding of the ecosystem and then changing forestry practices in the woods. Whereas staff described old growth as "storing wood on a stump" and "cellulose cemeteries," most researchers viewed old growth with awe and reverence.

Jerry Franklin's 1981 publication "Ecological Characteristics of Old Growth Douglas-Fir Forests" led to a much-changed understanding of the vital role old-growth forests played in a well-functioning forest ecosystem. One of the traditional arguments that Franklin took on was that old-growth trees were decadent and needed to be removed to make way for more virile, faster-growing trees. Most importantly, he was able to demonstrate that the overall primary productivity—photosynthetic production of biomass—of old growth was maintained at high levels and that the amount of organic matter actually increased with the accumulation of dead tree boles. Old-growth forests require roughly 150–250 years to develop under natural conditions in the Cascades and are recognized by four distinctive features: large, live old trees; large snags; large logs on the ground; and large logs in streams. Standing snags and downed logs provide important habitat for a wide range of species from northern spotted owls to flying squirrels. The logs found in streams provide both stability for streambanks and, importantly, a range of habitats for insects, invertebrates, and fish. Large decaying logs on the ground play a succession of roles in the forest over hundreds of years as they progress from towering giants to, ultimately, unrecognizable bits of the forest floor. One of the most important benefits of old-growth forests is that they serve as one of the most valuable carbon sinks on the planet.

The research that Franklin led resulted in understandings of just how extraordinary the Pacific Northwest's Douglas-firs are. William Dietrich in *The Final Forests: The Battle for the Last Great Trees of the Pacific Northwest* (1992) described one of those remarkable features: "A mature

Douglas-fir can contain 70 million tiny needles, which together represent an acre of surface area to the atmosphere. The trees are mighty combs, brushing the air to collect moisture and sunlight and to cleanse the atmosphere of the grit of pollutants. Their height of 200 to 300 feet is near the limit of a plant's ability to pull water against the force of gravity from its roots to its tops." Old growth that previously was viewed as a biological desert was found to be teeming with life: over one hundred species of birds, fish, reptiles, and mammals were dependent on old growth and up to fifteen hundred species of invertebrates. Some tree voles were even found to spend their entire lives in old-growth canopies eating fir or hemlock needles and never coming down to the ground.

Old-growth stands in which wind, decay, and natural thinning have led to wider spacing of trees than plantations provide flying room for predators such as northern spotted owls and sunlight for an understory of young trees. The overall effect is of a multilayered English cottage garden on steroids, with plants occurring at all levels of the forest from ground hugging to mid-story to the tops of the towering patriarchs of the forest. Dietrich also described how "old growth is warmer and more snow-free in winter, providing animals with better shelter and feed. It is cooler in spring and summer, conserving snow and soaking up rain, preventing flooding and erosion. As a result, old-growth streams also tend to make better fish habitat . . . a stream in old-growth forest raises seven times the fish of a counterpart in a harvested area."

Franklin recognized that old-growth stands were being rapidly cut, and although they were protected in such places as designated wilderness areas and national parks, they represented only 5 percent of the original landscape. In 1981, he wrote that "the end of unreserved old growth forests is in sight. The public, scientists, and land managers are increasingly concerned about whether species, communities, and functions are in danger of being eliminated." This assertion by Franklin directly challenged the previous thirty-five years of practices of most Forest Service leaders.

Franklin's full description of the characteristics of an old-growth forest, which is both pragmatic and poetic, deserves to be repeated here:

> Trees typically vary in species and size; dominant species are truly impressive. Some large species differ in color and texture as well as in size. The multilayer canopy produces a heavily filtered light, and the feeling of shade is accentuated by shafts of sunlight on clear days. The understory of

shrubs, herbs, and tree seedlings is often moderate and is almost always patchy in distribution and abundance. Numerous logs, often large and in various stages of decay, litter the forest floor, creating some travel routes for wildlife and blocking others. Standing dead trees, snags, and rotted stumps are common, although a visitor gazing toward the ground will often mistake dead trees in early stage of decay for live trees. It is quiet; few birds or mammals are seen or heard except perhaps the melody of a winter wren, the faint songs of golden-crowned kinglets in the tree canopies, or a chickaree.

In *The Hidden Forest,* Jon Luoma, who followed closely the work of scientists like Jerry Franklin and his peers, captured well another facet of old-growth forests, their unlikeness to crops: "One constant sensation in the ancient forests is indeed of disorder, and of rot. Busted snags, dead remnants of huge trees lance upward, here and there, debarked, sun-bleached, rotting on the stump, and riddled with holes—ranging from tiny holes that mark part of the decaying bole look like it was used for shotgun practice to big, oblong holes that look like someone took a heavy chisel to the tree."

One of the more surprising discoveries in the Andrews Forest was that the forest itself moves—that over their lifespan these behemoths moved root mass and all several feet in what amounted to a very slow landslide. Remarkable!

Old-growth forests are complex, and, although scientists do not use the term, they are magical, as magical as those described by J. R. R. Tolkien in his *Lord of the Rings* trilogy. Franklin contrasts the almost mystical old growth with the antiseptic plantations of largely Douglas-fir forests that were replacing them by noting that "the most sterile successional stage, in diversity of both plant and animal species, is a dense, rapidly growing young conifer forest." A nonscientist might have described these uniform plantations as sterile deserts. One of the most important assessments made by Franklin was the recognition that while it was unclear whether any particular species was entirely dependent on old growth for its survival, the fact that a species could survive in younger forests did not mean it could survive once old growth was gone. This assessment would be later confirmed by other researchers and would be the determining factor in bringing the high-production phase of national forestry in the Pacific Northwest to a sudden close.

William Dietrich, writing in *The Final Forest* also captured well the awe and inspiration that old-growth forests arouse: "I don't know why humans are so fascinated by creatures that are big, such as dinosaurs and elephants and whales, but instinctual awe certainly extends to these forests. The idea that something that big is alive, pumping water more than 20 stories high, grasping the sun with 70 million needles and showering the ground with up to 8 million seeds per acre each year remind us how unbelievable our planet is. To ramble along the mossy mat of a big old growth log—using it as a sidewalk to look down at the garden of fern and wood sorrel and salal and skunk cabbage and mushroom and salmon berry and fairy bells and lady slipper and huckleberry—to do that is to walk across the breast of a giant, sleeping mother."

Within a stone's throw of my cabin rise a dozen or more of what I consider elders of the forest, Douglas-firs and western red cedars from four to six feet in diameter, likely 250 to 300 years or more old, here more than a century before Pinchot roamed near these woods, here even before Lewis and Clark glided by 20 miles south in their canoes on the Columbia River. Recently, one of these elders was cut down, as it was close to a neighbor's cabin and, after its top blew off, it was deemed a hazard tree. I counted the rings: it was more than six hundred years old. It had been growing here for more than half a millennium, well before even Columbus first visited this continent. My first reaction on seeing this tree cut down was tremendous anger. Later, when I had determined the age, I simply felt sad as so few elders of our forest remain.

These ancient forests around my cabin exude peace, grace, solidity, resilience. They help us cope with the climate crisis: holding more snow in the winter and thus releasing more water in drier summers; staying cooler in the hotter summers in stark contrast to the urban heat islands (though the temperature was still above 100 degrees at my cabin during the "heat dome" summer, 2021, when the temperature reached 117 in Portland). More than any other aspect, what this ancient forest provides me is spiritual solace. These ancient forests have withstood over hundreds of years whatever nature has thrown at them: powerful winds, long droughts, wildfires. In their silence and grandeur, in the increased water flows, in the cooler conditions they provide during the summer, one can almost imagine them as sentient beings who offer compassion to all creatures found among them, from endangered salmon to the northern spotted owl.

In her book *Finding the Mother Tree*, Suzanne Simard has captured well this extraordinary aspect of old growth, their Buddha-like loving kindness and compassion toward their smaller, weaker kin. Making observations based on hard science conducted in her lab and in the field, she writes, "The older trees are able to discern which seedlings are their own kin. The old trees nurture the young ones and provide them food and water just as we do with our own children." She describes how, most astonishingly, when older trees die, "they pass their wisdom to their kin, generation after generation, sharing the knowledge of what helps and what harms, who is friend and who is foe, and how to adapt and survive in an ever-changing landscape." When we consider passing wisdom from one generation to the next, we are speaking of thirty- to sixty-year time frames. With old Douglas-firs, like the one near my cabin recently cut down, we are talking about five hundred- to one thousand-year time frames.

This magical aspect of old-growth forest, described so well by Simard, is one that Pinchot came to appreciate. Pinchot lived for another twenty-five years after he was Forest Service chief, and his thinking and values transformed over time. He gained a much stronger sense of the role that diversity plays in keeping forest healthy. He recognized the importance of the conservation of native species and called for more research on forest wildlife and urged caution in how we used our forests so as to not harm our "animal citizens." Pinchot later in his life wrote that the greatest good cannot be measured solely in board feet and cords, that the forests were important because they uplifted our inner selves. He wrote simply that "woodlands are beautiful."

Pinchot wrote in *The Use of the National Forests* that forests "exist today because the people want them . . . the officers are paid by the people to act as their agents and to see that all the resources of the Forests are used in the best interest of everyone concerned. What the people as a whole want will be done." Eventually, what the people wanted, which to a great extent became a clarion call for preserving the remaining old growth, was decisively recognized by the courts in the early 1990s. The leaders of the Forest Service had for over forty years failed to listen to the public and certainly failed to follow Pinchot's advice and act in the "best interest of everyone concerned."

Gifford Pinchot developed eleven maxims meant to guide Forest Service managers in all their actions, especially in the context of service to the many, diverse stakeholders the agency was to serve.

1. **A public official is there to serve** the public and not run them.
2. **Public support of acts affecting public rights** is absolutely required.
3. **It is more trouble to consult the public than to ignore them,** but that is what you are hired for.
4. **Find out in advance what the public will stand for.** If it is right and they won't stand for it, postpone action and educate them.
5. **Use the press** first, last, and all the time if you want to reach the public.
6. **Get rid of an attitude of personal arrogance** or pride of attainment or superior knowledge.
7. **Don't try any sly, or foxy politics.** A forester is not a politician.
8. **Learn tact simply by being absolutely honest and sincere,** and by learning to recognize the point of view of the other man and meet him with arguments he will understand.
9. **Don't be afraid to give credit to someone else even when it belongs to you.** Not to do so is the sure mark of a weak man, but to do so is the hardest lesson to learn. Encourage others to do things; you may accomplish many things through others that you can't get done on your single initiative.
10. **Don't be a knocker.** Use persuasion rather than force, when possible. [There are] plenty of knockers to be had. Your job is to promote unity.
11. **Don't make enemies unnecessarily and for trivial reasons.** If you are any good you will make plenty of them on matters of straight honesty and public policy and will need all the support you can get.

These maxims represent the underlying assumptions, values, and behaviors that Pinchot sought to develop in his agency and, importantly, the kind of organizational culture that was needed if that agency were to, like the forest he wanted to manage, endure. These maxims are quite extraordinary in that they have strong application to most governmental organizations that are designed to serve a citizenry that is never of one mind. Service is the first priority. Listening and engaging the public are next in importance. Most of his maxims relate to acts of leadership and identify essential behaviors—honesty, authenticity, recognition, persuasion—that are core to effective leadership

The culture of the Forest Service lost sight of many of these maxims during the high-production phase, especially the need to avoid arrogance and "superior knowledge." And, without a doubt, agency leaders viewed consulting the public as a nuisance. Their failure to listen and understand the changing values of a more environmentally sensitive public led them to ignore "what the public will stand for." The failure of the Forest Service to respond to the public's changing values, to recognize the inherent value of old-growth forest, to acknowledge the harms resulting from transforming a rich ecosystem into a uniform "crop" led to the last course available to the public, the courts.

The 1980s represented the most critical decade for the Forest Service since its inception in 1905. The agency was under siege from the environmental community while experiencing forceful pressures from a highly conservative executive branch to maintain high levels of cut. These expectations were generally reinforced by the legislative branch, although louder voices were emerging in Congress questioning the sustainability of the ongoing high levels of logging and their impact on endangered species. Would the Forest Service listen and change, or would it ignore the public and continue its obsession to realize the highest level of allowable cut possible? Unsurprisingly, the agency chose the latter. Actions on Pinchot's namesake forest demonstrate clearly the extent to which the culture circled the wagons, adopted a defensive stance in response to public pressures, and pressed ever ahead with what it felt it could best do, get the cut out.

In 1987, the GPNF issued a draft Environmental Impact Statement on its Proposed Land and Resource Management Plan. The full GPNF plan was issued in 1990 and was the last national forest plan published in the Northwest as all the other national forests in the region had published their plans earlier. In the "Current Situation" section at the beginning of the GPNF plan, the writers noted that "the volume of timber produced on the Forest is one of the highest in the National Forest System." For seemingly the first time, at least on the GPNF, mention is made that "old-growth trees provide spiritual, aesthetic, and recreational values." This statement does mark a change from previous documents about the GPNF and represents an acknowledgment of the public's changing values. It did not, however, lead to any real change in practices on the ground. The plan further stated that the GPNF "contains some of the most important commercial stands of timber within the National Forest System" and that these stands were essential to meet regional and national demands for lumber. In addition, it noted the importance of these stands to nearby timber-dependent communities and the revenue provided to county governments. While some of the lands on the forest were withdrawn from timber production as a result of wilderness or national monument designation, the plan stated that nearly 1 million acres, the vast majority of Pinchot's namesake forest, was "suitable for timber production."

The GPNF plan went on to state that about 231,000 acres of old growth were present on the land as of 1981. What is most notable about this figure is how low it is. One might have expected it to be much higher given the total of 1.3 million acres across the entire Gifford Pinchot National Forest. This low number resulted from two processes, one natural and the other unnatural, fires and logging. The GPNF was heavily impacted by fires in the latter part of the nineteenth century and early twentieth century, particularly the Yacolt fire. The Yacolt fire burned over 200,000 acres of heavily timbered land that later became part of the GPNF. By the late 1920s, roughly an additional 70,000 acres of forest had also burned within the GPNF, then known as the Columbia National Forest. So much of the GPNF had burned during the early part of the twentieth century that H. O. Stabler stated in his annual fire report for 1910 that "The term 'Columbia National Burn,' is, I regret to say, somewhat applicable. . . ." Taken together, these burns represented about 21 percent of the area of GPNF. If one assumes that the entire GPNF originally was covered by old growth, that would have represented, minus the burns, a little over 1 million acres. Thus, not including burned lands, the amount of old growth that was logged in the GPNF by 1981 was close to 750,000 acres. These are remarkable numbers and document the fact that the agency was committed to the removal of virtually all of the old-growth forest, outside of wilderness areas, in Pinchot's namesake forest.

15

The Spotted Owl:
The Beginning of the End

When we are in the old growth, we are literally experiencing a meaningful feature of the body of the owl. We are within the owl's insulative layer: the protection from wind and snow we enjoy among the trees on a cold winter's day makes the forest our feathers too.

—Tim Fox

The 1990 Land and Management Plan for the GPNF recognized three old-growth and mature forest indicator species: spotted owls, pileated woodpeckers, and pine martens. The plan acknowledged that past timber harvest reduced habitat for spotted owls as a result of the "removal of mature and old-growth stands and fragmentation of habitat areas." Given how much old growth each spotted owl pair was projected to need (and those acreage numbers were much in dispute, with the Forest Service consistently using numbers in the lower range), the plan estimated that on the 1.3 million acres of the GPNF, habitat capability existed for 101 pairs. Remarkably, the plan then stated plainly, "Under this Plan, the owl habitat capability will decrease to a level of 58 pairs by the end of the fifth decade (of the Plan)." What the plan did not say is that prior to the beginning of the high-production phase some forty-five years earlier, many hundreds of pairs of spotted owl habitat existed on the GPNF as old-growth stands covered much of the forest. The next statement in the plan is even more remarkable: "This level [58 pairs] does not leave the margin considered necessary in order to take into account the possible loss of habitat due to fire, insects, disease, or windthrow, and possible unsuitability of some habitat areas due to factors not known at this time." In addition, "The actual reduction, however, will probably be larger because of increased fragmentation in habitat areas not managed for spotted owls." Fragmentation of the forest was inherent in the goal—build more roads, access more roadless

155

areas, harvest higher in the watersheds, and reduce connectivity. Just as a host of assumptions needed to be true for the hopes of intensive management of the forest to be realized in enabling higher levels of cut, so too did a host of assumptions need to be met to realize the future viability of the threatened spotted owl. Once again, the Forest Service was going out on the proverbial limb hoping for the best. And time and time again, their assumptions were proven wrong.

With this radical decrease in the amount of old-growth forest planned between 1990 and 2040, other old-growth-dependent species were affected as well. Pileated woodpeckers' habitat capability was expected to decline from 648 pairs to 168 pairs, a 74 percent reduction. Pine marten habitat capability would decrease from 1,321 females to 365 females over 50 years, a 72 percent reduction. The public was supposed to take solace in these numbers as the Forest Service communicated that unlike spotted owls, these other two species could also survive in "mature forest stands" that could "develop more quickly than old growth." To enable continued harvesting of increasingly difficult-to-reach old growth, the plan described the need for even more roads to be constructed—a projected 120 miles of roads annually over the next ten years.

Although the needs for primitive recreation were documented, no additional wilderness areas were recommended over the next fifty years. And while the forest contained 208,000 acres of roadless areas in 1990, the plan recommended that 127,000 of those acres be removed from roadless designation, as that would have prevented timber harvest. Even though the plan identified recreation demand in non-wilderness roadless areas at about 5.5 million recreation visitor days by 2040, it also acknowledged that the supply would only equal about 2.3 million recreation visitor days. Time and time again, the Forest Service made clear that regardless of the Multiple-Use Sustained-Yield Act, regardless of the National Forest Management Act, one use remained dominant: logging. That is what the culture rewarded; that is what most Presidential administrations rewarded; that is what most Congresses rewarded; that is what most local, resource-dependent communities wanted; that is certainly what the nearby mills wanted. However, that is not what most people across the entire country wanted. And what about all the animals in the woods and the many plants that depended on mature and old-growth forests—that is not what they needed to survive.

The 1990 GPNF Land and Resource Management Plan identified four general goals:

- "Resolve as many issues as possible."
- "Incorporate necessary changes to existing Forest programs . . . to cause the least amount of disruption to the current social and economic situation."
- "Provide for stability in resource outputs and services over time. Radical changes from one decade to the next should be avoided," and
- "Operate within all laws, regulations, and rules."

The Forest Service utterly failed to meet these four goals. This was the forest that had been renamed after its founder to honor his legacy. And yet, in a remarkably short time period, the leaders of the GPNF and the Forest Service as a whole lost sight of his vision. This failure to achieve what the plan set out as the most important goals for those 1.3 million acres did lead to one change. No longer would the GPNF be the "forgotten forest." No longer would it be the "sacrificial forest." No longer would the national forests throughout the Pacific Northwest be treated as they had been during the high-production phase. Just three years after the GPNF Management Plan was issued, the President of the United States, not a regional leader of the Forest Service, not the chief of the Forest Service, not the secretary of agriculture, but President Clinton and his vice president, Al Gore, recognized the fundamental dysfunction of this nearly ninety-year-old agency and spent precious days early in their new administration working to clean up the mess.

The northern spotted owl changed everything. Just as Rachel Carson's book *Silent Spring* (1962) opened the public's eyes to the harms of pesticides like DDT, and just as the disappearing eagles and ospreys in the 1960s opened their eyes to the need to both eliminate use of harmful chemicals that were causing treasured species to go extinct and protect the habitats on which they depend, so too were the public's eyes opened by the plight of the spotted owl and other wildlife that called older forests home. One year after the issuance of the GPNF Land and Resource Management Plan, District Judge William Dwyer issued an injunction that blocked all national timber sales involving owl habitat. This ruling virtually brought to a halt all logging across most of the central Cascades in Washington and Oregon. Almost all logging in Pinchot's namesake forest ceased as well.

The GPNF plan, which called for close to 400 million board feet to be harvested annually for the next fifty years, became a worthless stack of paper. Some five years after the plan was issued, rather than harvesting 400 million board feet, the GPNF harvested about 20 million board feet, a reduction of 95 percent. Toward the end of the 1990s, not a single board foot of timber came off the forest. Dwyer wrote: "The most recent violation of the NFMA exemplifies a deliberate and systematic refusal by the Forest Service and Fish and Wildlife Service to comply with the laws protecting wildlife. This is not the doing of the scientists, foresters, rangers, and others at the working levels of these agencies; it reflects decisions made by higher authorities in the executive branch of the government." Without a doubt, the executive branch was ultimately the accountable part of government toward which Dwyer directed his scorn. Leaders at almost all levels of the Forest Service, from chief to supervisors, had a similar mindset to that of senior leaders in the executive branch: maximize, to the extent possible, the level of cut on the Pacific Northwest forests.

Not all Forest Service employees working in the Pacific Northwest were aligned with their leaders. Compared to the 1950s and 1960s, the agency in the late 1980s looked considerably different. This was largely a result of the NFMA, which required a workforce with skills that were much more diverse than those of the foresters and engineers who had previously dominated the agency. After the passage of the NFMA, over the period of a generation, the Forest Service staff went from 284 to 688 wildlife biologists, 75 to 236 fisheries biologists, 47 to 206 archaeologists, and 7 to 84 ecologists. Affirmative action programs also led to changes. As a result of both these programs and many socioeconomic pressures, the agency became much more diverse, with a younger cohort that included more women. Not only had it become more diverse as a result of these changes, but the dominant culture of the Forest Service was no longer seen as viable by many of this younger cohort. More and more voices within the agency were calling for change. One voice especially emerged that represented well this sense of unease with the status quo—that of Jeff DeBonis.

Before moving to work with the Forest Service in the Northwest, DeBonis had worked on the Kootenai National Forest in Idaho. There, he was given considerable discretion in writing the environmental assessments that were required for timber sales and found support from his manager when the volume of timber sales needed to be reduced to address the needs of endangered species. He then left Idaho and moved to Oregon to begin work on the Willamette National Forest.

In the late 1980s, DeBonis encountered the attitude that Dwyer later castigated. One of the early projects he took on was to finalize an environmental assessment for a proposed timber sale on the Willamette, which, he discovered, contained several spotted owl habitat areas (SOHAs) and which he knew needed to be protected based on the Forest Service's own guidelines. He also discovered that a new road was to be built directly above the McKenzie River, an important salmon-bearing stream, which the staff hydrologist said had a 90 percent chance of failing and thus potentially causing significant sedimentation of the river and interfering with salmon spawning. He then revised the environmental assessment, reduced the size of the cuts, and took it to the district ranger to be signed. In an interview I conducted with DeBonis, he related that the district ranger's response was, "I can't sign this; I am the signing authority, you put it back the way it was; if you don't fix it, then you will be insubordinate." This Willamette National Forest ranger was likely representative of many rangers throughout the Pacific Northwest. Had DeBonis acted similarly with a proposed sale in the GPNF, he clearly would have been seen as insubordinate. At the time, this incident simply represented the ongoing tension between many Forest Service leaders and their staff. Within a very short period of time, however, the incident would lead to actions that would have a profound impact on the Forest Service.

A growing number of Forest Service employees were becoming increasingly distressed by what they recognized as unsustainable levels of cut and the impact of those cuts on important animal species, especially the spotted owl. Two years before the Dwyer injunction, DeBonis wrote a lengthy, heartfelt letter to the chief of the Forest Service, Dale Robertson. DeBonis's action was a radical act, as Robertson was four organizational levels above him. Writing a letter to someone significantly higher up the organizational chain of command was simply not done; in the military-like structure of the Forest Service, one was supposed to work within the chain of command.

DeBonis wrote in his letter: "These are troubling times for many of us. The values of our public and our employees have been rapidly changing and have become increasingly divergent, increasing the level of controversy surrounding management of the National Forests. . . . Many people, internally as well as externally, believe the current emphasis of National Forest programs do not reflect the land stewardship values embodied in our forest plans. Congressional emphasis and our traditional methods and practices continue to focus on commodity resources. We are not meeting the quality land management expectations of our public and our employees. We are not being viewed as the conservation leaders Gifford Pinchot would have us become." Once again, we see one cohort of employees placing heavy emphasis on Pinchot as one who, were he alive, would have argued for conservation and sustainability over production.

DeBonis did not expect much from this letter; he simply felt the need to communicate his frustrations and disappointments. When he did not receive a response from the chief—which did not surprise him—he sent the letter to *High Country News* and soon thereafter it was reprinted in the *New York Times*. Now he had the attention of not only the chief of the Forest Service but also many members of the public who cared passionately about preserving old growth. In my interview with DeBonis, he recalled how he was called into his forest supervisor's office and told, "you can't talk about this stuff if you want to keep your job. We may have to send you to a place like Siberia." The timber industry demanded that the Forest Service fire DeBonis. DeBonis defended his actions as a free speech issue, and that defense was "bulletproofed" when Chief Robertson stated that, while he did not agree with him, he agreed with his right to say it.

His previous supervisor on the Kootenai National Forest had called DeBonis a revolutionary and himself a change agent—that change agents live for another day while revolutionaries die on their sword. DeBonis had chosen to die on his sword. Within two years of writing his letter, he left the Forest Service. What he crystalized in the letter, however, grew from a seed of discontent held by many of his peers to a powerful movement both inside and outside the Forest Service that demanded change. Many arrows were being fired at the Forest Service, and like a beast that only knows to keep charging its victim no matter how much blood is flowing, the agency continued blindly down the path it had trodden for forty-five years. By the end of President Reagan's second term in office in the late 1980s, old growth was being eliminated at record rates: up to 62,000 acres a year, which translates into 172 acres per day. Finally, the checks and balances so wisely put in place by this country's founders functioned as they were intended. The judicial branch held the executive branch accountable for not upholding the laws of the land. Judge Dwyer shouted unequivocally, STOP! And, finally, the Forest Service stopped. The timber beast, spilling copious amounts of blood, suddenly and finally died. Only with this death came the possibility of the rebirth of old growth.

Not only had people like DeBonis come along to challenge the culture of the Forest Service, but the many "ologists" who were hired in the 1970s and 1980s spoke with a stronger voice. While leaders in the Forest Service did their best to silence them, these professionals represented a new perspective that became identified as "new forestry" in contrast to the "old forestry." They recognized both the trees and the forest as part of a tapestry in the broader landscape. Well before these two schools of forestry emerged, Aldo Leopold described clearly the distinctions between them: "One group (A) regards the land as soil, and its function as commodity production; another group (B) regards the land as biota, and its function as something broader. How much broader is, admittedly, in a state of doubt and confusion. In my own field, forestry, group A is quite content to grow trees like 'cabbages,' with cellulose as the basic forest commodity. It feels no inhibition against violence, its ideology is agronomic. Group B, on the other hand, sees forestry as fundamentally different from agronomics because it employs natural species, and manages a natural environment rather than creating an artificial one." New forestry rejected the principle that national forests needed to be highly regulated and intensively managed. New forestry refused to see the forest primarily as "cellulose," as a commodity. Rather, it valued what many were recognizing, simply, as natural forests. It recognized an ecosystem unique on this planet, one that had endured for thousands of years since the last ice age. Unfortunately, natural forests throughout the Pacific Northwest remained primarily only in a few disparate pockets of wilderness, roadless areas, and national monuments and national parks. The Forest Service, in its unalloyed zeal and its righteous sense of doing what was right, had largely succeeded in doing what it set out to do in 1945: radically transform most of the natural forest in the Pacific Northwest into a tree plantation. Hirt recognized the juncture that the nation faced in its management of the Pacific Northwest forest: "Ironically, reform may now be feasible only because America's vast reservoir of valuable old growth timber has been mostly liquidated. There is relatively little left of America's pre-Columbian forest to exploit. The government-sponsored 'Great Barbecue is over.'"

Aldo Leopold stressed a distinctive perspective in which humans are a part of the greater ecological community. He recognized that only then will people treat that community with love and respect. Other values had to be considered if people were to treat the natural world not as existing solely for economic gain but rather as a source of inspiration, of renewal, of spiritual awakening, of potential transcendence, and as a home for wolves, bears, and even the lowliest creatures that live in the duff and forest litter, without which the forest cannot remain healthy. Perhaps the greatest failing of Pinchot's Forest Service heirs was their inflexibility and their inability, or unwillingness, to recognize the astonishing complexity that existed in the forest. Many of the agency's leaders acted in ways that were terribly destructive even though many believed they were working to fulfill Pinchot's vision for the forest. Foresters' strengths had transformed into weaknesses. The beliefs in intensive management and a fully regulated forest, and the actions based on those beliefs, led to disastrous, catastrophic results, the virtual elimination of a vibrant, unique, and complex ecosystem that had evolved over many millennia.

While Pinchot may have questioned the term, he surely would have appreciated the principles undergirding what in the early 1990s was called new forestry. Once again, Jerry Franklin was at the center of this new approach. While he recognized that there may have been economic reasons for clear-cutting large sections of the Pacific Northwest forests, his research proved that there were no ecological reasons. He and many other forest scientists concluded that "economic and social considerations, rather than ecological considerations, determined the choice of cutting." This view directly challenged the guiding Forest Service paradigm of the past forty-five years: that clear-cutting was required for the successful regeneration of Douglas-firs.

One of the terrible ironies of forestry during the forty years after WWII was that, by viewing old growth as decadent, foresters failed to recognize the importance of dead wood, snags, and decomposition to ensuring a healthy functioning forest. While old-growth Douglas-firs may live five hundred to six hundred years or more, they continue to play a vital role in the forest as they die and become standing snags, home to many threatened species, and finally as decaying organic material on the forest floor. Their vitality, in essence, extends at least one thousand years. This new and fundamental understanding changed significantly the public's view of old-growth forests and how we need to manage them in the future. With farsighted policies, with an aroused public, with more humble forest managers who recognize these other values present in old-growth forest, these elders of the woods may be restored to the splendor and magnificence they represented in pre-Columbian times. After forty-five years of emphasis on the death of the forest, rebirth became possible. Not in fifty years, not even in one hundred years, but, perhaps, in two hundred years. Just as ancient towering medieval cathedrals have been destroyed by unmindful marauders and then restored to their grandeur with much effort and persistence, so too can the ancient forests of the Pacific Northwest be restored to their former glory. Rebirth of old growth is certainly possible with this new mindset and recognition that the very health of our planet may depend partly on the extraordinary potential of old growth to capture carbon.

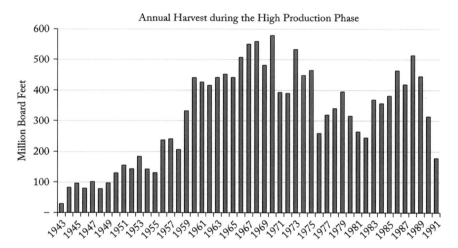

Figure 2. Annual harvest during the high-production phase on the Gifford Pinchot National Forest. From USFS, Region 6

Part III

Ecological Management: The Rebirth of the Forest

16

A Turning Point: From Production to Ecological Management

The works of naturalists, a full range of biologists, forest scientists, and geomorphologists—all the inquiries of honest science—continue to refine our insights and inform our efforts to preserve and recover forests.

—Bill Yake

Just five years after the first Land and Resource Management Plan for Pinchot's namesake forest was issued, calling for nearly half a billion board feet of timber to be cut on the GPNF annually for the foreseeable future, the GPNF supervisor in 1995 issued an amendment to the 1990 original plan in response to the earlier report by the Forest Ecosystem Management Assessment Team (FEMAT). This amendment "provided new goals, objectives, standards, and guidelines for resource management." Although the writers called the new document an "amendment," it was a stark contrast to the original plan. Not only had the bathwater been thrown out, but the baby had been, also. The old guard in Pinchot's namesake forest must have felt that a revolution had taken place, although they did not have to march to the guillotines and were still nominally in charge. Of the 1.3 million acres in the GPNF, almost 470,000 acres became off-limits to logging of old growth. Less than one-third—the now designated matrix lands—remained open to timber harvesting. Over a third of the GPNF was designated as late successional reserves (LSRs). LSRs contained some existing old-growth forests, which would henceforth be protected in their natural condition, and younger stands with the potential to take on the characteristics of their elders: multiple species and layers; large logs and snags; imperfections such as tree cavities, broken tops, and large deformed limbs and masses of fungi, lichens, and bryophytes. The hope is that while these young stands may not duplicate existing old-growth forests, they could provide "adequate habitat for species in the long term." Finally, the leaders of the GPNF recognized that the forest was not intended to be treated as a crop and that providing habitat for endangered and at-risk species was a necessary priority. In essence, they recognized that a messy, complex forest, not an orderly, highly regulated one, was a good thing.

In the past, GPNF supervisors had a high level of autonomy in the silvicultural practices deployed. Beginning in 1994, that autonomy was greatly reduced as a reflection of the loss of trust that was identified by FEMAT. Under the FEMAT report's heading "Silviculture" was a note-worthy statement: "Thinning or other silvicultural treatments inside reserves are subject to review by the Regional Ecosystem Office to ensure that the treatments are beneficial to the creation of late-successional forest conditions." The regional office made clear they would be looking over the shoulder of the "old guard" to ensure that they abided by the requirements identified by the Northwest Forest Plan (NFP). Perhaps one of the most galling requirements for the old guard was that in the LSRs no harvest was allowed in stands over eighty years old. Not only was true old growth off-limits, but also trees that within one hundred years or more had the potential to take on old-growth characteristics. The new plan stated clearly that "the purpose of these silvicultural treatments is to benefit the creation and maintenance of late-successional forest conditions." One other rec-ognition in the new plan is likely to have raised the ire of the old guard: in LSRs, management planning needed to recognize the value of keeping dead and dying trees in the forest. Natural forests contain the continuum from life and death to rebirth, and that continuum provides all the con-ditions necessary for biodiversity. This amended plan was the first official planning document out of the GPNF to lay the necessary foundation that potentially enables the rebirth of old-growth forests in the Gifford Pin-chot National Forest and the rest of the Pacific Northwest.

The matrix lands in the GPNF were those targeted for timber produc-tion. Even these lands, however, were to be treated in vastly different ways from how they had been treated before the FEMAT report. The impor-tance of coarse woody debris was especially highlighted: "A renewable supply of large down logs is critical for maintaining populations of fungi, arthropods, bryophytes, and various other organisms that use this habitat structure"; and woody debris was also seen as essential to martens, fishers, and amphibians. "Coarse woody debris that is already on the ground needs to be retained and protected from disturbance to the greatest extent possi-ble during logging and other land management activities."

One of the crucial discoveries of the 1980s, that of biological legacies, was now directly influencing the management of all Forest Service lands. Disturbances to the ecosystem, whether from fire, wind or other natural phenomena, generally left conditions on the ground that could be described as "gappy, patchy and clumpy." Most major forest fires did not burn all parts of the forest severely. Rather, uneven patches were almost inevitably left in which some patches were skipped over entirely and remained green, some were burned moderately and were left with a mix of dead and green trees, and some were burned entirely where a new forest would emerge. Gaps between and within patches occurred. Clumps of thick, young growth were also left undisturbed. Timber harvesting needed to learn from the models that resulted from the concepts undergirding biological legacies. The 1994 report stated: "For many species, benefits will be greatest if trees are retained in patches rather than singly," and that "70 percent of the total area to be retained should be aggregates of moderate to larger size (one half to two and a half acres) with the remainder as dispersed structures (individual trees . . . including smaller *clumps* less than a half-acre) . . . to the extent possible patches and dispersed retention should include the largest, oldest live trees . . . and snags occurring in the unit. Patches should be retained indefinitely." The report further provided explicit requirements for the amounts of snags that needed to be retained in timber harvest areas. Not only were actual snags required to be left at a certain density but also green trees, which may be converted to snags, had to be considered. Gifford's namesake forest had rewritten the rules for the greatest good for the greatest number in the long run. What an extraordinary change in attitude toward snags from the earlier view that they all needed to be eliminated from the landscape.

Three years after issuing the amendment to the first GPNF Land and Resource Management Plan, the GPNF published a 1997 Monitoring and Evaluation Report. One of the greatest challenges for anyone experiencing a significant change, and especially so for leaders, is to effectively let go of some of the things they cherished before the change. FEMAT marked that moment of change for national forests in the Northwest and their leaders.

Changes like those called for by the FEMAT report are a moment in time. What follows change is the transition, which is a psychological adjustment to the new environment. Transitions are often uncomfortable for those experiencing them and inevitably engender resistance as they are periods of letting go and taking on new perspectives, new values, and new practices; ultimately new assumptions are adopted about what works. Ted Stubblefield was the supervisor responsible for the first Land and Resource Management Plan issued in 1990. He was the supervisor at the time that the so-called Gang of Four (Jerry Franklin, Jack Ward Thomas, Norm Thompson, and John Gordon, all well-known forests scientists) did its groundbreaking work when FEMAT issued its report and the NFP was developed. What becomes clear on reading the introduction to the 1997 report, designed to communicate how the GPNF was faring under the guidance of the Northwest Forest Report, is that Stubblefield was stuck in the past and resistant to the call for change. He had barely begun to acknowledge the transition. The last sentence in the first paragraph of the Monitoring and Evaluation Report makes clear his resistance: "this document reflects the seventh full year of implementing the GPNF Plan which was approved on June 1, 1990." Judge Dwyer effectively blocked the GPNF plan a little over a year after it was issued. All timber sales were brought to an immediate halt. Dwyer's injunction was followed by the Gang of Four and FEMAT reports, which declared emphatically that the practices of the past were dead. The original GPNF plan was no longer a viable document. The 1994 amendment, which was developed in response to the NFP, was the new plan. Yet Stubblefield characterized the amendment as though it represented a few changes to the 1990 plan. Some twenty years after this 1997 report, he seemed to still harbor anger toward the environmental community. I approached him to be interviewed for this book; he declined, and I believe he was unwilling to meet with me because of my past environmental associations. Ecological management, in his eyes, was simply wrong.

Lynn Burditt was a forester who, unlike Stubblefield, was influenced greatly by the FEMAT report and by research conducted on the Andrews Forest. Burditt joined the GPNF as deputy supervisor soon after Stubblefield retired as supervisor. She represented a stark departure from the old guard. She had a significant and distinctive role in shaping policy after the development of the NFP and, specifically, how that would play out on the GPNF. Burditt received her early training in forestry engineering and was one of the few women working in that area in the Forest Service beginning in the 1970s. At the time she joined the GPNF in 2000, the staffing level of that forest was one-quarter of its level compared to 1990—wrenching changes for those experiencing those sizeable reductions in personnel. The GPNF, which she now helped supervise, went from producing close to 500 million board feet annually just prior to the NWP to selling zero timber the year she joined the GPNF in 2000.

Burditt was one of those rare leaders within the Forest Service who recognized the need for culture change. She was also part of the cohort that began to be hired in the 1970s and 1980s that, as she noted, "set out to institutionalize a different set of values." She described in an interview I conducted with her how she would hear some peers comment that "things would still be as they had been [pre NWFP] if we had not hired women and 'people of color,' though that is not the term they used." These old guard members then added, "that is when everything started going downhill." Burditt was acknowledging that sexism and racism were not uncommon in the Forest Service. The old guard's most important values were loyalty, productivity, and obedience. The new cohort that represented diversity both in terms of race and gender as well as background possessed a very different set of values: interdependence, open-mindedness, and empathy. They rejected the symbiotic relationship between the Forest Service and the timber industry and Congress. They were much more open to the research discoveries that highlighted the complexity and wealth of diversity in old-growth forest.

Burditt appreciated many of the old guard and their commitment to the agency while disagreeing with some, if not many, of their beliefs. She appreciated such practices as calling meetings between line and staff "family meetings," while recognizing that that term was likely galling to those being downsized. She appreciated treating people fairly while recognizing that calling the new group that handled such things as recruitment, hiring, compensation, and employee relations "human capital management" was not likely to increase employee morale.

The 1990s represented the end of the old culture of the Forest Service. The beginning of the twenty-first century marked the transition from that which represented the past to something new yet to be named and yet to clearly and decisively emerge. Burditt was a product of the old culture while not being fully merged with it. By the time she took on her leadership role in the GPNF, she and others like her were no longer a small minority. More and more of those diverse hires from the 1970s and 1980s had emerged as leaders, decision-makers, and shapers of culture.

The clearest example of the distinction between the old and new culture is what the former called for in terms of annual cut and what the later latter viewed as more reasonable levels of cut. The old guard that shaped the GPNF plan of 1990 called for almost a half billion board feet to be cut off the forest annually well into the future. For most of the first decade of the twenty-first century, the annual cut coming off the GPNF in fact averaged about 25 million board feet annually, 4 percent of what the old guard had called for. The new cohort, which Burditt was so representative of, recognized that they were in a transition period and that transitions were marked by uncertainties, ambiguities, and lack of clarity about the future, qualities that the old guard abhorred.

Two 1997 timber sales in the GPNF that were monitored for adherence to the standards of the Northwest Forest Plan provide examples of some of those ambiguities and how they played out in the forest. These sales had been approved by Stubblefield before Burditt arrived in the GPNF. In both cases, the sales failed to meet standards for green trees, snags, and downed logs. Managers had failed to verify that layout and marking guidelines ensured sufficient trees were marked for retention. Another failure that was recognized was that streams in one timber sale area were not adequately buffered from the cutting area. The report downplayed these difficulties by stating that "these minor deviations are expected as the Forest transitions to new management standards and guidelines." Corrective actions were identified that called on fish biologists, hydrologists, and soil scientists to participate in classifying and locating streams prior to completion of a timber sale. The ecological specialists had an important role to play in ensuring that the new rules were being adhered to. While they were given more influence, they were not able to stop completely some harvesting of old growth. The old guard represented by supervisors like Stubblefield continued to exert power, and they still had harvesting of old growth in their sights. One of those timber sales was called the Walupt Cispus Timber Sale, which included old growth. A rationalization of the sale was to reduce fragmentation. This undoubtedly could have been accomplished without logging old growth. Fortunately, the sale received no bids, which may in part have been a result of protest by the environmental community.

One change that did occur in response to the NFP was that the GPNF no longer compared current accomplishments against the 1990 projections, but rather to the projections made for the 1994 NFP. The reason for this was simple and political. Had the accomplishment been measured against 1990 projections, the report would have read that 334 million board feet were projected to be logged annually throughout the 1990s, whereas 41 million board feet were actually harvested in the mid-1990s, an extraordinarily high level of reduction, one without precedence. Stubblefield acquiesced to the new reality in reporting that the goal was 64 million board feet and that 41 million board feet were harvested. In the prior year, as the GPNF struggled to make an adjustment to the new realities it faced under the NFP, the GPNF had the lowest level of timber harvested since the depths of the Great Depression, a little over 11 million board feet.

The most significant impact from this low level of timber sales on the GPNF was on local communities that depended on timber receipts. Rural counties like Skamania County had little worries about funding public services like schools during the high-production phase. In Skamania County, 30 percent of its funding for schools came from timber receipts, the highest in the nation. With the stark reduction in logging, those receipts were greatly reduced. Rural counties quite suddenly often faced the necessity of learning how to make do with less. In the long run, achieving sustainable harvest levels would provide a more reliable benefit to the community and to the mills and their workers. In the short run, the transition often proved to be challenging.

While Gifford Pinchot's goal of ensuring the health of small, rural, resource-dependent communities did not disappear, what did increase in scope and focus was environmental protection and restoration. The Forest Service began to view community well-being as less dependent on traditional timber harvest and more on attracting tourists for outdoor recreation, forest and watershed restoration, and harvesting of non-timber forest products like matsutake mushrooms and huckleberries. From the 1940s through the 1980s, a Forest Service report on socioeconomic impacts from the Northwest Forest Plan noted that "contributing to community stability through a policy of sustained-yield timber harvesting to provide a non-declining, even flow of forest products and associated jobs and income was a central goal of national forest management." "Non-declining flow" as a goal was no longer viable when the NFP was implemented. For many communities, however, several new terms came into being: "amenity values" "amenity migration," and "amenity-driven economic development."

The reality for resource-dependent communities close to the GPNF varied highly. "Studies also found that the Northwest Forest Plan impacts on communities differed at the community and county scales, and depended on local social, cultural, economic, and environmental contexts." Communities dependent on timber mills that closed during the 1990s suffered more. What was greatly misunderstood about those closures was that many, if not most, were not a result of the reduction of flow of logs from the woods. In Washington state between 1968 and 2002, the number of timber mills declined from more than two hundred to seventy-five. Surprisingly, mill capacity actually increased as the mills that remained adopted new technology. One result of these advances and reliance on new technology was that fewer mill workers were needed. Increases in automation were a much greater driver of job losses in rural communities than the reduction of timber harvest as a result of the Northwest Forest Plan. By 2000, Forest Service and Bureau of Land Management (BLM) lands provided less than 5 percent of the total timber supply in areas impacted by the plan. This percentage in fact mirrored the percentage of timber supplied by Forest Service lands in 1931 when most mills relied on timber coming off private lands and the Forest Service was concerned about a timber famine. The timber economy had come full circle in eighty years.

My cabin sits in Skamania County, which is 1.3 million in acres in size. About 78 percent of those acres is in the Gifford Pinchot National Forest. Not surprisingly, the county was initially negatively impacted by the NFP. As described by the regional labor economist Scott Bailey in 2021, "Skamania County's economy went through a wrenching transition" as the county was "long dependent upon timber for jobs and income." "Ten percent of the county's job base disappeared, and unemployment topped 22 percent in February 1992." In 1993, however, a major new employer—the Skamania Lodge—appeared, subsidized by federal funds, which provided almost the same number of jobs as had been lost. Bailey wrote some thirty years after the plan was implemented, "Almost overnight, Skamania had shifted from a timber economy to a tourist economy." This shift well represents the transition that took place across the region with amenity migration and amenity-driven economic development.

One of the very positive effects of the reduced budgets for the ecology of the GPNF was road closure. The roaded system in the forest had grown to 4,508 miles by 1991. With the NFP in effect, which called for no net increase in roads in key watersheds, the number of roads in the GPNF declined to 4,275 miles in 1997. Once again, a turning point had been reached. The seemingly inexorable increase in road miles, which began with the end of WWII, had finally been halted. Roads were being decommissioned.

The turn away from post-WWII high production to ecological management in the early 1990s in the GPNF and national forests throughout the Pacific Northwest resulted from the actions of one person, Judge William Dwyer, when he ruled on a case involving a little-known bird, the northern spotted owl. With the Dwyer ruling, foresters were finally coming to terms with the reality that the policies that had guided them for forty-five years after WWII were no longer viable, either politically or ecologically. They slowly began to recognize that other values the public held were ascendant: protection of habitat for endangered species; appreciation of the complexity and immensity of old-growth forests; concern for the aesthetic and spiritual values inherent in old-growth forests. Ecologists had seized the high ground in the debate between those wanting to continue to log and those wanting to protect habitat. Concern for the ecosystem emerged as a driver for change. This new thinking, according to William Dietrich in *The Final Forest*, shifted the focus toward "how to manage the entire landscape to preserve ecosystems . . . and the spotted owl proved crucial to this transformation . . . because it required large blocks of native habitat . . . if the owl disappeared, it meant the forest system was collapsing; that a prehistoric ecosystem inherited by the pioneers was in danger of being entirely wiped out. The owl came to symbolize first an entire kind of forest, and then a worldview: a way of seeing nature, and man's role in it, different from anything the general public had accepted before." This paradigm shift in how people viewed the forest had enormous repercussions for the many stakeholders in our national forests. The Forest Service, which cut 1 billion board feet on Pacific Northwest forest in 1946, had increased that cut to a record 5.7 billion board feet in 1986, with most of that cut coming from old growth in the Pacific Northwest. More than a million acres of old growth were cut in the Pacific Northwest in the 1970s and 1980s alone.

The "decadent" wood that foresters had viewed with disdain for almost one hundred years in fact served a critical purpose. Woodpeckers cannot find their prey in healthy young trees; they depend on dead snags where wood is softer. Researchers learned that simply leaving dead snags in a tree stand increased bird numbers by 30 percent. Deadwood is equally important on the ground as "70 percent of northwest amphibians and 85 percent of the region's reptiles need downed logs to survive."

While two disparate groups existed uneasily within the Forest Service, one holding on tenaciously to the old culture and one pushing for change, one individual emerged who appeared to bridge the two groups, Jack Ward Thomas. At the time of the Dwyer ruling on the spotted owl, Thomas had worked for the Forest Service for over twenty-five years and had moved up the ranks of the Forest Service as a wildlife biologist and became known as the elk specialist within the agency. He was not viewed as one of the "get out the cut" guys, and at the same time, he strongly identified with the culture of his agency. As someone who worked at the margins of his organization, he was not viewed with suspicion by the old guard, and thus had the capability of acting as an internal change agent. In 1989, Thomas was called to lead an Interagency Scientific Committee (ISC) to develop a scientifically credible strategy for ensuring the long-term health of the spotted owl. The report that emerged from this committee challenged much of the dogma that the Forest Service had lived by for the previous forty-five years. The key strategic shift was from the requirements for an ongoing supply of timber to the habitat requirements of wildlife species.

The Thomas report served as a flashpoint in the midst of the timber wars and the battle over protection of the spotted owl. On one side of the debate were environmentalists, adept at using the courts to challenge timber sales, and on the other side were loggers, who had been cutting trees for several generations, who saw no reason to change, and who feared the loss of their livelihood. In the midst of the often heated and tense stand-off between these various groups, two scientists from the Andrews Forest, Art McKee and Chris Maser, came to a groundbreaking understanding regarding the needs of spotted owls: owl pairs needed immense reserves, as large as 1,000 acres, to thrive as a species. McKee and Maser recognized that the Forest Service needed to consider not only how much old growth remained in the Pacific Northwest but also the ecological condition of an entire landscape. This understanding directly challenged the practices of the previous forty-five years, especially that of clear-cutting.

In the Pacific Northwest, clear-cuts had been limited to 40 acres largely because that was thought to be the largest amount that people would accept on public lands. The actual result of that policy was a highly fragmented landscape, one that was well documented by environmentalists who took pictures of these dispersed clear-cuts from low-flying planes and used them effectively to turn the public against the Forest Service. The results of this fragmentation were both a decline in diversity and the loss of the necessary amount of habitat for a number of species, including the spotted owl. It also resulted in dispersed islands. Maser made clear the impact of this fragmentation: "Each tenfold decrease in island area led to an approximate halving of the number of species that could survive there."

One of the critical questions that remained unanswered at this time was just how much old growth remained in the Pacific Northwest. Not surprisingly, the answer that came from the Forest Service was quite different from the answer that came from the environmental community. The Forest Service said that 6.2 million acres of old growth remained. The Wilderness Society commissioned Peter Morrison, a forest ecologist, to answer the question using the understanding developed by the scientists of the Andrews Forest. His answer: 2.4 million acres. How could these answers differ so significantly? The Forest Service, when it presented its findings to Congress and the public, made a significant edit. The initial report prepared by a contractor was titled "Potential Old Growth Map." A 1997 article from the *University of Washington News* related that when the report was presented to Congress, the word "potential" was dropped from the report. That "potential" likely accounted for the nearly 4-million-acre discrepancy. The Forest Service distorted its findings; the agency refused to admit that the vast old-growth forests of the Pacific Northwest, which, based on Forest Service assessments was about 33 million acres in the early 1930s, had been reduced to just 2.4 million acres by the late 1980s.

While the Thomas report captured the attention of policymakers and the public in the Pacific Northwest with its focus on the northern spotted owl, it did not address the broader biodiversity issue. Congress then commissioned another study "to suggest forest management strategies to protect old growth forests, the species associated with these forests, and threatened fish stocks." The report that resulted from this study became known as the Gang of Four report (named after the panel of four scientists involved). Critics of this effort called the group charged by Congress to develop recommendations the "Gang of Four" due to their intense dislike for Congress's willingness to seek scientific guidance on an issue they had previously dominated through political pressure. (The term "Gang of Four" soon became a badge of honor for the four scientists.) To develop the report, the lead scientists, including Jerry Franklin, Norm Johnson, and Jack Ward Thomas, had convened a group of scientists and ecological specialists from the many affected national forests in the Northwest and Northern California. Only staff experts were engaged, while forest supervisors and managers were not allowed to participate. Franklin was especially concerned about the safety of the staff experts working with the Gang of Four and potential adverse career consequences. At one point during their work, Franklin noticed that Ted Stubblefield, GPNF supervisor at the time, and several other forest supervisors had wandered into the work area. Franklin related to me that he approached them and forcefully told them, "Supervisors are not allowed here—you need to leave now!" Franklin later acknowledged that "they were extremely upset that they were unable to influence the work of the Gang of Four" and that "Ted Stubblefield hated my guts." From the line managers' perspective, the world had turned upside down. They had always been the decision-makers, the deciders, the ones on the inside with all the authority. Suddenly they were on the outside looking in. They were both incredulous and angry about this turn of events.

At the outset, the lead scientists were unsure how exactly they would achieve Congress's mandate to "map and grade the old-growth forest." So they brought the experts together in Portland for two weeks and arranged them in a large room by geography with staff from Mount Baker National Forest at one end of the room next to staff from the GPNF next to those from Mount Hood National Forest and so on—each group arranged geographically in relation to their neighbors so they could easily look around and see what was going on with each working group and how well their work fit together. Jerry Franklin later commented in one of our interviews, "We wanted as neutral an environment as possible for the participants, where they could feel safe, where they could be asked to provide their best information. They were beautiful. They were professional. They were great people. The agency professionals were empowered to do their job. They did it and they did it beautifully. They were the magic ingredient in the Gang of Four process."

What especially stands out in this assessment of the work accomplished by the Gang of Four is that for the first time the greatest good for the greatest number was not being addressed solely by forest supervisors largely guided by the timber industry and Congress. No longer were scientists quarantined to the back rooms. They were now the ones leading. The Gang of Four report concluded that a significant reduction in timber harvest was required beyond what was recommended by the Thomas report. This recommendation, not surprisingly, was simply ignored by the George H. W. Bush administration in the early 1990s and the US Forest Service under that administration. Rather, the Forest Service chose to implement the Thomas report, which in turn was successfully challenged in court because it failed to protect the biodiversity of the forest.

The significance of the Gang of Four's report, led largely by Jerry Franklin and based on his earlier research on old-growth forests, was that it provided the first comprehensive look at old-growth forests across the entire landscape of the Pacific Northwest. Scientists finally had a primary role in actively shaping policy. They were asked to show how their theories of ecosystem management could be put into practice and thus reform the management of old-growth forests in the Pacific Northwest. However, gridlock in Congress led to inaction, and the spotted owl and timber management became a national issue in the 1992 presidential campaign, which resulted in the election of Bill Clinton. Because Clinton had identified the timber wars in the Pacific Northwest as a national problem needing a national solution, in the first half year of his presidency he convened a daylong conference in Portland with a wide range of stakeholders to find a solution to the timber wars.

Clinton communicated that he wanted a solution within sixty days, and he followed the recommendation of one of the scientific panels that urged him to rely on the knowledge and expertise of those with evidence and facts on what was happening to habitat, wildlife, and biodiversity. Clinton charged FEMAT to produce a range of options for him to consider. They did so, and eventually Clinton chose what became known as Option 9, largely developed by Jerry Franklin, which integrated many of the elements of the other alternatives as well as information from previous reports. Option 9 became the basis for what was soon established and approved by Judge Dwyer as the Northwest Forest Plan. Under this plan, designed to ensure the viability of not only the spotted owl but also other at-risk species in Pacific Northwest forests, timber harvest from federal forests in the Pacific Northwest was expected to fall more than 75 percent against the levels harvested in the 1980s.

One of the reports generated by FEMAT soon after the meeting in Portland was "An Ecological, Economic, and Social Assessment." The section titled "Overview: Social Assessment of the Options" leads with the statement, "Not all is well in the forests and communities of the Pacific Northwest." One can read that opening sentence as a simple statement of fact or an extraordinary admission by an agency that was once blind and now could see. Reading further, one gains a greater sense of what was not well; where, in "many forest-dependent rural communities, unemployment is high, hope is low, and despair common. People living in communities long dependent on the forests near them, are reeling under the effects of the changes sweeping across the region." Certainly, timber-dependent communities surrounding the GPNF were in a state of shock when they began to understand the extent to which timber harvest were going to be reduced. The "changes" mentioned in the FEMAT report were a direct result of the Forest Service's failure over the previous several decades to acknowledge all the varied ecological values provided by Pacific Northwest forests.

Repeatedly the report refers to trust as the missing ingredient. The writers, who had witnessed years of animosity between opposing camps—and who observed the ongoing intransigence of a government agency with the word "service" in its name, implying above all service to the people of this country— recognized a fundamental truth. This agency, the US Forest Service founded by Gifford Pinchot, had lost the trust of those it was intended to serve. A simple declaration was made: "Trust must be recreated."

A key question was asked, how did we get here? And a startling acknowledgment was made: "The lesson of the last 100 years is clear: a tyranny of incremental decisions has led us to the current gridlock. We have yet to find the right way to deal with either our forests or the people who depend on them." Quite an astonishing description, "a tyranny of incremental decisions." Is it true that a grand plan to decimate a natural, wild ecosystem containing millions of acres of trees up to five hundred years old did not exist? Had what occurred been a slow-moving disaster whose scale and severity were recognized only when the damage was done and something irretrievable had been destroyed? Even in this report by FEMAT, which acknowledged that a turning point had been reached and that significant changes must take place in Forest Service practices, the writers failed to point a finger at agency leaders who for forty-five years loudly and forcefully called for the removal of all the "decadent" trees—that is, old growth—in the Northwest. Forest Service leaders, especially those in the Pacific Northwest, who were in lockstep formation with their superiors in Washington, DC, were still not being held fully accountable for their past actions. They had not acted as Pinchot's legitimate heirs. Rather, their actions to "liquidate the old growth" were more akin to the cut-and-run loggers of the nineteenth century whom Pinchot despised. Pinchot had created the Forest Service primarily as a means of ensuring that cut-and-run logging and the resultant destruction of rural communities would be a relic of the past.

The most damning assertions in the FEMAT report identified multiple failures on the part of the agency that had failed to live up to Gifford Pinchot's vision of the greatest good for the greatest number in the long run. The report poignantly listed the many reasons for the crisis that resulted in judicial intervention: "It is caused by not practicing multiple use management wherein all of the resources are valued and managed on a sustained yield basis. It is caused by not providing an adequate rationale for liquidation of old-growth trees when the 'allowable cut effect' was discredited as silviculturally impossible. It is caused by not embracing a vision of the federal forests as repositories of diverse resource values but rather holding a narrow definition of the value of forest as commercial timber lands. It is caused by ignoring the comments of people around the country on forest plans, Wilderness designations, Wild and Scenic River designations." The writers were emphatically and vigorously castigating the old culture, the dominant leaders of the previous forty-five years, for their many failures. Pinchot's heirs in his namesake forest and across the Pacific Northwest were finally being held to account. They failed Pinchot. They failed the public they served. They failed the forest.

One of the more disturbing assertions of the FEMAT report was the recognition that the range of options for responding to the crisis was greatly limited by the Forest Service's failure to address the many social, economic, and ecological problems resulting from decades of mismanagement of the nation's forests. Past attempts to change Forest Service practices under the headings of New Perspectives and then New Forestry had failed. A new approach, Ecosystem Management, heralded a paradigm shift with profound impacts on the future management of the nation's forests. Rather than view trees as crops and promote single-aged plantations,

Ecosystem Management called for an integrated conservation strategy. This strategy addressed the needs of northern spotted owls, marbled murrelets, old-growth forests, and watersheds and the at-risk fish species that live in them. In recognition that the movements of most species are not constrained by artificial boundaries, the FEMAT report called for planning at the landscape level.

The FEMAT report identified three new categories of national forestlands in the Pacific Northwest: late successional reserves, matrix lands, and adaptive management lands. Importantly, LSRs are recognized as the "result of a unique interaction of disturbance, regeneration, succession, and climate that can never be recreated in their entirety through management." The plan recognizes that spotted owls and marbled murrelets will not thrive in younger forests. Because so little old growth was left in the Pacific Northwest, LSRs were viewed as vital to restoring a more natural forest. In contrast to LSRs, matrix lands were those identified as suitable for timber harvests, while adaptive management areas were identified as areas where new approaches to forest management could be tested.

In addition, the report noted that late successional reserves will be regenerated by "different processes during a different period from that of the existing late successional forests. It is highly likely that silviculturally created stands will function differently from current old stands that developed over the last 1,000 years. Consequently, conserving a network of natural old-growth stands is imperative for preserving biodiversity into the future." What is poignantly recognized here is that focused management actions designed to do the right thing from a biodiversity perspective cannot restore that which has been destroyed. Given the untold number of remaining mysteries of what makes for a healthy functioning old-growth forest and given the exceptional complexity of those forests, the trees that will exist in a thousand years may look like old trees, but they may not operate as true old growth with all its miraculous complexity and multiple functions.

For the first time, a host of federal agencies, including the Forest Service, BLM, Fish and Wildlife, National Fisheries Service, and the Environmental Protection Agency (EPA), all agreed to a common management approach. Rather than focus on disparate tracts of land, they recognized the entire Pacific Northwest as an ecosystem. This was a significant paradigm shift. A holistic view based on solid science was finally being applied to Pinchot's utilitarian "greatest good" ethic. As a professional forester who believed in a sustainable approach to forestry, Pinchot would likely have been delighted to incorporate genuine scientific findings into how his national forests were managed. In the 1970s and 1980s, his heirs chose to ignore what their scientists were telling them until the courts forced them to listen. Only then did change happen.

Most forest supervisors in the Pacific Northwest were aligned with the timber industry; however, not all of them were onboard. One of those latter was Jim Furnish, who became supervisor of the Siuslaw National Forest in 1991. Furnish joined the agency in 1965 and made his way up the ranks like many of his peers, and like most of them he did not question the high level of cut throughout the 1970s and 1980s. He did, however, have an open mind and willingness to listen to agency scientists. He eloquently described the cognitive dissonance he experienced on first listening to Chris Maser, the forest ecologist who specialized in understanding the functioning of old-growth forests: "I sat enraptured as Maser talked about old growth forest, squirrels and their poop, fungal spores, mycorrhizae (fungi that grow symbiotically with tree roots and dramatically improve a tree's uptake of water and soil nutrients), lichens, soil-dwelling insects, forest productivity, and by inference, how just about every aspect of our forest management was naïve and simplistic—in a word, wrong. Forests were incredibly complex biotic systems, Maser said; simple notions of just managing trees actually involved significant risks of upsetting the delicate balance of important forest relationships."

Another of the more significant discoveries scientists at the Andrews Forest made was how important mycorrhizae were to the health of old-growth forest. Mycorrhizae are part of an extraordinary symbiosis between 300-foot-tall trees and their fungal bodies found underground. The fungi process sugars from the trees and in return help the trees greatly increase their intake of water and critical nutrients, including nitrogen and phosphorous, while supporting the transfer of significant amounts of carbon between trees. This surprising discovery led scientists to understand that mycorrhizae played a critical role in promoting coexistence and biodiversity. The biologically rich zone surrounding roots is called the rhizosphere, and a single gram of that soil contains 100 million bacteria and many miles of fungi. Scientists were now confirming what many early foresters intuited, that the soil itself was crucial to forest health. Foresters had ignored what was happening high in the canopy; they had ignored what was below their feet. Both were critical to the healthy functioning of a forest.

Furnish initially felt confused and upset as his fundamental beliefs about forestry were challenged by his own agency scientists. He began to question the deeply held values that he had developed as a young forester in the 1960s. Why did the Forest Service treat the timber industry as the power to always be placated? How did this state of affairs come into being? How did the agency lose sight of the values most of the public held dear? After much deep reflection, Furnish began to recognize that the greatest good was grounded more in environmental values like scenery, clean water, healthy fisheries and wildlife, and outdoor recreation—that many in the public he served were more interested in the forests in their natural state rather than logs on logging trucks. "I began to understand the distinction between dollar and values . . . that environmental services flowed from forested, mountainous landscapes . . . that will always far exceed the value of logging and grazing."

Furnish was part of a cohort of managers within the agency who believed that the culture itself needed to change. The chief at the time, Dale Robertson, was presented with a recommendation to adopt a new approach, what some were calling "A New Perspective." Rather than choose to act boldly as a transformational leader, Robertson took the safer choice and remained a transactional leader. He refused to lead the agency in a different direction; he refused to take on the challenge of culture change. Several years later, Clinton acted against precedent and fired Robertson and replaced him with the man he relied on to bring an ecosystem management approach to the agency, Jack Ward Thomas. For the first time, the agency had a scientist as its chief, and a leader who fully supported the direction that Jim Furnish wanted to take the Siuslaw. In a matter of years, the Siuslaw National Forest timber harvest declined from 215 million to 23 million board feet a year, a 92 percent reduction. Furnish put in place policies designed to achieve the intent of the Northwest Forest Plan: to enable more of his forest to attain old-growth characteristics and move from uniform plantations designed to be cut every forty to seventy years to a more natural forest where diversity, complexity, resilience could take hold.

Furnish was one of the few members of the old guard who called on his peers to acknowledge that the "timber is king" approach needed to be rejected and replaced with a fresh one that recognized the importance of restoration. He recognized the significance of the transition that he was in the midst of. For forty-five years, the Forest Service served as custodians of national forests, the "life" of our forests, and that was followed by forty-five years in which high production of timber was the overriding goal, the "death" of our forests. In the early 1990s, the Forest Service began transitioning to a new phase in which it needed to "explicitly embrace the mandate of ecosystem management with the goal of maintaining or achieving naturalness. Primary values should be clean water and air, abundant fish and wildlife, quality recreation opportunities, and sustaining landscape function." Furnish very eloquently, and simply, called for a return to a more natural forest, to the "rebirth" of our forests.

One of the distinctions that set the GPNF apart from many of the other national forests in the Pacific Northwest was that large sections of it had been burned in the late nineteenth and early twentieth centuries. In both the Siouxon watershed and the Cispus watershed could be found vast tracts of young forests that were eighty to ninety years old, which the Forest Service, in its zeal for cutting old growth, ignored. Not only were these areas not cut, but they also were not roaded. One of the discoveries made by the FEMAT group was that some of the most intact watersheds were those that had been burned over and then left alone. While most of the GPNF was, as Jerry Franklin characterized it in an interview, "whacked" and largely fragmented by clear-cuts, some drainages like the Siouxon that had earlier burned and thus were viewed as less valuable, needed only to be treated with patience. Some forests, like those in the Siouxon watershed, if left alone, could grow into a true old-growth forest.

The new emerging culture, among other values, recognized that in some cases the best action is no action. Let it be. And so the Forest Service let the Siouxon be, not logged, for almost a century. Nature, however, chose otherwise. In the fall of 2020, the Big Hollow Fire burned through much of the Siouxon watershed. As a result of climate change and the increased drying out of the Pacific Northwest forests, fires on the wetter west side of Washington are occurring on a more frequent basis than was historically the case. And the result of this fire was the loss of a significant amount of mature forest, an entire watershed that was poised, with time, to take on the many characteristics of old growth.

The Dwyer ruling and the development and implementation of the NFP established a clear demarcation for the US Forest Service. Most organizational cultures change only in response to changes in the external environment. Insightful and reflective leaders in organizations that recognize those existential threats lead their organizations to change their cultures using diverse methods. Over time, new values and new assumptions around what determines success emerge. Interestingly, this model, which is true for for-profit organizations, did not apply to the Forest Service. Rather, the agency's culture changed as a result of actions from the bottom and middle as well as at the edges. People like Jeff DeBonis, who represented the new and younger, more environmentally sensitive employees in the agency, were key catalysts to this change. People like Jim Furnish, who had risen up through the ranks with an openness to learning that set him apart from most of his peers, and then acted on that learning and changed his approach to forest management. People like Lynn Burditt, who was one of the first women to work side by side with the male-dominated engineers and foresters, and who, because she witnessed the catastrophic impacts of the Mount St. Helens eruption on the forest and then its stunning rebirth, viewed the forest with a vastly new understanding. People like Jerry Franklin, who had been kept at arm's length for decades, who was tolerated but not taken seriously, and who then acquired real power and acted on that power. Franklin captured well what many of his peers were feeling when he wrote just prior to the Dwyer ruling, "Let us adopt a forest ethic. Let us approach forest ecosystems with the respect that their complexity deserves. And, considering our current level of knowledge, let us approach the forest with appropriate humility."

While people like Franklin, Furnish, DeBonis, and Burditt pushed for change from within the Forest Service, their efforts would likely have failed without forces pressing for change from outside. The most significant pressure influencing Forest Service culture was the result of a powerful outside force, the judiciary, which declared emphatically and powerfully that past actions and practices could not continue into the future. The 1990s marked the transition from the old to the new and represented a tumultuous time of uncertainty and ambiguity, which is so typical of major organizational transitions. By the end of that decade, the Forest Service had embarked on a new era, one that can best be described as ecological restoration.

17

Ecological Restoration

> The wood wide web has been mapped, traced, monitored, and coaxed to reveal the beautiful structures and finely adapted languages of the forest network. . . . Mother trees recognize and talk with their kin, shaping future generations. . . . These understandings have transformed our understanding of trees from competitive crusaders of the self to members of a connected, relating, communication system.
>
> —Dr. Suzanne Simard

Emily Platt has had a unique role in influencing ecological restoration on the Gifford Pinchot National Forest. Her early influence was as executive director of the Gifford Pinchot Task Force, now Cascade Forest Conservancy, a nonprofit organization established to "protect and sustain forests, streams, wildlife, and communities" in the GPNF. Later, after obtaining a PhD in forestry, she joined the Forest Service and became a district ranger in Pinchot's namesake forest. As district ranger she had a direct role in shaping policy on the ground. This change in roles from outside advocate to inside leader represents well the extraordinary culture shift for the Forest Service.

As an advocate acting to protect the GPNF, Platt noted in an interview I conducted with her that the old guard, well after the implementation of the NFP, was still targeting old growth: "The GPNF was still planning for old-growth logging at the beginning of the 2000s, and they no longer are planning that now—this has been a huge transition for them. That has been the most dramatic change. They were not only inclined to go into those matrix lands, that is what they did. They did ancient forest logging—when I first begin work here, every single timber sale had old-growth logging as a part of it."

Platt as an advocate observed firsthand the transition under way within the Forest Service. In our interview, while she was an executive director, she noted that:

> Some of the Staff are still very traditional and focused on getting the timber out. They are given these targets by Congress every year and are

given money to make it happen. That is their job, and they take that seriously. On the other hand, many more younger people are progressive and focused on restoration. They have a more holistic view of their job—not just to get out timber sales but also to restore fish and wildlife habitat. There are more people in the Agency now supportive of a restoration agenda. . . . That was such a huge thing that came of the Northwest Forest Plan to take an ecosystem approach. It certainly clashes with the old way they were doing things. It is a part now of how they view business—to look at the forest as a landscape—to see it at a larger scale.

Platt emphasized the need for more ecologists to ensure that fish and wildlife needs are met, that those needs should be the drivers, not silvicultural needs. As the father of the conservation movement, Pinchot almost surely would have agreed with Platt the advocate who related during the interview that "it is a new era for Forest Conservation—an exciting time. Most people have accepted that restoration needs to be our focus, and figuring out how to make that happen on the ground is a huge challenge."

In a 2018 interview I conducted with Platt, when she was a district ranger on the GPNF, I asked her about the old "get out the cut" culture. She observed, "No, the old guard is not gone—that sentiment is still strong in some places. But all of our forest plans now are written up and founded on ecological science and restoration—so that is a real shift, and the leadership of the agency is now supportive of that agenda. I would never thin in old-growth forest—does not make any sense. But in a plantation—up to eighty, even a hundred-plus years—stand thinning makes lots of sense. We probably have thirty years or so to do this work." Platt is highly representative of the new culture that recognizes that ecological restoration needs to be the focus during this phase of the Forest Service's life. It sets the stage for the rebirth of the forest and, over time, a forest with extensive old growth.

As a Forest Service employee, Platt acknowledged that old growth could still be cut on Pinchot's namesake forest, that the Northwest Forest Plan did not preclude cutting old growth. The Forest Service finally recognized that the greater good did not include going after old growth. Platt stated, "The social and political madness that would ensue from cutting old growth do not make it a real option for us . . . you do not want to spend years in litigation. That is the primary reason we focus on thinning—probably 99 percent."

One of the many projects planned for the GPNF that well represents this need for ecological restoration is one that Platt had a strong influence on, the Upper Wind Big Hollow project. The project targeted some 3,000 acres of forest plantations with the intent of opening "the forest canopy, allowing increased sunlight and space in the plantation, fostering development of an understory . . . and *allowing larger trees to develop more rapidly* (author's emphasis). Over time, thinning is expected to result in a more structurally and functionally diverse forest with a greater diversity of species represented."

One of the more controversial aspects of this project is to create some limited early seral habitat through "regeneration harvest," that is, clear-cutting. In the stages of forest succession, seral habitat is the habitat that results after a major forest disturbance such as a severe burn. The project proposes to create open conditions in the forest and to include "legacy structure within the treatment." This is a reference to the biological legacies that result from major forest disturbances, legacies that promote a "rich biodiversity because the remaining biomass provides resources to many life forms and because of habitat heterogeneity provided by the disturbances that generated them."

The project proposal addressed past silvicultural practices by noting that "Clear-cut logging on National Forest land returned in earnest in the 1950s. These clear-cuts targeted the older, large-tree forests, and created many even-aged stands between 20 and 80 acres in size. Clear-cutting on National forest lands essentially stopped in the late 1990s. Since then, the trees planted in these clear-cuts have advanced these stands to a mid-seral condition." Here we have the Forest Service acknowledging that old growth was targeted for cuts and that the result was a plantation forest lacking complexity. The project goes on to recognize that "differentiation from an even-aged stand to a more structurally complex and species diverse un-even-aged stand" is the desired future condition. What becomes clear from the language throughout the project proposal is the importance of biological legacies in promoting biodiversity and that one result is a forest that is more patchy, gappy, and clumpy. The recognition that this forest in the GPNF needs to transition from "even-aged" to "structurally complex" represents the true possibility for the rebirth of more natural forest.

A table in the project proposal highlights the distribution of forest seral stages over time for the entire Wind River watershed in the southern end

Table 1. Forest seral class distribution at select years over the entire Wind
River Watershed

Year	Non-Forest	Early Seral	Mid-Seral	Late-Seral & Old-Growth
Circa 1850	5%	28%	9%	58%
Circa 1900	5%	15%	36%	44%
1996	7%	24%	47%	22%
2017	0%	4%	51%	45%

of Pinchot's namesake forest (Table 1). One of the most notable changes
is how, since the NFP was implemented, that late seral and old growth in
the Wind River Watershed more than doubled from 1996 to 2017 from
22 percent to 45 percent.

As part of the restoration effort, this project seeks to enhance huckleberry resources and forage for wildlife species. The proposal noted that
road density has led to "wildlife harassment"; and that while in the past
these roads were built to access timber to cut, the opportunity now is to
assess which roads to close or decommission. The proposal states that "the
desire is to reduce tree density in the young stands to speed the development toward old-growth and add the complexity such as species diversity
and larger snags and down logs common to older forests." Such an extraordinary statement, "to speed the development toward old growth," was so
unlike anything that the Forest Service would have proposed before the
Northwest Forest Plan.

Platt recognized that restoration does not mean that the forests will
simply look like they did before logging began on Pinchot's namesake
forest. In my interview with her, she described how "we have to think
about more things today like the climate, the ecological changes that have
happened. How things were in the past regarding forest structure and the
like can inform what we do in the future but not determine it. Our target is
not to replicate what was. Especially with climate change . . . our new plans
do address climate change. At project scale it is almost too small a scale. It
is much easier to address at a much larger scale. In thinking about carbon
storage, we have to address that in the context of a whole host of ecological
factors—it does not make sense to do plans with the idea of only maximizing carbon storage, especially as there are ecological reasons for thinning

our plantations." Too much has changed to simply seek to return to how things were one hundred years ago. Restoration must consider the diverse changes that have impacted forest, and no change is more significant than climate change. In December 2023, the chief of the USFS, Randy Moore, announced that all our national forests would amend their forest plans in response to the threat of climate change. He declared that old growth needed to be protected and the conditions developed so that more mature forest could develop into old growth. The extraordinary capacity of our older forests to store carbon is finally being fully acknowledged.

This culture of the Forest Service that emerged in the 2000s, which Platt so well represents, stands in sharp contrast to the old culture of the Forest Service, which was dominated by a homogenous workforce of mostly White men in their fifties and sixties. The most visible representation of that homogeneity can be seen at the GPNF Training Center, a historic log building in the southern GPNF. A large portrait of Gifford Pinchot, who appears rather stern and as a patriarch of a growing clan, rests on a wall above the fireplace, the place of honor. On the walls throughout the Training Center are pictures of the many groups who held training sessions there beginning in the 1920s and into the 1930s, the stewardship phase. All are of White men, mostly young, with a few elders among them. These were the future leaders of the Forest Service. Many of these men became Forest Service leaders during the forty-five years after WWII and thus were responsible for eliminating old growth and replacing them with even-aged plantations of Douglas-firs. They made the forest look much more like them: less diversity, more sameness. The Northwest Forest Plan marked the reversal of that seemingly inexorable march to the sameness of uniform plantations of the previous forty-five years.

The NFP was applied to 25 million acres of national forests in Washington, Oregon, and Northern California, including all 1.3 million acres of the GPNF. The new premises that guided foresters were grounded in two concepts, ecosystem management and biodiversity conservation. Ecosystem management recognizes the total forest and all its elements as an interconnected whole, a web of life that can be readily unraveled by a failure to understand and respond to those uncountable interconnections. Biodiversity conservation recognizes the interdependence of all species with the forest and the importance of conserving the whole natural forest in ensuring the viability of all those species dependent on a natural forest.

One of the most influential insights that helped guide the development of ecological restoration and emerging Forest Service leaders who agreed wholeheartedly with the recommendations of the NFP, was probably best captured as a concept by John Muir in the nineteenth century: "When we try to pick out anything by itself, we find it hitched to everything else in the Universe." Another insight that influenced this emerging group of leaders was the Native American concept of seven generations. Any action taken should consider the impacts seven generations out. Any action taken should consider the interconnected strands of the web of life we all live within, and how actions may have unintended consequences because of our failure to recognize those many connections.

The most notable characteristic of old-growth forests in the Pacific Northwest is their diversity. Diversity of structure, of composition, and of species. Diversity on both horizontal and vertical levels. Diversity of species below ground, on the ground, and in the canopy, in the air. Diversity at all levels of life from birth, adolescence, maturity, elderhood, and finally, death. Diversity in health from vigor to decapitation—standing snags—to senescence, and decaying logs on the forest floor. The emerging culture of the Forest Service beginning in the 1990s recognized the importance and value of these many forms of diversity and adopted the understanding that promoting forest diversity was key to ecological restoration.

Dominick DellaSala in *The Northwest Forest Plan: Still the Best Science of the Day* documented that prior to the establishment of the Northwest Forest Plan, "older forests were being clear-cut at a rate that would have virtually eliminated all old growth by 2020." The result would have been the extinction of the northern spotted owl and the marbled murrelet within an astonishingly short period of time. The efficacy of the plan depended on the application of both a coarse and a fine filter to the forests throughout the Pacific Northwest. The coarse filter was the primary tool for enabling an ecosystem approach to the forest, while a fine filter was applied to ensure biodiversity conservation. The coarse filter recognized that considering individual units across each national forest as independent of each other and treating them to their own independent silvicultural treatments was the surest way to kill the forests with a thousand cuts. The forests in the Cascades, from northern Washington through Oregon and into Northern California, needed to be viewed and managed as an interconnected landscape. The creation of late successional reserves became the centerpiece of the NWP; this network of reserves, stretching north to south for over 300 miles, was the basis for a conservation strategy for old-growth-dependent species. DellaSala summarized the importance of these connected reserves, "Globally, scientists have recognized that large, interconnected reserves maintained in perpetuity (i.e., fixed on the landscape) are fundamental to the future of life on the planet."

One of the most essential benefits these reserves provide, beyond ensuring the survival of old-growth-dependent species, is that of carbon sinks. Prior to the establishment of the Northwest Forest Plan, given the high level of logging, Northwest forests were a net source of CO_2. When those forests were logged, they quickly released about half of their carbon stores as CO_2. Now with logging levels reduced by some 80 percent, and with the rapid regrowth of these fertile forests, the national forests in the Pacific Northwest have been transformed from a contributor to the climate crisis to a contributor to climate mitigation. These forests are now a net sink for carbon and are needed to help reverse the buildup of greenhouse gases in our atmosphere. As a result of the high levels of cut during the high-production phase of forestry, foresters were unwittingly contributing to the climate crisis. While most of the attention on deforestation's contribution to climate change was centered on Brazil and Indonesia, our own forests over the past twenty years can be held up as a model for the benefits of forest restoration. Jerry Franklin and others in "The Northwest Forest Plan: Origins, Components, Implementation Experience, and Suggestions for Change" affirm the value of old-growth forest as carbon sinks: "The storage of carbon on federal lands is especially noteworthy because the region's high biomass forests are among the world's most carbon dense forest ecosystems."

Myriad other benefits are provided by these reserves such as climate refugia and high-quality water. Temperatures worldwide over the previous hundred years increased by 0.7 degrees Celsius. Over the next eight decades, temperatures in the Pacific Northwest are projected to increase by two to six degrees Celsius. The lower estimate is based on the slim hope that the Paris Climate agreements to reduce greenhouse gases will be achieved. The higher projections are based on a more realistic assessment that those agreements will not be adhered to. What does this mean for wildlife, whether flying squirrels, wolves, salamanders, or frogs? What does it mean for plants and plant associates whether mycorrhizae, lichen, salal, or ferns? With all the uncertainties about the rate and extent of climate change, we have more questions than answers.

A highly likely scenario is that we will see migrations of wildlife and plants both northward and toward higher elevations. A simple illustration shows the magnitude of these temperature changes. Jerry Franklin writes, "The climate at 500 feet elevation would migrate 1,500 to 3,500 feet up the mountain slopes. The zone of major snow could almost disappear. Climates would move 200–300 kilometers north of their current location. The climate of southwestern Oregon would be in northern Oregon and that of northern California in southern Oregon."

Migrations across landscapes would be made extremely challenging if not impossible without the interconnected reserves running north to south throughout the Cascades as animals and plants seek out the cooler and more moist conditions on which they depend. In addition to providing climate refugia, the forest reserves will also ensure we have a much more reliable source of high-quality water both for ourselves and for water-dependent aquatic species (from salmon to the smallest invertebrates). Civilizations ranging from the Maya in Central America to the Hopi in the southwest of North America have collapsed as a result of prolonged droughts. While the founders of our national forests stressed the need for a sustainable supply of timber as a primary reason for protecting these forests, the other driver was water. Healthy forests act as sponges and are vital to water storage, reduced flooding, and the overall integrity of aquatic systems. Aquatic reserves, which are designed to ensure high-quality water throughout the Cascades, also contribute to the functional connectivity of late successional reserves. The aquatic reserves in many ways function in a way similar to the human circulatory blood system with its many arteries and veins carrying essential life-giving elements to all parts of our body.

While the coarse filter of ecosystem management is applied across the landscape, a fine filter of biodiversity conservation is applied on a much smaller scale. Because logging will inevitably continue on our national forests, a fine filter of "survey and manage" was applied by the Northwest Forest Plan. DellaSala in "Building on Two Decades of Ecosystem Management and Biodiversity Conservation under the Northwest Management Plan" notes how this fine filter will ensure the future viability of "some 400 species of amphibians, bryophytes, fungi, lichens, mollusks, vascular plants, arthropod functional groups, and one mammal, including many endemics that otherwise may not persist outside the reserve network." Survey and manage, which is accomplished by pre-logging surveys, essentially acknowledges that the forest needs to be approached with a much greater sense of humility. The Forest Service was conceding the reality of "unknown unknowns." Especially in light of climate change, the need is even greater to understand, at a more refined level, the risks that proposed management policies and practices pose to poorly understood or rare species. The most vital function that the fine filter approach of survey and manage provides is that of minimizing the chance that rare species do not become endangered species as a result of unanticipated population declines, whether from climate change or catastrophic disruptions resulting from severe fires or other major disturbances.

The poster child and impetus for an ecosystem management and biodiversity conservation approach to national forests in the Pacific Northwest is the northern spotted owl. Logging of most of the national forests in that region was dramatically reduced directly as a result of the spotted owl. The spotted owl became, for our national forests and all the species that reside in them, not only a symbol but also, like the canary in the coal mine, a warning of potential dangers ahead. Dangers, especially, of extinction. Unfortunately, even with this heightened awareness, spotted owl populations on federal lands have continued to decline.

Research has provided some heartening discoveries that do show the positive effects of the NFP and, in particular, the setting aside of large reserves. Greater spotted owl population decreases were found in matrix lands, where logging continued, in contrast to late successional reserves. DellaSala reported, "The decline in spotted owls was steepest on study areas not managed under the Northwest Forest Plan, and therefore the downward trajectory of owl populations might have been much worse without the Northwest Forest Plan." Unfortunately, some logging of old-growth habitat, by both the USFS and BLM, on which spotted owls depend, while at a much-reduced level from the pre-Northwest Forest Plan period, has continued. This decrease in old-forest areas along with competition from the barred owl has continued to adversely affect spotted owl populations. DellaSala's research has led to some reassuring findings: "The barred owl's competitive advantage over the spotted owl diminishes in spotted owl territories with a greater proportion of late-successional habitat. Conservation of large tracts of contiguous, old-forest habitat is well justified in any attempt to maintain northern spotted owls in the landscape."

The greatest good not just for the spotted owl but for all older-forest-dependent species was never elimination of what foresters viewed as decadent forest. Rather, it now means not only preserving every single old tree across the landscape, but also transforming the millions of acres of single-aged, single-species plantations into rich, diverse, chaotic, wild, natural old-growth forests. The next few decades are crucial to realizing this noble and hope-restoring goal.

Just as we eliminated DDT from the environment beginning in the 1970s and nurtured the return of eagles and ospreys to the landscape, so too can we create the conditions for the return of old-growth forests, for the rebirth of our ancient forests across the Cascades from Washington to Northern California. This effort cannot be one spanning a few decades, but rather must be sustained for centuries. The most essential first step as described by DellaSala is to ensure, "Every acre of mature and old-growth forest on federal lands, including when those areas eventually burn or are reset by natural disturbances, must be protected in perpetuity." Because the vast majority of old-growth forests were hauled off the landscape in logging trucks, we must now protect all remaining old growth trees. In a recent essay sent to the author, Jerry Franklin echoed this sentiment: "At this point in time and given their special nature, all remaining naturally regenerated mature and old-growth forests should be left to continue their natural development." What is especially remarkable in that declaration by Franklin is the word "all." This need to protect all that is left of the mature and old-growth forest in the Pacific Northwest is a poignant recognition simply of how little is left.

A one hundred-piece picture puzzle may challenge a ten-year-old. A five hundred-piece picture puzzle may challenge an adolescent. A one thousand-piece picture puzzle will challenge most adults. Old-growth forests are probably best viewed as a one hundred thousand-piece picture puzzle. Where does one begin? The most fundamental understanding is knowing that the whole puzzle will not be put together unless every piece is safeguarded. Just as puzzlers look at the picture of the whole puzzle on the cover of the box, so too people will benefit from spending time in a wilderness or long-protected preserve to know what an old-growth forest looks like. Through the work of many researchers, the Forest Service has gained some critical understandings about the biodiversity of old-growth Pacific Northwest forests. These include:

- Hidden species play key ecological roles.
- Large reserves alone do not suffice to ensure conservation of the entire legacy of natural biological diversity.
- Providing some old-forest elements between reserves is vital—tiny remnant islands of old-growth forests are important for species refugia and centers of dispersal.
- Riparian areas and wetlands, as well as rare and tiny environments, play key roles in conservation of biodiversity.
- How forests are connected over time and across space greatly affects biodiversity.

The insights that have derived from the Northwest Forest Plan have put us on a path that, if we continue down, can allow our descendants to experience the Pacific Northwest forests as they were experienced by Indigenous peoples who had been living there for over ten thousand years before the arrival of early settlers—as a landscape of grandeur and wildness that provided for many of the necessities of life. Just as no man is an island, so too no forest is an island. Forests exist across landscapes, and so we must protect forest across landscapes. Linked forests provide critical pathways for wildlife over time and space whether the predator wolf or the ground-dwelling salamander. Only by protecting these linked and interconnected forests can we also protect biological diversity. In many cases, this diversity is comprised of those hidden species below our feet and out of sight high in the canopy. While most of our attention is directed toward what we can see, we also must attend to the health of the soil through which old growth send their roots for the nutrients without which they would perish.

The path Pinchot's namesake forest was on as well as all national forests in the Pacific Northwest prior to the 1990s was one that resulted in single-species-dominated plantations. One example of the results of that sterility well illustrates the harms to the entire ecosystem: mature forests produce thirty times more truffles per acre than plantations and have nearly twice as many truffle species. Flying squirrels and red-backed tree voles depend for their survival on these truffles especially during summer draughts. Predators like spotted owls in turn depend on those flying squirrels and voles if they are to have a healthy population. Once again, we see how the strands of the web of life are connected.

The overarching goal for the next century must be restoration. Many people view restoration as simply bringing back the old-growth forests as they existed at the time of Lewis and Clark. Regrettably, that is not a realistic goal. The conditions that existed for many centuries prior to settlement of the Pacific Northwest by settlers beginning in the mid-1800s cannot be replicated. Restoration can set the forest on a path that will lead to a healthier, functioning, natural forest that provides a home to all species that depend on them. One of the key measures going forward for determining the well-being of the forests is whether biodiversity is at a minimum maintained. An understanding and realization of several conservation principles is essential:

- Species that are widely distributed are less prone to extinction than those with more restricted ranges.
- Large patches of habitat supporting many individuals are more likely to sustain those populations than small patches.
- Populations residing in habitat patches in close proximity are less extinction prone than those in widely separated patches.

A helpful view of restoration is described in *Creating a Forestry for the 21st Century: The Science of Ecosystem Management,* edited by Jerry Franklin and Kathryn Kohm. They describe restoration as "the process of encouraging a system to maintain its function and organization without continued human intervention. If a system has been shifted outside its range of performance under natural conditions, restoration attempts to move the system toward that range of performance in the future. . . . The goal of restoration is to reestablish the ability of the system to maintain its function and organization without continued human intervention."

Most of the forests throughout the Pacific Northwest were radically shifted outside their normal "range of performance" as a result of human intervention. The key to restoration is function and organization. Those two terms, as applied to old-growth forest, sound like simple concepts yet are quite complex. Function or that which is functional is defined by Webster's as whatever is "used to contribute to the development or maintenance of a larger whole." All the myriad pieces of the forest make up a whole. Because we can never fully understand how all the pieces interact and support the whole, we can never simply replicate the conditions that led to the development of old-growth forests as we now know them. We can protect the pieces and provide the conditions that will, over time, contribute to the "development or maintenance of a larger whole." Organization or to organize is defined by Webster's as to "arrange or form into a coherent unity or functional whole." In some ways these two terms almost appear as a snake eating its tail—a circularity that returns us repeatedly to some ineffable whole. The higher purpose, then, of restoration is to restore the whole, the whole forest, the natural forest.

Application of the principles of conservation biodiversity will help ensure protection of the pieces, which Aldo Leopold presciently wrote about much earlier. Application of the principles of ecosystem management will help ensure protection of the whole. Both are needed to achieve the restoration of Pinchot's namesake forest and forests throughout the Pacific Northwest. Both are needed if the Cascades in 2300 are to resemble the Cascades as they were in 1900. What was destroyed in a period of forty-five years will take centuries to be restored.

One of the most vital questions that can be asked is: to restore natural forest, do we simply let mother nature do her work and leave forests alone, or will active forest management facilitate the transformation of plantations more quickly into forests with old-growth characteristics? Much disagreement exists on the right answer to this question. As a wise person might respond, "it depends." The concept of equifinality has much relevance given the conditions in which Northwest forests currently exist and the hundreds of years of history and varied conditions over which old-growth forests developed.

Not all old-growth forests developed in the same fashion. Significant amounts of these forests in the Pacific Northwest developed after major disturbances, especially catastrophic fires and major windstorms. These disturbances left many biological legacies: patches of live trees, standing dead trees, fallen trees across the land, and small numbers of living old growth. The trees that survived these disturbances grew rapidly afterward. All of these conditions set the stage for the development of old-growth forest across vast tracts of the Pacific Northwest. What did not often occur was the dense, uniform regeneration of single-aged, single-species conifers, the results from clear-cuts during the high-production phase after WWII. Because the conditions after major disturbances were highly variable, they led to the kind of complexity that is highly characteristic of old growth: large live trees, large dead trees, large fallen trees, and trees of diverse sizes, ages, and species.

Some old-growth stands likely did develop more as even-aged stands, especially after severe disturbances such as stand-replacing catastrophic fires. Unlike the disturbance created by clear-cuts with slash burning and planting of single species of trees, these even-aged stands did contain a variety of biological legacies such as snags and fallen logs. These even-aged stands developed into characteristically old-growth forests as a result of a wide variety of small to intermediate disturbances including windstorms, ice storms, insect infestations, root rot, and fire that, over time, led to structural complexity, which is the key to its biological diversity.

Our understandings about the variable pathways by which old-growth forests developed provide at least a partial answer to the "how" of restoration forestry. Given the diverse pathways along which-old growth forests developed, foresters must recognize that they need to allow for a diversity of pathways rather than assume that only one approach, such as thinning, is needed. By using multiple approaches, risks to forest health are reduced. One size does not fit all. Perhaps the most important way of thinking that our future stewards will need, not just for the next few decades but for centuries, is that of a learner. A learner is one who approaches the forest with curiosity, with openness, with more questions than answers. A learner approaches the forest with humility, with awe at the complexity of the whole. A learner approaches the forest with patience knowing that hundreds of years were required to achieve the stunning majesty of old-growth forests.

Some of the key principles underlying restoration include focusing on the entire ecosystem, restoring resilience, and prioritizing the most degraded environments. To consider the entire ecosystem means to consider the diversity of successional forests across the landscape. Franklin and his peers confirm, "Every successional or structural stage of forest development makes unique and important contributions to biological diversity and ecological function." One of the ironies that resulted from forestry practices during the forty-five years after WWII was not only a loss of old growth but also a loss of early successional ecosystems. Suppression of fires was one of the primary contributors to this lack of early seral forests.

Early successional forests, which largely resulted from stand replacement events like fires and windstorms, are characterized by Franklin as having "open non-tree dominated environments." In addition, he notes that they have "high levels of structural complexity and spatial heterogeneity and retain legacy materials." The microclimate in these post-disturbance environments is radically different from that in older forests. Much more sunlight reaches the forest floor, temperatures are more extreme, wind speed is greater, and humidity is lower with reduced moisture in litter and soils. These environmental changes favor some species while creating adverse conditions for others. The biodiversity of early seral systems is quite distinctive from that of old-growth forests. Both are needed for a healthy ecosystem as are the interim stages. Franklin summarizes the value of what many consider forest catastrophes, "Many species and ecological processes are strongly favored by conditions that develop after stand-replacement disturbances."

To ensure the maintenance of these rich early seral forest ecosystems (ESFEs), the Forest Service needs to recognize major disturbances to the landscape as opportunities, not catastrophes. Biological legacies— for example, snags and downed trees left after a disturbance—need to be maintained and natural stand development processes allowed to unfold naturally. Salvage logging must be eliminated entirely. Franklin affirms that the best option is to simply let nature alone, to not manage the forest: "Naturally generated ESFEs are likely to be better adapted to present day climate and may be more adaptable to future climate change." The adoption of this leave-it-alone strategy after major disturbances is especially important now as the West experiences ever-increasing major forest fires as a result of climate change. Increasingly, many of these fires are now recognized as "climate fires." Ecological restoration argues that the best approach to restoration is to simply leave it as it is found after the fire— nature knows best.

Increasing the resilience of our Pacific Northwest forests is the second principle underlying effective restoration. Resilience is the ability to bounce back after harms have been inflicted. Resilience is the capacity to endure and surmount adverse events and processes. These harms include fires, insect infestations, wind and hailstorms, root rot, and climate change. The most consequential harm inflicted on our Pacific Northwest forests was the conversion of old growth into even-aged, single-species plantations. One choice we can make is to leave these plantations alone and view time as the great healer. Over time, competitive mortality and a variety of natural disturbances will inevitability occur in these forests, and, with some luck, an old growth forest will evolve in place of that plantation. Another option is to seek to accelerate the development of old-growth characteristics in plantations through thinning. To achieve the complex structure of old-growth forest, thinning must be done in a way very distinctive from the kind of thinning done solely to maximize timber productivity. Variability is the key: variable spacing, variable densities, variable patches, variable gaps. These small gaps encourage the growth of herbs, shrubs, and understory trees as well as allow for some scattered dominant trees. Franklin notes, "Studies show that when variable-density thinning is used, thinned stands usually have better developed understories, higher shrub densities, a greater richness of understory plant species, and more plant cover than un-thinned stands."

To optimize resilience while reducing risks, the Forest Service needs to apply both approaches—leave some percentage of plantations alone and apply variable density thinning to others. Monitoring over time will be essential with the mindset always of the learner. Research has shown that plantations are most responsive to thinning when they are young, less than eighty years old, and will likely increase the development of structural complexity and biological diversity in young forests. Thus, appropriate thinning of some Pacific Northwest plantations during the next several decades will be crucial to long-term forest health.

One of the least controversial aspects of restoration is focusing on and prioritizing the most degraded environments. Of course, single-aged, single-species plantations represent some of the most degraded environments in the Pacific Northwest as they are biologically sterile compared to early seral or old-growth forests. Roads, which in almost all of our national forests appear like the webs made by a drunken spider, have seriously degraded much of the landscape across the Pacific Northwest. In the GPNF, over 4,000 miles of roads extend across 1.3 million acres. Given lack of budgets to maintain those roads, many are failing and eroding. One of the direct impacts of these failures is the degradation of aquatic ecosystems. Streams are silting up and salmon populations decline as a result.

In Washington state, the Department of Fish and Wildlife has recommended that two-thirds of national forest roads in the state need to be removed. While the need for access to recreation areas and for future thinning requires the maintenance of some roads, priority needs to be given to road removal. With all the uncertainties regarding the impact of climate change, the need is greater than ever to significantly enlarge late successional reserves, roadless areas, and aquatic reserves. Larger reserves will in turn increase connectivity and provide climate refugia. Cattle need to be removed especially from all riparian areas and much larger no-grazing zones established. Given the increased amount of precipitation falling as rain in the winter, riparian areas need increased protection to reduce erosion and sedimentation from flooding. These protections will improve natural summer storage and lead to an increase of a closed forest canopy.

Finally, one of the keys to restoration is how we manage wildfires. We know now that much of the biodiversity we have across landscapes in the Pacific Northwest is a direct result of fire. Fires are occurring much more frequently and with greater severity as a result of climate change across the West. These fires will be part of the natural process of helping those untreated plantations develop old-growth characteristics. DellaSala elaborates on the role of fires: "Notably, burned forests successionally link complex early seral forests to future old-forest development and are not ecological disasters as often claimed." Smokey the Bear has led most of the public to view fires as tragic occurrences. The Forest Service needs to reinvent Smokey the Bear to promote a healthier view of fires as important in the long term for the development of natural forests.

Fortunately, restoration of Northwest forests will also help us save the planet from the oncoming and worsening climate crisis. All of the restoration actions previously described by Franklin and DellaSala will result in optimizing carbon sequestration and storage. The changes that Pacific Northwest forests will experience are dramatic. Edward Parson in "Preparing for Climatic Change: Water, Salmon, and Forest of the Pacific Northwest" notes that by the middle of this century, "The pattern of snow in any given month during the snowmelt period is projected to be similar to present snow-cover a full month later." The Columbia River will have much greater flow in winter and much reduced flow in summer. Warmer stream and estuary temperatures will make salmon recovery even more tenuous. Lower elevations will experience reduced water storage as a result of reductions in snowpack and increased fire frequency and severity. These climate change–related impacts are another strong reason for increasing the size of LSRs, which will enhance ecosystem resilience to climate change. The carbon storage capacity of Pacific Northwest forests will be greatly increased as our older, high biomass forests are protected and our younger forests are allowed to develop into older forests. A side benefit of this increase in carbon sequestration and storage, writes DellaSala, is that "carbon dense forests are associated with high levels of biodiversity and numerous other ecosystem services."

Because what can be measured is, typically, what gets done, the Forest Service must adopt and be held accountable to a diversity of metrics including carbon sequestration and storage, recovery of threatened species, viability of wildlife and salmon populations, clean air and water, and contributions to a restoration- and recreation-based economy. One clear indicator of an adherence to these metrics will be increasing numbers of fishers denning in old-growth trees and repopulating the forest and hearing wolves howling in the Cascades by mid-century. Jerry Franklin in "Understanding and Managing Forests as Ecosystems" best captures this need to attend to multiple values and needs: "A key lesson we have learned about managing forests as ecosystems is that attempting to maximize management of any individual output will result in marginalization or elimination of other important functions. . . . Natural forest ecosystems—our models for sustainable management—provide multiple values but maximize none." Once again, the old-growth forest guru captures the essential understanding that Forest Service leaders need to have going forward, a simple yet profound understanding—that the model for achieving Pinchot's vision of providing the greatest good for the greatest number in the long term is the natural forest ecosystem. Attending to the pieces only offers peril; attending to the whole brings ecological well-being.

Old-growth Douglas-fir. Friends and volunteers with the Cascade Forest Conservancy admire an especially magnificent Douglas-fir. *Courtesy of Jurgen Hess Photography.*

Old-growth forest in the Gifford Pinchot National Forest with mixed understory and decaying logs on the ground. *Courtesy of Jurgen Hess Photography.*

Old-growth forest in the Gifford Pinchot National Forest with snag in the foreground. *Courtesy of Jurgen Hess Photography.*

Old-growth Douglas-fir with fall maple leaves very close to my cabin. *Courtesy of Lis Silliman.*

Old-growth Douglas-fir forest in the Gifford Pinchot National Forest. *Courtesy of Jurgen Hess Photography.*

Nurse log. Douglas-firs six hundred to eight hundred years old are not uncommon. A nurse log may take up to two hundred years to fully decay. *Courtesy of Jurgen Hess Photography.*

A trail in the Trapper Creek Wilderness near my cabin in the Gifford Pinchot National Forest. *Courtesy of Jurgen Hess Photography.*

Old-growth Douglas-fir with vine maple in the understory in the Gifford Pinchot National Forest. *Courtesy of Jurgen Hess Photography.*

Decaying old-growth stump in the Gifford Pinchot National Forest. *Courtesy of Jurgen Hess Photography.*

18

Gifford Pinchot and the Next Hundred Years

Research reminds us that the old growth Pacific Northwest forests that have been logged away in recent years cannot return to a climax, old-growth state until A.D. 2500 to A.D. 2800 even if they are left alone. Climax forest is one that has reached its end state of development.

—Richard Preston

About one hundred years before the Northwest Forest Plan was developed, Gifford Pinchot spent several weeks in the Cascades and took a close look at the old-growth forest there. He saw the same forest that Lewis and Clark saw some eighty years earlier. Pinchot marveled at the immensity of the old-growth trees he observed. Although he was a forester, his role at that time was as an assessor. In the 1890s, less than 5 percent of the US population lived in the Western part of the country. Most of the people in the United States had no idea of the remarkable natural resources that spanned three states and contained more biomass per square mile than any other place on earth. Gifford Pinchot was one of the few persons living at that time who did recognize the value of those forests and their diverse ecological services. The Forest Service that emerged after the Northwest Forest Plan has taken to heart the need for ecological restoration.

Pinchot wanted those forests for workers in rural areas and small towns. He wanted those forests for townspeople who needed forest products to build their homes and towns. He wanted the wealth those forests represented to be shared and to improve the economic well-being of people across the country. To achieve those ends, he and Theodore Roosevelt protected the vast majority of those forests by creating the US Forest Service, thus transforming the forests of the Cascades into national forests.

Had Gifford Pinchot magically returned a hundred years after tramping through the forests of the Cascades in the early 1890s and flown in a small plane over his namesake forest, he almost certainly would have been terribly dismayed on seeing immense clear-cuts and disturbing fragmentation across the landscape. He would have been distressed by the loss of jobs. He would have been unsettled by the lack of old growth. He would have been mystified by how the agency he was so proud of could have gone so far off the rails and away from his vision.

Pinchot's grandson, Gifford Pinchot III, understands the founder of the US Forest Service in a way that surpasses many of those who have written about the original Pinchot. In an interview I conducted with him, he stated, "My grandfather really had two primary legacies—both an environmental and social legacy. Most people just think about the environmental legacy when they think about my grandfather. The way he saw conservation was both as an environmental and social cause. It was about preserving the forest for the benefit of the common people as opposed to the benefit of a few rich people. He was very concerned about the concentration of wealth. When people compare him to John Muir, they leave out what he was trying to do for people as well as for the land which was equally about being a Progressive, whereas Muir essentially just wanted to leave it the way it was."

Gifford Pinchot III recognized that one of his grandfather's greatest gifts, beyond his capacity for hard work, organization, and public relations, was also an ability to always keep a focus on doing the right thing and persisting through whatever obstacles were thrown in his way. In our interview, he elaborated:

> He had a degree of focus on what he considered to be right; he was an extremely high-minded individual. He was loyal to his dead fiancée, Laura Houghteling, until he was 47, when he married Cornelia. This could lead a man to be somewhat obsessive. That level of commitment is not usual with people. Secondly, he had good family connections to people in power globally and an amount of chutzpah that is hard to imagine now—he felt that he could go and talk to anybody about anything. When he went to France as a young man, the first thing he did was go and see Louis Pasteur. He was incredibly good at making connections even though he felt rather socially inept. He just never backed off on anything, always went forward. He was determined, and he believed he could succeed. He was clever and strategic as well. He had this high-minded thing

going, but he was always a player and with no restraints on making the right things happen. There was a purity of focus to him that was hard to resist. What he wanted was forests that remained as forest, that supplied a steady supply of timber to small companies run by ordinary people. He loved those beautiful places and did not want to destroy them. He thought you could take trees out of the forest without destroying them.

One question I asked about the first Gifford Pinchot was: how did he become a forester and one who was so committed to a sustainable approach to forestry a hundred years before that term came into popular parlance? Gifford Pinchot III provided this understanding: "First of all Gifford Pinchot did not have to make a living—it was easier for him to be high-minded as he never had to think about survival and day-to-day living. The family history of having stripped the land bare probably was an object lesson—they had been loggers and used the resources to achieve wealth and they were ready to move on. When he was a young man, his father realized that we could do this to the entire country and then where would we be. So, there was some remorse from the family history. My guess is that Laura had something to do with that. Often where there is a man who is concerned with social justice it is because there has been a woman who has had his ear for quite a while."

Laura Houghteling, whom Gifford Pinchot met while working as a forester on the Biltmore Estate, was his first love. They were engaged to be married, but she died of tuberculosis not long after their engagement. Pinchot "communicated" with her for over twenty years after her death and undoubtedly sought her spiritual counsel as he fought to establish millions of acres as national forests. As a Progressive, social justice was an important outcome of his efforts, and he was no doubt assured that Laura would have affirmed all he was doing for the common good. Gifford Pinchot III reflected further on their unusual relationship. "If you are going home every night and experiencing spiritual conversations, you might very well respond to a sense of having a higher calling. Also, there was a revulsion at the way people of wealth were treating natural resources, especially if you had decided to do something about the forest and went out west and saw the rampant corruption there." This sense of a higher calling was an attribute which Gifford Pinchot, the organizer, the pragmatist, the achiever, kept hidden from almost everyone. Yet this higher calling was fundamental to his way of being.

Perhaps the dominant view that emerged of Gifford Pinchot after his death was that he was solely interested in the forest as something that existed primarily for utilitarian purposes, in contrast to John Muir who cared only that the forest be preserved. Gifford Pinchot's grandson provides a different perspective.

> John Muir could not have worked in DC and accomplished what Pinchot did. The west would have seceded had the rest of the country agreed to what Muir was advocating. There was an unremitting desire to save the forests that drove Gifford Pinchot throughout his life, and he did a much better job of that than Muir. Muir created a love of wilderness which is an important thread in making all this work, and he is the father of the preservation movement, which is different from conservation. Conservation was not an easy sale, but it was more achievable than setting aside 200 million acres of wilderness. My grandfather appreciated the beauty of forests and their spiritual impact on people—seeing the forests as a place where people can go to be restored was part of who he was. That was not a sellable concept in those days. Yet that was very much a fundamental aspect of who he was. He took advantage of every opportunity he had to be in the woods. He would head to the wilderness—camping, just being there, wandering about, traipsing through the wilderness.

Gifford Pinchot III believes that his own reflections on what the greater good means today would resonate fully with his grandfather's beliefs.

> Logic does not explain the way we feel after spending time in the forest. You go into the wilds—feel this is beautiful—and yet you are not really there and then something clicks and you realize the connection you have with nature and suddenly the benefit becomes an order of magnitude greater. That is not rational. Rather it is about being a human animal in the kind of environment that we were designed for. We connect to a part of ourselves that gets lost in the city. That is an important part of what was driving my grandfather. Even when he and Teddy were in DC and busy with the work of the government, they took off on long walks, went to the Potomac River, took off their clothes, and went for swims. They kept reconnecting to nature. That is not a data-driven approach to life. Rather it is a seizing of what is a deeper part of our nature.

During our current era of uncertainty—given the magnitude of the climate crisis—about whether we will have a habitable planet in a hundred years, when millions of people are fleeing their native lands in response to severe droughts, this period when the threats of terrorism and pandemics magnify so many people's anxiety, the need is greater than ever to have natural, awe-inspiring forests where we can reconnect with nature. Yes, we need to use all the tools of ecosystem management and biodiversity conservation at our disposal. Yes, we need to use always the best science available to guide us. Yes, we need to protect our Pacific Northwest forests as they are such an important element in addressing the climate crisis. Above all we need to act with humility given how much we do not know and to act with great patience and caution given future unanticipated changes. We cannot know how our Pacific Northwest forests will evolve, and thus we must work to keep all our options open, so we have even more flexibility in our decisions and actions in the future. Beyond carbon sequestration and storage, beyond recreation pursuits, beyond providing life-giving water, we need to restore our forests to allow us to, as Gifford Pinchot III so eloquently stated, "seize what is a deeper part of our nature." We need the forests more than ever for the spiritual solace they provide us.

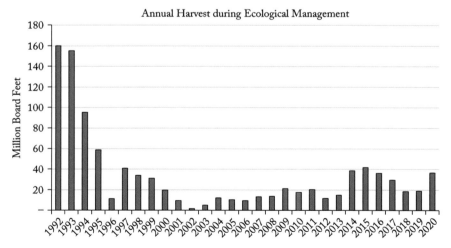

Figure 3. Annual harvest during the ecological management phase on the Gifford Pinchot National Forest. From USGS, Region 6.

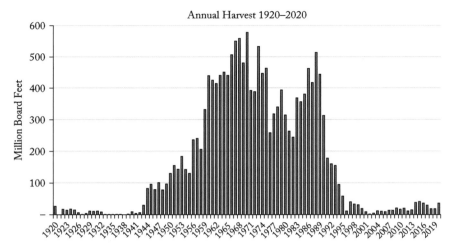

Figure 4. Annual harvest from 1920 to 2020 on the Gifford Pinchot National Forest. From USFS, Region 6.

Epilogue

Philosophical Discourse between Gifford Pinchot and John Muir: Early Twenty-First Century

I wrote this epilogue to illustrate how these two men, who were more influential than any others in the creation of our public lands, had they been able to put the angst of the Hetch Hetchy controversy behind them, would likely have been lifetime friends. Muir wrote in 1895, "The battle we have fought and are still fighting for the forests is a part of the eternal conflict between right and wrong, and we cannot expect to see the end of it." These two men with their distinctive talents and accomplishments had tremendous respect and appreciation for each other and fundamentally agreed on what was right and wrong. John Clayton captures well the key distinctions between the two men in his book Natural Rivals: *"Muir aspired to be nature's prophet. Pinchot aspired to be its statesman. Muir's assignment required a one-in-a-million talent. . . . Pinchot's assignment was thornier."*

Gifford Pinchot: Well, John, you have been observing life down there almost a hundred years now, and I know that you are not just keeping an eye on Yosemite.

John Muir: That's right, Giff, it's the whole dang blue marble—I do love that picture that the astronauts gave us, which shows this whole living planet hanging gloriously in the black abyss—but what you are hinting at certainly is true as well; for me, ultimately, it's about the forests, the wild landscapes, the rocky spires, the wolves and grizzlies.

GP: The forests are what brought us together. The forests are what sustained us both. Imagine, John, if I had your literary gifts and you had my analytical and administrative talents what we each might have accomplished. Perhaps you could have made the difference on Hetch Hetchy even though I opposed you, and me, perhaps, well, perhaps I could have moved people the way you so eloquently did. I admit it, John, what some people observed as the cold utilitarian in me did get in the way.

JM: Well, Giff, since you brought it up, let me make an analogy. You were like the "managed forests" that your beloved Forest Service created after WWII—ordered and orderly, organized and productive, focused and thrifty. While I was like the wilderness, unruly and chaotic, unbound and complex, untamed and intemperate. But you are right in that the forests are what brought us together and what has kept us in conversation since you joined me those many years ago.

GP: Conservation and preservation. Conservationist and preservationist. That represents the core characterizations that I suppose neither of us will ever elude. Frankly, I feel rather burned by it all. You are the knight in shining armor always held up as the Great Preserver. For environmentalists you represent the Holy Grail, while me, I have been tagged as the man behind what became the dictum that became the Forest Services' holy grail, Get the Cut Out. It's just not fair. You are venerated, while for many environmentalists, I am if not disregarded then reviled.

JM: No Giff, it's not fair, I agree. I have my Yosemite, one of the most glorious landscapes on earth that I will never tire observing from these lofty heights. That's true. Whenever I feel discouraged, I simply return to Half Dome, to the Falls, to the Merced. Ahhh, such restorative powers they have for me. I have always had Yosemite to return to—my magical home that can only be magical when you possess that ineffable sense of place, that glorious connection to the land and the forests. But Giff, you have 190 million acres of national forests that you can rightly call yours. Surely that is comforting. Don't be so hard on yourself. Misunderstood, perhaps, but certainly not reviled.

GP: I never imagined when Teddy and I first began drawing up our maps that our national forests would become so encompassing and extensive. We had the luxury of vast forests in the West that were practically untouched and because of the cut-and-run ethics in the east and Midwest, we knew that we could gain the public's acceptance by drawing the contrasts. And I admit it, I did have a damned good public relations gift. And what we started simply kept growing through adolescence and then even into adulthood, like those athletes on steroids. Of course, some of the additions back east like the Smokies were only possible because they were so damaged that most people viewed them as a wasteland and with the depression in full swing, well, a real value for the dollar. And then all of the Alaskan lands—again, timing was the key. Most folks simply had no idea: out of sight, out of mind. But give Carter his due: his most important legacy without a doubt.

JM: Well, Giff, which place down there most renews you? You can find a national forest in just about all of the states. Each of us needs that special place—someplace you can get lost in and yet feel renewed. We traveled together and camped together in quite a few of those special places across the West: the Grand Canyon, the Sierras, the Cascades. I was working overtime trying to convince you, trying to reach your heart through those glorious landscapes. As usual, you were in your head, ruminating on possibilities, mulling over the political landscapes rather than the one right before your eyes. What about that forest they named after you? The Gifford Pinchot National Forest? Quite a bit of land too, 1.3 million acres. Makes my Muir Woods seem tiny, although the redwoods there make your big Douglas-firs look like little brothers, at least what few are left of them.

GP: Truth be told, my special place, the place that renews me, is the pond near Grey Towers, the home my father built, which I inherited. Fishing, thinking, reflecting, planning. They all went together for me. There you have, perhaps, the real distinction between the two of us. I am standing next to a manmade pond with a fishing pole in a developed landscape that two hundred years ago was a primeval hardwood forest that my forebears harvested, while you are standing on that crazy rock jutting out into Yosemite Valley surveying what appears to be your wilderness realm, all yours, no one else's.

JM: Tell me, Giff, how did you arrive at that vision of yours for the national forests, "the greatest good for the greatest number in the long run?" A lot of wiggle room in that; perhaps that gave it legs that could run the long race. I mean, that phrase is still seemingly a guiding light. But, good God, what a mess they made of it after WWII. They were doing a fine job for about forty years and then the switch—from holding true to your vision to killing it. Right about the time you died. I always wondered about that. What was behind the switch? We know, though, what resulted. Forty years of wreckage, of devastation to the forest, the near wiping out of an entire species, the genocide of old growth. And then a little bird came along.

GP: At my core it seems that I have always been a political animal. I absolutely believed that we needed to manage forest for the long term. Today they call it sustainable forestry. I was never naive about man's willingness to destroy that which sustains him. I wanted to protect our forests for the long term, and I knew that those forest resources were essential to people's and this nation's health and well-being. And, of course, it had to be something that Teddy would like, would champion. Resulted from one of my quiet moments by the pond. I am proud of it, I admit it. But you are right. Something switched. I had instilled a culture in the Forest Service that endured and stayed true to my vision for nearly forty years and then, whoosh, it fell away like the big trees before the chainsaw. Broke my heart.

JM: Cultures do change, even ones like the Forest Service that you so assiduously shaped. In some ways you were lucky—the Roaring Twenties were dominated by the private timber beasts. They did not want competition, so your people were happy to be stewards patiently waiting for what they were sure was to be a timber famine. Never came. And then the Depression. Despair and no demand. More opportunity for stewards to prevail. What the academics refer to as the socioeconomic political reality. A lining up of forces well beyond anyone's control but lucky for the forests. But there was simply too much wiggle room in your "the greatest good." The greatest generation came along after WWII, and they had very different ideas. The "can do" crowd. It all began to break apart in the 1940s, and then in the 1950s, both preservation and even your vaunted conservation crumbled like sandcastles before the tides. Gone. And forty years later, almost all the old growth was gone too. Unbelievable!

GP: You are right—the culture changed. People's values; their mind-set. It all slowly morphed into something I could not recognize. They ignored the incredible complexity of our forests. Humility was replaced with arrogance. They believed that they understood the forest best. When the reality was that we were all vastly ignorant. So much that we did not know. What they now refer to as the unknown unknowns. And what we admitted we knew that we did not know was embarrassingly tiny. Too proud to admit it. Blinded perhaps. That is what arrogance will do. No, John, your blessed humility before the glory of the wild could have at least nudged us to reconsider what became the prevailing value—get the cut out—for the four decades after WWII. After my death, my brother Brice toured through our national forests and saw vast clear-cuts, especially in the Pacific Northwest, and he commented at the time that those clear-cuts would have been anathema to me. And that is true. They were a tear in my spirit.

JM: And then the northern spotted owl came along. For me a wondrous irony. One of my favorite birds was the ouzel, the American dipper. A bird of the creeks and rivers. One with the water, ever moving, bobbing, yielding, searching. Impatient like me. Yet the birds of the forest that were my favorites were always the owls. They seemed to have supernatural powers—of sight, of sound, of movement, of ease and of grace. Now the great horned owl was certainly my favorite of the favorites. The epitome of their virtues while also a pillar of strength, a depthless pool of wisdom, an unerring sense of equanimity. The northern spotted owl is like a long-lost cousin who has appeared after just winning the lottery. A generous, giving, kind cousin with boundless love and compassion. Open-hearted and yet also a deep thinker. He quietly shouted at them, "stop this madness." And in a few years, it ground to a halt. The healing began.

GP: That bird and what she wrought, John, has given me hope. No sure thing. Never is with "the long run." At least now they are admitting that there was so much that they did not know, so little real understanding. From simplicity to complexity. From arrogance to humility. From trees to forest—seeing the whole rather than just the parts. Maybe seeing that blue planet hanging alone in the blackness birthed a new awareness. Serendipity was at work, it's true, but what a miraculous serendipity it was. Again, a switch. Values and mindset once again changing. I do believe people are now beginning to realize that the greatest good was never simply about the trees, John, but was truly about the forest. Hope is displacing despair. The forests will endure.

Acknowledgments

Writing this book has been a labor of love. The book would not have been completed without the help of friends and family. Of course, having a cabin in the woods, where I could think and write in a quiet environment without distraction, was immensely helpful.

My first reader of, at that time, a very rough manuscript was Peter Molienecki. I am grateful that he took the time to read the manuscript and offer encouragement and helpful feedback. I am especially grateful to Jerry Franklin, who served as my informal mentor on all things related to old-growth forest. Early in my writing, he allowed me to join him on a weeklong educational program in the Gifford Pinchot National Forest (GPNF). More importantly, he let me interview him on several occasions, provided immensely helpful insights into how the Forest Service worked, and gave me ongoing support and feedback. I am particularly indebted to Gifford Pinchot III, grandson of Gifford Pinchot, the founder of the US Forest Service. He helped me especially in my understanding of his grandfather as someone who was an extraordinary leader but also someone with powerful and quite unique motivations. Ed Monnig, who spent most of his career with the Forest Service and is a good friend and fellow adventurer, provided much support early on in this project and much advice throughout the process of doing research and finally on framing of the book.

I interviewed a wide range of people who provided diverse perspectives on forestry and the USFS generally and actions on the ground in the GPNF specifically. I am grateful to Emily Platt, who first provided her perspective as an executive director of the Gifford Pinchot Task Force, an environmental organization, and then some years later as the district ranger for the Mt. Adams District of the GPNF. I really appreciated that two former GPNF supervisors, now retired—Bob Williams and Bob Takaryck—were willing to meet with me and share their stories and experiences in what was then a very challenging role. One Forest Service leader who offered a unique perspective was Lynn Burditt. She moved up the ranks from individual contributor to a number of critical leader roles. Most importantly, she was one of those leaders who recognized the changes around her, listened to the scientists, and over time became much more willing to help the Forest Service move toward ecological management. Barbara Hollenbeck, a historian with the Forest Service, shared insight on why the Columbia National Forest was chosen to be renamed for Gifford Pinchot.

Two conservationists who, beginning in the 1980s, began to pay much closer attention to the "Forgotten Forest" and who provided me with their perspectives are David Jennings and Susan Saul. They were both founding members of the Gifford Pinchot Task Force, now the Cascade Forest Conservancy. Susan Jane Brown provided a lawyer's understanding of the many dynamics at play impacting Forest Service policies. Lisa Moscinski, on the staff of the Gifford Pinchot Task Force at the time of our interview, provided some quite insightful assessments of the Forest Service, perhaps most importantly that they focused on outputs rather than outcomes. I am especially appreciative of the insider (then later outsider) view of the Forest Service provided to me by Jeff Debonis.

I am extremely indebted to Rick McClure, now retired from the USFS, who spent most of his career working in the GPNF. Rick provided me a wealth of photographs, many of which were historical, that captured well two of the periods that I focused on: stewardship and high production. He also pointed me to a cabin in back of the main Mt. Adams District Office, where I found, among many other resources, the annual reports that were first published in the 1950s. Patty McNamee with the National Archives in Seattle was quite helpful, as she aided me in discovering the many annual general inspection reports that were so enlightening on what mattered to the Forest Service leaders and determining what was happening on the ground in the Columbia National Forest. Jamie Lewis with the Forest History Society provided guidance very early on regarding resources to consult and later provided some of the historical photographs. Joe Gates with Region 6 provided all the data that allowed me to develop the graphs for each of the three phases in the GPNF and to demonstrate how over one hundred years the forest went "back to the future."

The executive directors of two leading environmental organizations in the Pacific Northwest—Sean Stevens with Oregon Wild and Molly Whitney of the Cascade Forest Conservancy—read earlier versions of my book and provided much-appreciated feedback. Shiloh Halsey, also with CFC, was helpful as well.

I am grateful to my editor with Washington State University Press, Linda Bathgate, who early on took an interest in my book. The book went through some very significant revisions as a result of the very helpful feedback I received on three different occasions from outside reviewers. Those reviewers provided me crucial understandings of how best to shape the book in a way that both made it more readable and provided a more logical focus and flow.

Heather Erickson, my partner, has been a critic when needed and a supporter when that too was needed. My two daughters, Katrina and Marta Schenck, have been steadfast in their support and in their belief in me. I am so proud of them and so appreciative of their regard and love. So wonderful to know that they have long enjoyed the pleasures offered by my cabin in the woods and to know that they are always up for a hike in the woods.

Notes on Sources

Introduction

Pinchot quote on conservation from Gifford Pinchot, *Breaking New Ground* (Washington, DC: Island Press, 1998), 505.

Restoration definition from Jerry F. Franklin, K. Norman Johnson, and Debora L. Johnson, *Ecological Forest Management* (Waveland Press, 2018), 10.

1. The Birth of Forests

Early deforestation from Robert Pogue Harrison, *Forests: The Shadow of Civilization* (Chicago: University of Chicago Press, 1992), 8.

Meaning of circles from Harrison, *Forests*, 8.

Our interdependence with forest from Harrison, *Forests*, 199.

2. The Early Years and Gifford Pinchot

Transformation of the landscape from William Robbins, *Landscapes of Promise: The Oregon Story 1800–1940* (Seattle: University of Washington Press, 1999), 25–43.

Native Americans living in area for twelve thousand years from Pat Courtney Gold, "The Long Narrows: The Forgotten Geographic and Cultural Wonder," *Oregon Historical Quarterly* 108, no. 4 (2007): 596.

Smohalla quote from https://www.azquotes.com/author/24447-Smohalla

Frequency of fires on west side from *"New Findings about Old Growth Forests,"* *Science Update 4*, US Department of Agriculture, Forest Service, Pacific Northwest Service Research Station (2003). https://www.fs.usda.gov/pnw/pubs/science-update-4.pdf

Utilitarian approach to forestry from Char Miller, *Gifford Pinchot and the Making of Modern Environmentalism* (Washington, DC: Island Press, 2001), 121.

Pinchot quote on false forestry claim from Miller, *Gifford Pinchot and the Making of Modern Environmentalism*, 115.

First below-cost timber sale from Miller, *Gifford Pinchot and the Making of Modern Environmentalism*, 112.

Carl Schenck quote from Miller, *Gifford Pinchot and the Making of Modern Environmentalism*, 115.

3. Muir and Pinchot: Protecting the Forests

Purpose of Timber and Stone Act from Robert E. Ficken, *The Forested Land: A History of Lumbering in Western Washington* (Seattle: University of Washington Press, 1987), 49.

Pinchot on changing country's mindset from Pinchot, *Breaking New Ground*, 29.

George Perkins Marsh quote on unsustainable logging from George Perkins Marsh, *Man and Nature: Or, Physical Geography as Modified by Human Action* (Cambridge, MA: Belknap Press, 1965), 280.

Authorizing legislation for forest reserves from Gerald W. Williams, *The U.S. Forest Service in the Pacific Northwest: A History* (Corvallis: Oregon State University Press, 2009), 37.

Pinchot quote on forest devastation from Pinchot, *Breaking New Ground*, 82.

Pinchot quotes on regulating use and wasteful lumbering from Pinchot, *Breaking New Ground*, 103.

Pinchot quote on monopolies from Pinchot, *Breaking New Ground*, 82.

Pinchot's mission for the Forest Service from Williams, *The U.S. Forest Service in the Pacific Northwest*, 60.

Pinchot's *Use Book* from Gifford Pinchot, *The Use of the National Forest Reserves*, 1905, US Department of Agriculture, Forest Service.

Pinchot quote on the small man from Pinchot, *Breaking New Ground*, 259.

Pinchot quote on Conservation from Pinchot, *Breaking New Ground*, 261.

Three questions for National Forest Commission from Pinchot, *Breaking New Ground*, 89.

Muir quote on forest providing a perennial supply, from Gerald W. Williams and Char Miller, "At the Creation: The National Forest Commission of 1896–97," *Forest History Today*, Spring/Fall 2005, 37.

Muir and Pinchot under the stars, from Miller, *Gifford Pinchot and the Making of Modern Environmentalism*, 133.

Camping and male bonding from Miller, *Gifford Pinchot and the Making of Modern Environmentalism*, 134.

Pinchot quote on Hetch Hetchy from Roderick Nash, *Wilderness and the American Mind*, 4th ed. (New Haven, CT: Yale University Press, 2001), 171.

4. Creation of the US Forest Service

Prediction of timber harvest by Bernhard Fernow from Char Miller, *American Forests: Nature, Culture, and Politics* (Lawrence: University Press of Kansas, 1997), 18.

Organic Act of 1897 from Williams, *The U.S. Forest Service in the Pacific Northwest*, 43.

Roosevelt quote praising Gifford Pinchot from Theodore Roosevelt, *The Autobiography of Theodore Roosevelt, Condensed from the Original Ed., Supplemented by Letters, Speeches, and Other Writings*. Centennial ed. Wayne Andrews, ed. (New York: Scribner, 1958), 210.

Roosevelt quote on importance of Pinchot to his administration from Roosevelt, *The Autobiography of Theodore Roosevelt*, 210.

On many facets of Pinchot from Charles Wilkinson, *Crossing the Next Meridian: Land, Water, and the Future of the West* (Washington, DC: Island Press, 1992), 125.

Increase in size of national forest to almost 151 million acres from Samuel Hays, *Conservation and the Gospel of Efficiency: The Progressive Conservation Movement, 1890–1920* (Cambridge, MA: Harvard University Press, 1959), 47.

Gifford Pinchot III's quote on his grandfather from interview with author.

Pinchot quote on being responsive to changing public needs from Gifford Pinchot, *The Fight for Conservation* (New York: Doubleday, Page and Co., 1910), 60.

Unwavering rules of Pinchotism from James Lewis, *The Forest Service and the Greatest Good: A Centennial History* (Durham, NC: Forest History Society, 2005), 131.

5. The Custodial Role

Recommended harvest cycle for Douglas-firs from Margaret Herring and Sarah Greene, *Forest of Time: A Century of Science at Wind River Experimental Forest* (Corvallis: Oregon State University Press, 2007), 21.

Munger's view of fire impacts on forest regeneration from Herring and Greene, *Forest of Time*, 27.

Munger's view on old forest from Herring and Greene, *Forest of Time*, 53.

Munger's quote depicting snags from Herring and Greene, *Forest of Time*, 63.

Amount of timber products in 1900 from John Fedkiw, *Managing Multiple Uses on National Forests, 1905–1995: A 90-Year Learning Experience and It Isn't Finished Yet* (US Department of Agriculture, Forest Service, 1995), https://foresthistory.org/wp-content/uploads/2017/01/ManagingMultipleUsesOnNationalForests.pdf

Annual timber harvest during custodial period from Fedkiw, *Managing Multiple Uses on National Forests, 1905–1995*, https://foresthistory.org/wp-content/uploads/2017/01/Managing MultipleUsesOnNationalForests.pdf

6. The Struggle to Make Conservation Work

Pinchot's Progressive concerns from David Clary, *Timber and the Forest Service* (Lawrence: University of Kansas Press, 1986), 10.

Pinchot's quote on monopoly, from Clary, *Timber and the Forest Service*, 25a.

Cutting of old growth from Nancy Langston, *Forest Dreams, Forest Nightmares: The Paradox of Old Growth in the Inland West* (Seattle: University of Washington Press, 1995), 259.

Dominant mindset for foresters from Langston, *Forest Dreams, Forest Nightmares*, 163.

Dominant narrative for foresters from Langston, *Forest Dreams, Forest Nightmares*, 146.

New formula for sustained yield from Langston, *Forest Dreams, Forest Nightmares*, 169.

Pinchot's quote on a forest's diverse attributes from Gifford Pinchot, *A Primer of Forestry* (Washington, DC: Government Printing Office, 1899), 53.

Forest rangers 'mix of values from Williams, *The U.S. Forest Service in the Pacific Northwest*, 56.

Creation of an agency with effective norms from Herbert Kaufman, *The Forest Ranger: A Study in Administrative Behavior* (Baltimore: Johns Hopkins Press, 1960), 235.

The emerging Forest Service culture from Kaufman, *The Forest Ranger*, 207.

Pinchot quote on destroying wildlife from Harold K. Steen, *The US Forest Service: A History* (Seattle: University of Washington Press, 1976), 87.

The importance of periodic inspections from Kaufman, *The Forest Ranger*, 139.

Descriptions from numerous inspection reports from National Archives Pacific Alaska Region, Seattle, Washington.

7. Tensions: Stewardship or Production

Epigraph from Peter Wohlleben, *The Hidden Life of Trees: What They Feel, How They Communicate*. Translated by Jane Billinghurst (Vancouver/Berkeley: Greystone Books, 2015).

Pinchot quote on the necessity of forest preservation from Pinchot, *The Use of the National Forest Reserves*, 8.

Early Forest Service leader quote on preserving supply from Forester Ames' 1907 Report, National Archives Pacific Alaska Region, Seattle, Washington.

Pinchot quotes in 1909 memo on managing forest sustainably from Gifford Pinchot, National Archives Pacific Alaska Region, Seattle, Washington.

Acting forester's letter on establishing level of cut from Forester Hall, National Archives Pacific Alaska Region, Seattle, Washington.

Quote from Ranger Cox on a conservative cut policy, Ranger Cox, National Archives Pacific Alaska Region, Seattle, Washington.

Quote from Ranger Cox on primacy of conservative policy, Ranger Cox, National Archives Pacific Alaska Region, Seattle, Washington.

Roosevelt quote linking forestry and conservation movement from Roosevelt, *The Autobiography of Theodore Roosevelt*, 218.

Charles Wilkinson's quotes on Pinchot's attributes, from Wilkinson, *Crossing the Next Meridian*, 65.

Pinchot quote on preserving the forest for homes from Hays, *Conservation and the Gospel of Efficiency*, 42.

C. S. Judd quote on getting rid of old growth from Langston, *Forest Dreams, Forest Nightmares*, 110.

Definition of allowable cut from Clary, *Timber and the Forest Service*, 343.

Early foresters' focus on fast-growing trees from Clary, *Timber and the Forest Service*, 35.

Early foresters' views on old-growth forest from Langston, *Forest Dreams, Forest Nightmares*, 35.

Henry Graves quote on converting old growth into "thrifty stands" from Langston, *Forest Dreams, Forest Nightmares*, 113.

8. Setting the Stage for Liquidation of Old Growth

E. T. Allen's early studies from Herring and Greene, *Forest of Time*, 21.

Reforestation crisis as a result of clear-cutting from Richard A. Rajala, *Clearcutting the Pacific Rain Forest: Production, Science, and Regulation* (Vancouver: University of British Columbia Press, 1998), 112.

Leo Isaac quote on need for seed trees from Leo A. Isaac, "Life of the Douglas-Fir Seed in the Forest Floor," *Journal of Forestry* 33, no. 1 (January 1935), 61–66.

Walt Lund quote on problems from clear-cutting from Lund, *Forestry Interviews, 1927–1965*, Regional Oral History Office.

Pinchot quote on clear-cuts from Gifford Pinchot, *The Conservation Diaries of Gifford Pinchot* (Durham, NC: Forest History Society, 2001).

Forester quote on value of strips from Assistant Ranger letter, National Archives Pacific Alaska Region, Seattle, Washington.

Pinchot quote on forest fires from Kaufman, *The Forest Ranger*, 18.

Timothy Egan quote on link of fires and Forest Service from Timothy Egan, *The Big Burn: Teddy Roosevelt and the Fire That Saved America* (Boston: Houghton Mifflin Harcourt, 2009), 227.

Forest Service chief Graves quote on producing timber perpetually from Chief Graves letter, National Archives Pacific Alaska Region, Seattle, Washington.

Forester George Cecil's quote on conserving timber for the future from Forester Cecil's letter, National Archives Pacific Alaska Region, Seattle, Washington.

Forester George Cecil's quote on "surplus" timber from Forester Cecil's letter, National Archives Pacific Alaska Region, Seattle, Washington.

Forester Park's quote on low annual cut level from Forester Park's letter, National Archives Pacific Alaska Region, Seattle, Washington.

Forester Sherman's quote on extent of old-growth forest from Forester's Sherman's letter, National Archives Pacific Alaska Region, Seattle, Washington.

9. The Beginning of Production

Mays quotes from 1947 General Inspection report, National Archives Pacific Alaska Region, Seattle, Washington.

Naming a national forest after Gifford Pinchot from 1947 General Inspection report.

Cornelia Pinchot quote at dedication ceremony on Pinchot's Conservation legacy from Miller, *Gifford Pinchot and the Making of Modern Environmentalism*, 11.

Cut-level increases after WWII from Fedkiw, *Managing Multiple Uses on National Forests*, 48.

Cut levels and miles of roads and trails in 1959 from Summary of Information, Gifford Pinchot National Forest, National Archives Pacific Alaska Region, Seattle, Washington.

Miles of roads and trails in Columbia National Forest from 1947 General Inspection report, National Archives Pacific Alaska Region, Seattle, Washington.

Timber sale increases from Fedkiw, *Managing Multiple Uses on National Forests*, 15.

Chief Forester Greely on end of virgin forests in the Western states from Williams, *The U.S. Forest Service in the Pacific Northwest*, 203.

Chief Forester Lyle Watts on timber-dependent communities from Clary, *Timber and the Forest Service*, 211.

Chris Maser on Forest Service losing touch with constituents from Chris Maser, *Forest Primeval: The Natural History of an Ancient Forest* (Sierra Club Books, 1989), 52.

Weyerhaeuser quote on cold war and wilderness from Kevin Marsh, *Drawing Lines in the Forest: Creating Wilderness Areas in the Pacific Northwest* (Seattle: University of Washington Press, 2007), 48.

Loyalty and culture of Forest Service from Marsh, *Drawing Lines in the Forest*, 84.

10. Culture Change

Quotes from A. R. Standing, Summary from Inspection Report, 1950, National Archives Pacific Alaska Region, Seattle, Washington.

Quote from 1954 Inspection Report, National Archives Pacific Alaska Region, Seattle, Washington.

Quote from Michael Frome on clear-cuts as a necessary tool from Michael Frome, *The Forest Service* (Santa Barbara, CA: Praeger, 1971), 97.

Jorgensen quotes on multiple use and cut levels from 1960 Summary of Information, National Archives Pacific Alaska Region, Seattle, Washington.

Preserving high-elevation regions from Marsh, *Drawing Lines in the Forest*, 64.

Inventory of roadless areas from *Road-less Area Report*, 1926, National Archives Pacific Alaska Region, Seattle, Washington.

Unsustainable level of logging from Charles McKinley, *Uncle Sam in the Pacific Northwest: Federal Management of Natural Resources in the Columbia River Valley* (Berkeley: University of California Press, 1952), 41.

Destruction of societies from Jared Diamond, *Collapse: How Societies Choose to Fail or Succeed* (New York: Penguin, 2004), 11.

Emphasis on timber production from Paul Hirt, *A Conspiracy of Optimism: Management of the National Forest Since World War Two* (Lincoln: University of Nebraska Press, 1994), 131.

Rural communities and impact of unsustainable logging from McKinley, *Uncle Sam in the Pacific Northwest*, 44.

Conversion of old growth to new stands from William G. Robbins, *Landscapes of Conflict: The Oregon Story, 1940–2000* (Seattle: University of Washington Press, 2004), 13.

Receipts for Skamania County from 1960 Summary of Information, Gifford Pinchot National Forest, National Archives Pacific Alaska Region, Seattle, Washington.

Leopold quote from Luna B. Leopold, ed., *Round River: From the Journals of Aldo Leopold* (Oxford, UK: Oxford University Press, 1972), 102.

Leopold quote from Aldo Leopold, *A Sand County Almanac: And Sketches Here and There* (Oxford, UK: Oxford University Press, 1949), 224–225.

11. Intensive Management

Tokarczyk quotes from interview with author.

Todd quotes from Oral History Project on Timber Management in Pacific Northwest, Bancroft Library, Berkeley, California.

Usher quotes from Oral History Project on Timber Management in Pacific Northwest, Bancroft Library, Berkeley, California.

Jorgensen quotes from Oral History Project on Timber Management in Pacific Northwest, Bancroft Library, Berkeley, California.

Granger quotes on intensively managing the forest and need for roads from National Archives Pacific Alaska Region, Seattle, Washington.

Chief Watts quote on ramping up production from National Archives Pacific Alaska Region, Seattle, Washington.

Chief McArdle on Region 6's importance from National Archives Pacific Alaska Region, Seattle, Washington.

Forest Service emphasis on timber production from Clary, *Timber and the Forest Service.*

Forecast for timber access roads from 1954 Inspection Report and 1964 Summary, National Archives Pacific Alaska Region, Seattle, Washington.

GPNF supervisor quotes on cutting older stands from National Archives Pacific Alaska Region, Seattle, Washington.

Need to double annual cut in Region 6 from National Archives Pacific Alaska Region, Seattle, Washington.

Manipulation of annual cut numbers from Hirt, *A Conspiracy of Optimism,* xxiii.

Dedication of Forest Service to market-oriented production from Hirt, *A Conspiracy of Optimism,* xxxiv.

Iron triangle at work from Hirt, *A Conspiracy of Optimism,* 144.

Need for more roads from Timber Resource Review, USDA, Forest Service, 1958.

Increase in timber production from Hirt, *A Conspiracy of Optimism,* 131.

Terrible business partners from Hirt, *A Conspiracy of Optimism,* 82.

Chief Jorgensen's quotes on multiple use from 1959 Annual Summary, National Archives Pacific Alaska Region, Seattle, Washington.

Secretary Benson on distinction between preservation and conservation, from Hirt, *A Conspiracy of Optimism,* 107.

Increases in allowable cut from GPNF Annual Summaries, National Archives Pacific Alaska Region, Seattle, Washington.

Need for inventory of timber resources in GPNF from 1960 Annual Summary, National Archives Pacific Alaska Region, Seattle, Washington.

Quotes on sustained yield and need to harvest older trees from 1961 Annual Summary, National Archives Pacific Alaska Region, Seattle, Washington.

Quote on harvesting full allowable cut from 1962 Annual Summary, National Archives Pacific Alaska Region, Seattle, Washington.

Chief Cliff on comparison of forestry to farming from Frome, *The Forest Service,* 179.

Logger quote on unstainable forestry from Wilkinson, *Crossing the Next Meridian,* 140.

Terracing in the GPNF from 1964 Annual Summary, National Archives Pacific Alaska Region, Seattle, Washington.

Actual cut in 1967 and one-log loads from 1967 Annual Summary, National Archives Pacific Alaska Region, Seattle, Washington.

Record cut in GPNF from 1968 Annual Summary, National Archives Pacific Alaska Region, Seattle, Washington.

Extent of cut in GPNF over thirty-year period from Hirt, *A Conspiracy of Optimism,* 135.

Quotes from Supervisor Williams on manipulating forest landscape environmental concerns from 1970 Annual Summary, National Archives Pacific Alaska Region, Seattle, Washington.

Chief Cliff's quote comparing clear-cutting to urban renewal from Frome, *The Forest Service,* 83.

Intensive management consequences from Hirt, *A Conspiracy of Optimism,* 141.

Absurdity of assumptions from Hirt, *A Conspiracy of Optimism,* 141.

12. New Environmental Policies

Shattering the basis of sustainable harvests from Fedkiw, *Managing Multiple Uses on National Forests, 1905–1995.*

Intensive management practices rationale to continue high levels of cut from GPNF 1984 Timber Management Plan, USDA, Forest Service, 1984.

Quote from Jack Usher, Oral History Project on Timber Management in Pacific Northwest, Bancroft Library.

Obsessive focus on timber from Clary, *Timber and the Forest Service,* 174.

Assistant Secretary, USDA, John Crowell on speeding harvest of old growth from *End of the Ancient Forest: A Report on National Forest Management Plan* (The Wilderness Society, 1988), 129.

13. The Eruption

Single most powerful disaster in US history from Steve Olsen, *Eruption: The Untold Story of Mount St. Helens* (New York: W. W. Norton, 2016), xi.

Susan Saul quote on Forest Service's lack of vison from interview by author.

Susan Saul quote on need to protect landscapes around Mount St. Helens from interview with author.

Most biologically diverse landscape from Jerry Franklin, "Biological Legacies: A Critical Management Concept from Mount St. Helens, 1990." *Transactions of the 55th North American Wildlife and Natural Resources Conference,* 1990, 216–219.

Importance of recovery processes from Franklin, *"Biological Legacies,"* 216–219.

Recovery of ecosystems after major disturbances from Franklin, "Biological Legacies," 216–219.

Failure of logged lands to regenerate from Max Geier, *Necessary Work: Discovering Old Forests, New Outlooks, and Community on the H. J. Experimental Forest, 1948–2000,* General Technical Report, Pacific Northwest Research Station, 2007.

14. Old Growth

High volume of timber coming off the GPNF from *Land and Resource Management Plan,* GPNF, USDA, Forest Service, 1990.

Acres of old growth left from *Land and Resource Management Plan.*

Timber logged at unsustainable levels from McKinley, *Uncle Sam in the Pacific Northwest,* 41.

The Columbia National Burn from Cheryl Mack, *The 'Columbia National Burn': A History of Fires and Firefighting on the Gifford Pinchot National Forest,* US Department of Agriculture, Forest Service, 1999. https://www.fs.usda.gov/Internet/FSE_DOCUMENTS/fsbdev3_004866.pdf

Rationale for supporting high levels of cut from *Draft EIS. Proposed Land and Resource Management Plan,* GPNF, USDA, Forest Service, 1987.

Dwindling of old-growth forest from *Draft EIS. Proposed Land and Resource Management Plan,* 1987.

Demand for timber in future decades *from Draft EIS. Proposed Land and Resource Management Plan,* 1987.

End of old growth from *Draft EIS. Proposed Land and Resource Management Plan,* 1987.

Quotes from Bob Williams from interview with author.

Acknowledgment of metropolitan areas near the GPNF from *Land and Resource Management Plan.*

Economic reasons to log old growth from *Land and Resource Management Plan.*

Intent to liquidate remaining old growth from *Land and Resource Management Plan.*

Conversion of old growth to young stands from *Land and Resource Management Plan*.

Importance of *Lobaria* to forest health from Jon Luoma, *The Hidden Forest: The Biography of an Ecosystem* (Corvallis: Oregon State University Press, 2006), 56.

Jerry Franklin quote on lack of knowledge about old growth from interview with author.

Jerry Franklin quote on a change in philosophy of the Forest Service from interview with author.

Distinctive features of old growth from Jerry Franklin et al., *Ecological Characteristics of Old-Growth Douglas-Fir Forests* (Portland, OR: USDA, Forest Service, 1981), 21.

Extraordinary nature of Douglas-firs from Franklin et al. *Ecological Characteristics of Old-Growth Douglas-Fir Forests*.

Importance of old growth for fish from William Dietrich, *The Final Forest: Big Trees, Forks, and the Pacific Northwest* (Seattle: University of Washington Press, 1992), 115.

Jerry Franklin quote on end of unreserved old growth from Franklin et al, *Ecological Characteristics of Old-Growth Douglas-fir Forests*, 1.

Jerry Franklin quote on characteristics of old-growth forest from Franklin et al, *Ecological Characteristics of Old-Growth Douglas-fir Forests*, 3.

Jon Luoma quote on disorder of old growth from Luoma, *The Hidden Forest*, 88.

Jerry Franklin quote on lack of diversity in young conifer forest from Franklin, *Ecological Characteristics of Old-Growth Douglas-fir Forests*, 4.

William Dietrich quote on human fascination with bigness, from Dietrich, *The Final Forest*, 114.

Mother trees caring for their kin from Suzanne Simard, *Finding the Mother Tree: Discovering the Wisdom of the Forest* (New York: Alfred A. Knopf, 2021), 259–261.

Pinchot quote on importance of forest to our inner selves from Miller, *Gifford Pinchot and the Making of Modern Environmentalism*, 338.

Pinchot on people making clear how they want the forest run from Miller, *Gifford Pinchot and the Making of Modern Environmentalism*, 360.

Pinchot's key maxims from Pinchot Institute for Conservation.

15. The Spotted Owl: The Beginning of the End

Planned reduction for spotted owls dependent on old growth from *Land and Resource Management Plan*.

Four general goals for the GPNF from *Land and Resource Management Plan*.

Dwyer quote on violation of the National Forest Management Act from Robbins, *Landscapes of Conflict*, 209.

Increase in numbers of "ologists" working for Forest Service from Dietrich, *The Final Forest*, 108.

Revision of environmental assessment in the Willamette National Forest from author interview with Jeff DeBonis.

DeBonis letter to Chief Robertson on troubling times for Forest Service employees from the *New York Times*, March 4, 1990, From Jim Furnish, *Toward A Natural Forest*, 87.

DeBonis quote on not talking from author from interview with Jeff DeBonis.

Elimination of old growth at record rates from Dietrich, *The Final Forest*, 246.

Distinctions between two divergent groups from Leopold, *Round River*, 221–222.

Jerry Franklin quote on economic considerations from Maser, *Forest Primeval*, 113.

16. A Turning Point: From Production to Ecological Management

New goals and objectives for the GPNF from *Amendment to Land and Resource Management Plan*, GPNF, USDA, Forest Service, 1994.

Designating LSRs to provide adequate habitat for at-risk species from *Amendment to Land and Resource Management Plan*.

Thinning inside reserves from *Amendment to Land and Resource Management Plan.*

Creating conditions for old growth from *Amendment to Land and Resource Management Plan.*

Importance of woody debris from *Amendment to Land and Resource Management Plan.*

Learning from biological legacies from *Amendment to Land and Resource Management Plan.*

Stubblefield stuck on endings from *Monitoring and Evaluation Report*, Gifford Pinchot National Forest, USDA, Forest Service, 1997.

A different set of values from author interview with Lynn Burditt.

Recognition of sexism and racism within the Forest Service from author interview with Lynn Burditt.

Failure to adhere to new standards from *Monitoring and Evaluation Report.*

Stubblefield and the new reality from *Monitoring and Evaluation Report.*

Non declining flow and amenity migration from Susan Charnley et al., *Socioeconomic Monitoring Results. Volume III: Rural Communities and Economics* (Washington, DC: USDA, Forest Service, 2006). https://www.researchgate.net/publication/240623918_Socioeconomic_Monitoring_Results _Volume_III_Rural_Communities_and_Economies

Impacts differ at community scale from Charnley et al., *Socioeconomic Monitoring Results. Volume III.*

Economic impacts in Skamania County from Skamania County Profile. https://www .skamaniacounty.org

Preserving ecosystems for the spotted owl from Dietrich, *The Final Forest*, 235–236.

A million acres of old growth cut from Dietrich, *The Final Forest*, 188–190.

Importance of deadwood from Dietrich, *The Final Forest*, 115.

Impacts of fragmentation from Maser, *Forest Primeval*, XX.

Fragmentation of landscape effects from Jon Luoma, *The Hidden Forest*, 154.

Remaining amount of old growth from Joel Schwarz, "How Much Old Growth Is There?," *University of Washington News*, April 8, 1997.

Jerry Franklin quotes on forest supervisors from author interview with Jerry Franklin.

Jerry Franklin quote on achieving Congressional mandate from author interview with Jerry Franklin.

"Not all is well in the forest" from *Forest Ecosystem Management: An Ecological, Environmental and Social Assessment*, USDA, Forest Service, 1993.

Trust, the missing ingredient from *Forest Ecosystem Management.*

Tyranny of incremental decisions from *Forest Ecosystem Management.*

Foresters' view of multiple use from *Forest Ecosystem Management.*

Divergence from the National Forest Management Act from *Forest Ecosystem Management.*

Reasons for judicial intervention from *Forest Ecosystem Management.*

Description of LSRs and matrix lands from *GPNF Land and Management Plan*, Amendment 11, 1995.

Experience of cognitive dissonance from Jim Furnish, *Toward a Natural Forest: The Forest Service in Transition* (Corvallis: Oregon State University Press, 2015), 74.

Importance of other environmental values other than logging from Furnish, *Toward a Natural Forest*, 79.

Decline of harvesting on the Siuslaw National Forest from Furnish, *Toward a Natural Forest*, 118–119.

Need for ecosystem management from Jim Furnish, *Toward a Natural Forest*, 115.

Jerry Franklin quote prior to Dwyer ruling from Jerry Franklin, "Toward a New Forestry," *American Forests* (November/December 1989): 1–8.

Learning from biological legacies from *Amendment to Land and Resource Management Plan.*

17. Ecological Restoration

Perspectives on forestry first as an advocate then as an insider from author interview with Emily Platt.

Descriptions of restoration efforts on GPNF from Upper Wind Big Hollow project.

Description of biological legacies from Wikipedia. https://en.wikipedia.org/wiki/Mount_St._Helens

Virtual elimination of old growth from Dominick A. DellaSala, *The Northwest Forest Plan: Still the Best Science of the Day* (Ashland, OR: Geos Institute, 2015), 4.

Importance of connected reserves from DellaSala, *The Northwest Forest Plan*, 17–18.

Other benefits of reserves from Thomas et al., "*The Northwest Forest Plan*," 281–284.

Impact of climate changes from Jerry Franklin, "An Ecologist's Perspective on Northwestern Forests in 2010," *Forest Watch* 10, no. 2 (1989): 69. https://andrewsforest.oregonstate.edu/sites/default/files/lter/pubs/pdf/pub1038.pdf

Importance of a fine filter for biodiversity conservation from Dominick A. DellaSala et al., "Building on Two Decades of Ecosystem Management and Biodiversity Conservation under the Northwest Forest Plan, USA," *Forests* 6, no. 9 (2015): 3332–3333.

Decline of spotted owls from DellaSala et al., "Building on Two Decades of Ecosystem Management and Biodiversity Conservation," 3329.

Diminishment of barred owls' competitive advantage from DellaSala et al., "Building on Two Decades of Ecosystem Management and Biodiversity Conservation," 3334.

Perpetual protection of remaining old growth from DellaSala et al., "Building on Two Decades of Ecosystem Management and Biodiversity Conservation," 3330.

Ensuring biodiversity of old growth for the long run from Kathryn A. Kohm and Jerry Franklin, *Creating a Forestry for the 21st Century: The Science of Ecosystem Management* (Washington, DC: Island Press, 1997), 49.

Key conservation principles from DellaSala et al., "Building on Two Decades of Ecosystem Management and Biodiversity Conservation," 3342–3344.

Importance of forest systems maintaining its function from Kohm and Franklin, *Creating a Forestry for the 21st Century*, 8.

Interdependence of the pieces of the forest from Kohm and Franklin, *Creating a Forestry for the 21st Century*, 8.

Development of old growth stands from "Restoring Complexity: Second-Growth Forests and Habitat Diversity," *Science Update*, Pacific Northwest Research Station, USDA, Forest Service, 2002.

Key restoration principles from Thomas et al., "The Northwest Forest Plan," 283.

Importance of structural complexity and spatial heterogeneity from Thomas et al., "The Northwest Forest Plan," 283–286.

Value of variable density thinning from "Restoring Complexity," 7.

Thinning young plantations from "Restoring Complexity," 8–9.

Importance of thinning for structural complexity from Jerry F. Franklin and K. Norman Johnson, "A Restoration Framework for Federal Forests in the Pacific Northwest," *Journal of Forestry* 110, no. 8 (2012): 433–435.

Role of fires from DellaSala et al., "Building on Two Decades of Ecosystem Management and Biodiversity Conservation," 3340.

Protecting mature and old-growth forests from January 2022 unpublished essay sent to author by Jerry Franklin.

Changes in Northwest forest resulting from climate change from Philip W. Mote et al., "Preparing for Climatic Change: The Water, Salmon, and Forests of Pacific Northwest," *Climatic Change* 61, no. 1 (2003): 66–67.

Increasing LSRs to enhance resilience from Mote et al., "Preparing for Climatic Change," 78.

A side benefit from Mote et al., "Preparing for Climatic Change," 68.

Attending to multiple values and needs from Jerry Franklin, *Understanding and Managing Forests as Ecosystems: A Reflection on 60 Years of Change and a View to the Anthropocene*, Pinchot Institute for Conservation, 2016.

18. Gifford Pinchot and the Next Hundred Years

Quotes from author interview with Gifford Pinchot III.

Epilogue

Quotes from John Clayton, *Natural Rivals: John Muir, Gifford Pinchot, and the Creation of America's Public Lands* (New York: Pegasus Books, 2019), 82.

Bibliography

Interviews

Burditt, Lynn. Interview with author, 2011.
DeBonis, Jeff. Interview with author, 2011.
Franklin, Jerry. Interview with author, 2011.
Pinchot, Gifford III. Interview with author, 2011.
Platt, Emily. Interview with author, 2018.
Saul, Susan. Interview with author, 2011.
Tokarczyk, Robert. Interview with author, 2011.
Williams, Bob. Interview with author, 2011.

Publications

Amendment to Land and Resource Management Plan. US Department of Agriculture, Forest Service, Gifford Pinchot National Forest, 1994. Pacific Northwest Regional Office, Portland, Oregon.

Cecil, George. Letter, 1921. Seattle: Forest Service, US Department of Agriculture.

Charnley, Susan, et al. *Rural Communities and Economics*. Vol. III of *Northwest Forest Plan, the First 10 Years (1994–2003): Socioeconomic Monitoring Results*. Portland, OR: US Department of Agriculture, Forest Service, Pacific Northwest Research Station, 2006. https://www.fs.usda.gov/pnw/pubs/pnw_gtr649.pdf

Clary, David A. *Timber and the Forest Service*. Lawrence: University Press of Kansas, 1986. https://doi.org/10.2307/j.ctv1p2gm62

Clayton, John. *Natural Rivals: John Muir, Gifford Pinchot, and the Creation of America's Public Lands*. New York: Pegasus Books, 2019.

Crowell, John B. Jr. *End of the Ancient Forest: A Report on National Forest Management Plan*. Washington, DC: The Wilderness Society, 1988.

DeBonis, Jeff. Letter to Chief Robertson. *New York Times*. March 4, 1990.

DellaSala, Dominick A. *The Northwest Forest Plan: Still the Best Science of the Day*. Ashland, OR: Geos Institute, April 15, 2015. https://geosinstitute.org/wp-content/uploads/2015/07/pnw-report-nwfp-still-best-science.pdf

DellaSala, Dominick A., Rowan Baker, Doug Heiken, Chris A. Frissell, James R. Karr, S. Kim Nelson, Barry R. Noon, David Olson, and James Strittholt. "Building on Two Decades of Eco-system Management and Biodiversity Conservation under the Northwest Forest Plan, USA." *Forests* 6, no. 9 (2015): 3326–3352. https://doi.org/10.3390/f6093326

Diamond, Jared. *Collapse: How Societies Choose to Fail or Succeed*. New York: Penguin, 2004.

Dietrich, William. *The Final Forest: Big Trees, Forks, and the Pacific Northwest*. Seattle: University of Washington Press, 1992.

Egan, Timothy. *The Big Burn: Teddy Roosevelt and the Fire That Saved America*. Boston: Houghton Mifflin Harcourt, 2009.

Fedkiw, John. *Managing Multiple Uses on National Forests, 1905–1995: A 90-Year Learning Experience and It Isn't Finished Yet*. Washington, DC: US Department of Agriculture, Forest Service, 1998. http://npshistory.com/publications/usfs/fs-628/index.htm

Ficken, Robert, E. *The Forested Land: A History of Lumbering in Western Washington*. Seattle: University of Washington Press, 1987.

Forest Ecosystem Management: An Ecological, Economic, and Social Assessment. Report of the Forest Ecosystem Management Assessment Team. Portland, OR: US Department of Agriculture, Forest Service, Pacific Northwest Research Station, 1993.

Franklin, Jerry. "Toward a New Forestry." *American Forests* 95 (November/December 1989): 1–8.

Franklin, Jerry. *Understanding and Managing Forests as Ecosystems: A Reflection on 60 Years of Change and a View to the Anthropocene*. Washington, DC: Pinchot Institute for Conservation, 2016.

Franklin, Jerry F. *An Ecologist's Perspective on Northwestern Forests in 2010*. US Department of Agriculture, Forest Service, Pacific Northwest Research Station, Plant Ecology, 1989.

Franklin, Jerry F. "Biological Legacies: A Critical Management Concept from Mount St. Helens." *Transactions of the 55th North American Wildlife and Natural Resources Conference*, March 16–21, 1990, Denver, Colorado: 216–219.

Franklin, Jerry F., and K. Norman Johnson. "A Restoration Framework for Federal Forests in the Pacific Northwest." *Journal of Forestry* 110, no. 8 (2012): 429–439. https://doi.org/10.5849/jof.10-006

Franklin, Jerry F., K. Norman Johnson, and Debora L. Johnson. *Ecological Forest Management*. Long Grove, IL: Waveland Press, 2018.

Franklin, Jerry F., Kermit Cromack Jr., et al. *Ecological Characteristics of Old-Growth Douglas-fir Forests*. Portland, OR: US Department of Agriculture, Forest Service, Pacific Northwest Research Station, 1981. https://doi.org/10.2737/PNW-GTR-118

Frome, Michael. *The Forest Service*. Santa Barbara, CA: Praeger, 1971.

Furnish, Jim. *Toward a Natural Forest: The Forest Service in Transition*. Corvallis: Oregon State University Press, 2015.

Geier, Max G. *Necessary Work: Discovering Old Forests, New Outlooks, and Community on the H. J. Andrews Experimental Forest, 1948–2000*. Portland, OR: US Department of Agriculture, Forest Service, Pacific Northwest Research Station, 2007.

General Inspection Reports. Seattle: Forest Service, US Department of Agriculture. 1923–1947.

Gifford Pinchot National Forest Supervisors. Summary of Information, 1958–1971. Seattle: Forest Service, US Department of Agriculture.

Gold, Pat Courtney. "The Long Narrows: The Forgotten Geographic and Cultural Wonder." *Oregon Historical Quarterly* 108, no. 4 (2007): 596–605. https://doi.org/10.1353/ohq.2007.0041

Graves, Henry. Correspondence. Seattle: Forest Service, US Department of Agriculture, 1915–1958.

Harrison, Robert Pogue. *Forests: The Shadow of Civilization*. Chicago: University of Chicago Press, 1992.

Hays, Samuel. *Conservation and the Gospel of Efficiency: The Progressive Conservation Movement, 1890–1920*. Cambridge, MA: Harvard University Press, 1959.

Herring, Margaret, and Sarah Greene. *Forest of Time: A Century of Science at Wind River Experimental Forest*. Corvallis: Oregon State University Press, 2007.

Hirt, Paul W. *A Conspiracy of Optimism: Management of the National Forests since World War Two*. Lincoln: University of Nebraska Press, 1994.

Kaufman, Herbert. *The Forest Ranger: A Study in Administrative Behavior*. Baltimore: Johns Hopkins Press for Resources for the Future, 1960.

Kohm, Kathryn A., and Jerry F. Franklin, eds. *Creating a Forestry for the 21st Century: The Science of Ecosystem Management*. Washington, DC: Island Press, 1997.

Land and Resource Management Plan. US Department of Agriculture, Forest Service, Gifford Pinchot National Forest, 1990.

Langston, Nancy. *Forest Dreams, Forest Nightmares: The Paradox of Old Growth in the Inland West*. Seattle: University of Washington Press, 1995.

Leopold, Aldo, *A Sand County Almanac: And Sketches Here and There*. Oxford, UK: Oxford University Press, 1949.

Leopold, Luna B., ed. *Round River: From the Journals of Aldo Leopold.* Oxford, UK: Oxford University Press, 1972.

Letters. Foresters Carter, Granger, Hall, McArdle, Parks, Sherman, Watts, 1920s. US Department of Agriculture, Forest Service.

Lewis, James G. *The Forest Service and the Greatest Good: A Centennial History.* Durham, NC: Forest History Society, 2005.

Lund, Walter. Interview by Amelia R. Fry. Transcript. Berkeley, CA: Forest History Society and Hill Family Foundation, 1967. https://digitalassets.lib.berkeley.edu/rohoia/ucb/text /timbermngpacnw00lundrich.pdf

Luoma, Jon R. *The Hidden Forest: The Biography of an Ecosystem.* Corvallis: Oregon State University Press, 2006.

Mack, Cheryl. *The "Columbia National Burn": A History of Fires and Firefighting on the Gifford Pinchot National Forest.* US Department of Agriculture, Forest Service, 1999.

Marsh, George Perkins. *Man and Nature: Or, Physical Geography as Modified by Human Action.* Cambridge, MA: Belknap Press edition of Harvard University Press, 1965.

Marsh, Kevin R. *Drawing Lines in the Forest: Creating Wilderness Areas in the Pacific Northwest.* Seattle: University of Washington Press, 2007.

Maser Chris. *Forest Primeval: The Natural History of an Ancient Forest.* San Francisco: Sierra Club Books, 1989.

Mays, L. K. General Inspection Report. US Department of Agriculture, Forest Service, 1947.

McKinley, Charles. *Uncle Sam in the Pacific Northwest: Federal Management of Natural Resources in the Columbia River Valley.* Berkeley: University of California Press, 1952.

Miller, Char. *American Forests: Nature, Culture, and Politics.* Lawrence: University Press of Kansas, 1997.

Miller, Char. *Gifford Pinchot and the Making of Modern Environmentalism.* Washington, DC: Island Press, 2001.

Monitoring and Evaluation Report. US Department of Agriculture, Forest Service, Gifford Pinchot National Forest, 1997.

Mote, Philip W., Edward A. Parson, Alan F. Hamlet, William S. Keeton, Dennis Lettenmaier, Nathan Mantua, Edward L. Miles, David W. Peterson, David L. Person, Richard Slaughter, and Amy K. Snover. "Preparing for Climatic Change: The Water, Salmon, and Forests of the Pacific Northwest." *Climatic Change* 61, no. 1 (2003): 45–88.

Nash, Roderick. *Wilderness and the American Mind,* 4th ed. New Haven, CT: Yale University Press, 2001.

Olson, Steve. *Eruption: The Untold Story of Mount St. Helens.* New York: W. W. Norton, 2016.

Pinchot, Gifford. *A Primer of Forestry.* Washington, DC: Government Printing Office, 1899.

Pinchot, Gifford. *Breaking New Ground.* New York: Harcourt, Brace and Co. 1947. Reprinted with new introduction by Char Miller and V. Alaric Sample. Washington, DC: Island Press, 1998.

Pinchot, Gifford. Key Maxims. Grey Towers, PA: Pinchot Institute for Conservation, 1910.

Pinchot, Gifford. Memo. US Department of Agriculture, Forest Service, 1909.

Pinchot, Gifford. *The Use of the National Forest Reserves.* US Department of Agriculture, Forest Service, 1905.

Pinchot, Gifford. *The Conservation Diaries of Gifford Pinchot.* Edited by Harold K. Steen. Durham, NC: Forest History Society, 2001.

Pinchot, Gifford. *The Fight for Conservation.* New York: Doubleday, Page and Co., 1910.

Rajala, Richard A. *Clearcutting the Pacific Rain Forest: Production, Science, and Regulation.* Vancouver: University of British Columbia Press, 1998.

Rapp, Valerie. "New Findings about Old-Growth Forests." *Science Update 4.* Portland, OR: US Department of Agriculture, Forest Service, Pacific Northwest Research Station, 2003.

"Restoring Complexity: Second-Growth Forests and Habitat Diversity." *Science Update*. Portland, OR: US Department of Agriculture, Forest Service, Pacific Northwest Research Station, 2002.

Road-less Area Report. US Department of Agriculture, Forest Service, 1926.

Robbins, William G. *Landscapes of Conflict: The Oregon Story, 1940–2000*. Seattle: University of Washington Press, 2004.

Robbins, William G. *Landscapes of Promise: The Oregon Story, 1800–1940*. Seattle: University of Washington Press, 1999.

Roosevelt, Theodore, and Wayne Andrews. *The Autobiography of Theodore Roosevelt: Condensed from the Original Ed., Supplemented by Letters, Speeches, and Other Writings*. Centennial ed. New York: Scribner, 1958.

Schwartz, Joel. "How Much Old-Growth Forest Is There?" *University of Washington News*, April 8, 1997. https://www.washington.edu/news/1997/04/08/how-much-old-growth-forest-is-there/

Simard, Suzanne. *Finding the Mother Tree: Discovering the Wisdom of the Forest*. New York: Allen Lane, 2021.

Standing, A. R. General Inspection Report. US Department of Agriculture, Forest Service, 1950.

Steen, Harold K. *The US Forest Service: A History*. Seattle: University of Washington Press, 1976.

Thomas, Jack Ward, Jerry F. Franklin, John Gordon, and K. Norman Johnson. "The Northwest Forest Plan: Origins, Components, Implementation Experience, and Suggestions for Change." *Conservation Biology* 20, no. 2 (April 2006): 277–87. https://doi.org/10.1111/j.1523-1739.2006.00385.x

Timber Management Plan. US Department of Agriculture, Forest Service, 1984.

Timber Resources for America's Future. US Department of Agriculture, Forest Service, 1958.

US Forest Service. Pacific Northwest Region. *Draft Environmental Impact Statement, Proposed Land and Resource Management Plan, Gifford Pinchot National Forest*. Portland, OR: US Department of Agriculture, Forest Service, Pacific Northwest Region, 1987.

Usher, Jack. Oral History Project on Timber Management in Pacific Northwest, Berkeley, CA, Bancroft Library, 2012.

Wilkinson, Charles F. *Crossing the Next Meridian: Land, Water, and the Future of the West*. Washington, DC: Island Press, 1992.

Williams, Gerald W. *The U.S. Forest Service in the Pacific Northwest: A History*. Corvallis: Oregon State University Press, 2009.

Williams, Gerald W., and Char Miller. "At the Creation: The National Forest Commission of 1896–97," *Forest History Today*, Spring/Fall 2005, 32–41.

Index

About the Author

Rand Schenck began his environmental activism focused on forestry in the late 1970s, with the Sierra Club in North Carolina. He served in a variety of leadership roles with the Sierra Club over the next fifteen years, with a major focus on designating more public lands as wilderness. After moving to Oregon in 1996, Rand joined the Board of Oregon Natural Resources Council, now Oregon Wild, and continued to focus on protecting Oregon's forests, wild waters, and wildlife.

Over the past decade Rand has focused his activism on climate change. He helped found 350PDX, a collective focused on climate justice, and Mobilizing Climate Action Together (MCAT), a community of volunteers working to ensure that Oregon builds a healthy climate and green-energy economy for future generations. He is the Forestry and Natural Lands Lead for MCAT, which seeks to implement climate-smart forestry, in which carbon sequestration and storage are optimized by protecting mature and old-growth trees, growing trees longer (which is by far the most effective natural climate solution), and ensuring a diversity of species, ages, and structures.

Professionally, Rand spent much of his career focused on helping large organizations be more humane and effective through executive coaching, building internal cultures, managing organizational change, and developing responsive leadership. Rand has a BA in History, MA in recreation administration, and MSW (master of social work). Now retired, he has even more time to spend in the forests he loves hiking and backpacking as well as enjoying the many benefits of living in the Pacific Northwest, which include skiing, rafting, canoeing, and sea kayaking.